SCM STUDYGUIDE TO CHRISTIAN DOCTRINE

Jeff Astley

scm press

Published in 2010 by SCM Press
Editorial office
13–17 Long Lane,
London, EC1A 9PN, UK

SCM Press is an imprint of Hymns Ancient and Modern Ltd (a
registered charity)
St Mary's Works, St Mary's Plain,
Norwich, NR3 3BH, UK
www.scm-canterburypress.co.uk

British Library Cataloguing in Publication data

A catalogue record for this book is available
from the British Library

978 0 334 04324 9

Typeset by Regent Typesetting, London
Printed and bound by
CPI Antony Rowe, Chippenham, SN14 6LH

Contents

Preface

The SCM Studyguide Series provides succinct introductions to key areas of study, exploring challenging concepts in an accessible way, and encouraging readers to think independently and interact with the text. This volume offers an introduction to Christian doctrine at undergraduate level 1.

The book begins with three chapters examining the general nature of Christian doctrine, its setting and sources, and the language it uses. It then surveys the major areas of doctrine – following a slightly unusual order. Embarking on the doctrinal journey, we first examine teaching related to concrete experiences, behaviour and belonging within the Church. We then travel through the themes of Christian salvation, responses to Christ and God's role in the world; before finally exploring the more abstract terrain of God's mysterious reality and our ultimate destiny.

While intended mainly as a textbook, the book encourages readers to engage in *theological conversations* between their own more 'ordinary theology', on the one hand, and the varied resources of ecclesiastical and academic theology, on the other. In this way, this primer in doctrine should help those who seek a form of Christian believing and spirituality true to their own life and reflection.

In writing this Studyguide I have drawn on my experience of teaching doctrine to a range of students and ordinands in colleges, universities, and on wider courses, especially in Lincoln and Durham. Some material from my *God's World* (Darton, Longman & Todd, 2000, now out of print) has been adapted for two of the present chapters.

In addition to the main discussion, some more technical or detailed *reference material* is provided in text boxes with a background tint – including a number of 'Coming to Terms with Theology' boxes – as well as in the footnotes. The details of the early history of Christology displayed in small print on pp. 141–5 fall into the same category. Prompts to stimulate theological conversation are included in the EXERCISE boxes, for use by individuals or (preferably) in group discussion.

Students of doctrine greatly benefit from listening to a variety of voices. The Further Reading section on pages 221–2 includes titles that survey most of the major doctrines, and their authors represent a wide spectrum of Christian denominations.

I am most grateful to Evelyn Jackson, Administrative Secretary to NEICE, for all her skilful work in preparing the manuscript for publication, and for help with the indexes.

Quotations from the Bible are from the *New Revised Standard Version* Bible, Anglicized Edition, copyright © 1989, by the Division of Christian Education of the National Council of the Churches of Christ in the USA, and are used by permission. All rights reserved.

1

Theology as Conversation: Thinking, Studying and Living Christian Doctrine

What is Christian Theology?

Although this book is a guide to the study of *doctrine*, I want to begin our reflections with the wider term *theology*. It is rather discouraging that both words are frequently used negatively – particularly by politicians and journalists – as labels for obscure or impractical ideas, to which a certain type of 'doctrinaire' person demands strict adherence. Needless to say, theologians don't recognize themselves in this description.

But who are 'theologians'? Well, you are one of them if you have ever engaged in reflective thinking or speaking about God, or about any topic that relates to the nature and activity of God. Theology is literally 'God-talk' or 'talk about God', from the Greek for 'God' (*theos*) and 'word' (*logos*). So, at one level, a theologian is just someone who speaks about God.

However, *logos* is also used in a more restricted way to indicate a 'study': that is, a rational discussion or an ordered investigation. (This is why theology is sometimes identified as 'a science', using the word in a very broad sense.) In universities and similar contexts, theology names a *field of study* or an academic department. This usage often embraces people who are not talking about God directly at all. They study religious people, and the literature, practices and artefacts associated with them, through the *disciplines* (forms of study and knowledge) of history, philosophy, sociology, anthropology and so on.

Alongside them, however, are also likely to be people who claim to be engaged in Christian 'systematic theology', 'dogmatic theology', 'philosophical theology' or 'historical theology'. Although they will spend a lot of their time *studying theology*, by poring over the arguments and claims of other people (mainly early and present-day Christians), they will often also be engaged in *doing theology* for themselves: that is, articulating and refining what they take to be the most accurate and defensible ways of speaking about God.

Few readers of this book are likely to identify themselves with *this* picture of theologians or theological scholars – not yet, anyway. But the word 'theology' did not begin life in the academy (as academics often refer to places of advanced study, particularly universities). It began in the Church, and the Church remains its natural and proper home. Theology *really* belongs in and to the Church. This is not to say that academics have no right to it, nor that the Church is not enormously in their debt for their theological research and thinking. But it does mean that Christians, as members of the Church, bear the prime responsibility for doing Christian theology. It is certainly not something that they can leave to universities.

In its earliest usage, the Greek word *theologia* referred to a form of speaking about God that was close to *speaking to God* in prayer, worship and religious encounter. Close, but not identical. Until the eighteenth century, 'theology was not just for the scholar or teacher but was the wisdom proper to the life of the believer' – of *all* believers – as an integral part of Christian life (Farley, 1988, p. 88). In this broader application, theology is a 'cognitive [knowing, believing, thinking] disposition and orientation of the soul' (Farley, 1983, p. 35); it is a capacity, inclination and aptitude for a personal knowledge of God. It springs from and is entailed by the practical knowledge or wisdom of faith, and has been described as that wisdom 'in a reflective mode' and as 'the cognitive component of piety' (David Kelsey, Richard Osmer), which shapes our apprehension of God and of the world in relation to God. Understood in this way, theology is not a body of information and theory *about* God; it is the reflective wisdom of the believer – *faith-become-reflective.*

Reflection in Theology

This implies, however, that we can't describe any old God-talk as theology. Sometimes, of course, it is just swearing – using 'God', 'Jesus' or 'Mary' simply to express the speaker's extreme feelings. These words can also be used in a wholly unreflective way in personal devotion and public ritual. In all these cases, the speakers may not be 'thinking what they are saying'.

We should reserve the word theology for *reflective* God-talk, using the adjective 'reflective' here in the broad sense of 'thoughtful' and 'considered'. I prefer it to 'rational', partly because that term often implies some sort of logical deduction; and I want to avoid the word 'reasonable', because it has similar overtones of defending views by evidence and arguments. Reflective God-talk includes these more rigorous and narrow types of disciplined thinking, but the idea of theology as a 'reflective exercise' also extends to people who are simply trying to think more deeply about their faith. Christians are rarely totally non-reflective, although few are engaged at the level of critical reflection expected of – and by – university scholars. Reflective believers may simply be seeking to uncover their faith's fuller and more profound meanings; and doing so in a way that values getting their own ideas clear and spotting weaknesses in their own thinking. Reflective believers also acknowledge the importance of having beliefs that are consistent with other ideas that they and others hold; and they realize the ever-present danger of their views falling apart because they are 'internally incoherent'. In these ways, faith is usually in *search of understanding*, which is another way of characterizing theology.

In brief, reflective God-talk is discourse about God in which people engage in an alert and self-critical manner, trying to make the best sense they can of the religious beliefs they hold. I take this to be the basic task of theology; and I agree that, to this extent, 'all believers can do theology' (Ritschl, 1986, p. 99). 'All Christians *who believe and who think about what they believe* are theologians', therefore; and this shared or general 'theology of all believers' serves as the foundation of academic theology (Moltmann, 2000, pp. 13–14). 'Students of theology, then, are not doing something that other Christians do not do, nor are they doing it for the first time' (Stiver, 2009, p. 3).

If you have not yet undertaken any kind of academic study of theology yourself, you probably fit into my category of 'ordinary theologian'. I describe *ordinary theology* as 'the theological beliefs and processes of believing that find expression in the God-talk of those believers who have received no scholarly theological education' (Astley, 2002, p. 1). But the differences between ordinary theology and *academic theology* are differences in degree – no pun intended! – rather than differences of kind. When ordinary theologians read books, write essays or attend talks, lectures and seminars, their own theological thinking and beliefs usually change in both style and content. This does not take place by the sudden replacement of their ordinary theology by a wholly different academic theology, but through a gradual learning process that is essentially a form of conversation between the two. And exactly the same process of conversational *dialogue* happens when your own theology – however ordinary or academic it is – encounters the traditional theology of the Church.

None of this means that the study of doctrine is reserved for Christian believers. I shall say something shortly to those readers who 'only want to study it', and profess no Christian faith of their own to which to relate their study. But perhaps I can say here that the category of ordinary theology can be broadened to include non-believers, since most people have *some* beliefs about the existence and nature of God, even if these are agnostic or atheistic. They, too, will find themselves engaging in a conversation with what they are learning about Christian doctrine.

What is Christian Doctrine?

One way of studying Christian theology is to adopt a historical approach, investigating how theology was done and has developed down the ages, in particular:

- in the New Testament period (about 50–100 CE);[1]
- in the patristic period (around 100–451) of the 'Greek Fathers' and 'Latin Fathers' of the Eastern and Western wings of the undivided Church;
- during the Middle Ages (up to about 1500);
- at the Reformation (mainly in the sixteenth century) and the later period of Protestant and Roman Catholic definitions of Christian orthodoxy;
- in the modern period (from the eighteenth-century Enlightenment, or Age of Reason, up to the present day).

---

1 CE is the abbreviation for the Common Era, now commonly used instead of AD (*Anno Domini*, 'in the year of the Lord').

(The last three periods are often studied solely with reference to Western, Roman Catholic and Protestant theology.)

Adopting a historical approach would involve learning a great deal about a number of key figures in the history of Christian thought: Athanasius and Augustine; Anselm and Aquinas; Luther and Calvin; Schleiermacher, Barth and Rahner; and many more. This book is not structured as a historical survey, however, but around particular theological themes, topics or ideas. One great advantage of this *thematic approach* is that the reader is challenged to respond more quickly and directly to the outcomes of historical and contemporary theological reflection. The danger of studying theology historically (or 'diachronically'), particularly in the beginning, is that the scholarly task of learning what other people said in different periods *may* encourage us to do theology 'at a distance', or at 'second-hand'. And that can prevent it from engaging with, challenging and changing our own theology. A topic-based course is more 'in-your-face' than that. It immediately forces a range of questions on us:

- Is this what I believe?   Is it what I should believe?
- What is wrong with it?   What is right about it?

However, we won't get away without *some* historical background to the theological themes that form the subject-matter of this book.

But we haven't yet explained what *doctrine* is. Basically, the word means 'teachings' (Latin *doctrina*, which comes from the same verb as the word 'doctor' – which originally simply meant 'teacher'). 'Christian doctrine' labels the way-of-putting-things and the way-of-believing-things that Christians have taught and still teach to one another. So doctrines are *communal* Christian understandings: the *shared* products of attempts by Christians to make sense of their beliefs, their experience, their literature and their world. 'The views of theologians are doctrinally significant, in so far as they have won acceptance within the community' (McGrath, 1997, p. 11). They are then treated as an acceptable standard, as *normative theology*.

I might sometimes speak of *my* (peculiar and idiosyncratic, perhaps some would say heretical) 'theology' – even of *my* 'Christian theology'. But it would be odd for me to call this 'my doctrine'; and even more odd to call these thoughts 'my Christian doctrine', even if I work energetically to teach them to others. Christian doctrine is wider than this; it is something learned from others. 'The faith is not, except secondarily, *mine* at all. It is something shared . . . a community's faith – the church's' (Norris, 1979, p. 7). Doctrine is 'communally authoritative teachings regarded as essential to the identity of the Christian community', and therefore represents 'an invitation to enter a new community and its associated conceptual and experiential world' (McGrath, 1997, pp. 12, 199).

Coming to Terms with Theology:
Doctrine and Dogma

While **doctrine** means Christian teaching(s) in a broad sense, **dogma** is reserved for teaching regarded by the Church as divinely revealed, and therefore binding. Dogmas have usually been defined by authoritative Church councils, expressing the consensus of the Churches. Examples include the dogmas of the two natures of Christ and the Trinity (see Chapters 7 and 9). All dogmas are doctrines, but not all doctrines are treated as dogmas.

The term *dogma* is most widely used in Roman Catholicism. Protestants do not think of dogmas as infallible ('without error'), as many Catholics do; but most regard them as authoritative if they are in accordance with Scripture. Some Protestants do not use the term at all, and others think of it simply as the prevailing expression of the Christian faith. The Orthodox Churches recognize no dogma after the year 787; whereas the (Roman) Catholic Church promulgated dogmas in the nineteenth and twentieth centuries.

Dogmatic theology (or 'dogmatics') is sometimes used of the exploration, critical examination and presentation of major Christian doctrines (including, but not restricted to, dogmas).

Systematic theology is a broader term, which can include moral theology, fundamental theology (considerations of the nature of theological sources and other general issues) and apologetics (defences of theology), as well as dogmatic theology proper. The adjective 'systematic' stresses the cross-links between doctrines, and the importance of consistency: 'to perceive connections between truths, and to know which belongs to which' (Brunner, 1934, p. 262).

Doing Doctrine

Doctrine – like 'theology' and 'faith' (see Chapter 2) – can be understood as both a noun and a verb. It is used of *what is taught* (the 'product') and of the *activity of teaching* (the 'process'). Understanding that 'Christian faith, Christian teaching, lives in and as *communication*' (Pattison, 2005, p. 7) helps us avoid an over-objective, detached or impersonal stance towards the *results* of Christian communication; especially when they are endorsed in the deliberations of individual theologians or Church councils. All teaching only 'works' when people *learn*; and people only properly learn when their minds and hearts are involved, and when their beliefs, values and dispositions to act and experience are *changed*. Whatever their source, doctrines too only come alive *for us* when they are really *shared* with us (*communicare* is Latin for 'to share'): when they truly communicate themselves to us personally, by engaging our own perspectives and ideas. God's truth is not to be thought of as neutral and impersonal 'information about', to be received disinterestedly; it is really communicated in an active encounter that demands decision and change in the recipient. And 'communicate' doesn't just mean sharing *ideas*; it can also mean conveying feelings and transmitting motion – even receiving communion.

Admittedly, doctrine has an *authority* that the individual learner cannot claim for her or his own theology, because it has been acknowledged by the wider Church spread out over the world and through time. Very often doctrine appeals to the authority of a *revelation*, a making-known that is said ultimately to derive from God, and mediated through the Church's Bible or her tradition (Chapter 2). Yet these things are themselves the products of a process of communication, in which God's inspiration and action changes people, sometimes so powerfully that they say things like, 'The word of the Lord came to me', or 'We have the mind of Christ'. But without the response of the recipient – whether that person is a prophet, apostle or bishop, or an ordinary, everyday Christian – even God's power of *effective* communication must fail.

Most theologians accept that God never speaks so loudly that God's hearers cannot also hear themselves think. It is only when I am ready to learn, and often only when what God says addresses *my* needs and concerns, that the circuit of communication is truly complete. Then the current flows and sparks, and I – with the Church down the ages – really jump; as I hear the word that is being discussed as an authoritative word, a 'word of God' to me. Yet even then, 'the learner does not lose or suppress his self for the sake of another. He finds himself in God' (Pattison, 2005, p. 26).

For these reasons, you should not expect these Christian teachings ever to be wholly alien to you; although I should caution that traditional doctrine can sometimes seem very strange indeed, a dish from which your taste buds may recoil. You will not, perhaps, be able to stomach all of it. But however exotic, unfamiliar or even repugnant it might seem on first acquaintance, remember that all Christian doctrine is the product of a process of effective communication and learning in which you yourself – as a Christian, or at least as someone who is sympathetic to Christianity – *already stand*. It is a diet you have (often unknowingly) absorbed, and by which you have been partly formed. After all, you are unlikely to be reading this unless the teachings of Christianity have in some sense fed you already, because you have been open to its taste.

This stuff is not foreign fare. We are at home in this kitchen.

Studying Doctrine

The activity of studying doctrine is an academically respectable academic subject which *requires* neither religious faith nor even much spiritual interest in what is being studied. Some readers will not wish to go beyond this exploration of 'what Christians believe'. Most, however, will want to be involved in both studying and *doing doctrine*. The study of the past and present teachings of the Church is an integral part of 'doing doctrine', but this *study of doctrine* should only be a preliminary task. The truly important exercise for Christian believers is that of interacting with this material so as to produce a theology that they can believe in and live by, in their own context and their own times. No one can do that sort of theology for you.

Many of the exercises in this book are designed to aid this interaction. Those who are only seeking material for a scholarly study of doctrine may not find them very useful. I hope that the other readers, however, will be encouraged by them – and by the other comments and questions in the text – to develop their own theological responses to the traditions of Christian teaching.

Theology in Conversation

My ultimate aim here is to help facilitate a (metaphorical) conversation. Accounts of the role of interpretation within Christianity draw heavily on our experience of what it is like to read a book, listen to a talk or watch a film. The fundamental point is that we never come to these activities with empty minds or hearts. Rather, we approach the 'other' (the text, talk or film) with a mind that already contains our own ideas, set in the perspective of our own 'viewpoint' or 'standpoint', and with a heart infused with our own feelings, values and concerns. We are not white sheets of paper waiting to be fed into a printer, or clear computer screens waiting for input. Nor (using a metaphor from an earlier technology) are we 'blank slates' ready for someone else to chalk their own words all over us.

Of course, we *receive* the traditional teachings of the Church. But this 'reception' is not like filling an empty jug at the tap, or (despite Rom. 9.20–1) moulding an unformed lump of clay on a potter's wheel – with one eye on a photograph of the last jug you made, to guide your hands. It is more like mixing two reactive chemicals in a test-tube; or carving a great tree trunk that already possesses a particular shape – as the Durham artist, Fenwick Lawson, does – and modifying and transforming it ('changing its form'). Its shape then expresses something else *as well*; for example, Mary mourning her crucified son.

For when we come to learn doctrine, we also have something to *contribute ourselves*: something to say on our own account. We are never, as it were, wholly silent listeners; but always 'talking back', even though some of us may rarely literally open our mouths. 'Emptying the mind' can be a valuable spiritual exercise. But it is not necessarily how we should – nor often how we can – prepare to read the Bible or any book, listen to sermons or talks, or watch what is portrayed on a cinema, TV or computer screen. (My image of good preaching, by the way, is a sermon that encourages – even goads – its listeners to respond by preaching their own, better and more relevant, sermon inside their own heads.)

What I hope will take place through this book, therefore, is a creative theological conversation between your own theology, on the one hand, and the shared theological resources of Christian doctrine, on the other. In this interactive process, it is extremely unlikely – and, in my view, not desirable – that the tradition erase all your own ideas in imprinting its own. It is much more likely that you will take some of it, perhaps a great deal of it, 'on board'; but that you will also resist and even reject certain elements that you receive. And it is almost inevitable that, when you do 'take over' or 'take up' a piece of traditional Christian teaching, it will be subtly *changed* in becoming part of your own belief- or value-system. As we address our doctrinal inheritance, its ideas converse and interact with our own: both moulding and reforming them, and eventually together transmuting into something rather different from either. And all this happens in ways that are often quite individual and personal to us.

After all, in the end we only believe what *we* can believe.

Theology and Interpretation

It is impossible to advance very far with our theological reflection without facing the challenge of interpreting the writings (and sometimes the speech) of others, in particular the texts of the Bible and of Christian thinkers down to the present day. Let's not be too daunted by this prospect. 'Interpretation' is not some mysterious task reserved for professional scholars; it is something that *anyone* who listens to other people speaking, or reads what they have written, is engaged in *all the time*. Interpretation is what we do when we try to make out the meaning of – to 'understand' – another person's words. Often we do this quite automatically, without thinking. But it sometimes proves to be a much harder task, prompting the puzzled question: 'What on earth did he/she mean by that?' It is important to make explicit two assumptions here.

1 *All meaning is interpreted meaning, and all texts become interpreted texts.* So it just won't wash to claim that a human act of interpretation is *not* involved when we are reading the Bible or the statements of a Church council.
2 *As readers or listeners we are always involved in 'making out meaning'*; and we can never absolve ourselves from responsibility for this activity. If we adopt the interpretations of academic or ecclesiastical experts – which is often a very reasonable thing to do – then their interpretations become *our* interpretation, and the way they see things becomes the way we see things. But *we* are still interpreting; we are still seeing these writings or ideas in a particular way.

The 'art of understanding' or 'theory of interpretation' (both phrases are captured by the term *hermeneutics*, from the Greek verb 'to interpret') was greatly influenced by the nineteenth-century scholar of the Romantic Movement, Friedrich Schleiermacher. For Schleiermacher, the interpretative task was essentially a matter of recovering the meaning that the author of a text intended. This involves a scholarly understanding of the grammar, use and context of the original language 'common to the author and his original public'. It also requires further scholarly study in comparing different expressions of the same idea. But it culminates in something else: a 'moment of immediate rapport with the text . . . in which we "divine" its inner meaning, the intention, the original creative act of the author that makes his product a unique and meaningful work' (Pattison 2001, p. 108). This is an act of *intuition* – that is, an insight that doesn't involve any steps of reasoning (and is therefore sometimes described as 'immediate'). It is the 'Got it!' moment of uncovering the writer's intended meaning, which comes as we use our own empathy and imagination to slip into the author's shoes.

> This is probably what most people mean by 'interpreting' someone else's writing, where the main responsibility of a reader lies in uncovering the *authorial intention* behind the text. During the course of the last century, however, this assumption was frequently challenged. It was argued, for example, that the text wasn't originally addressed to us anyway; and is now so distanced from the situation in which it originated that the author's intention is inaccessible. One result was a radical view of the 'death of the author'. This is often overblown; we don't always have to accept that 'what the text says now matters more than what the author meant to say' (Ricoeur, 1981, p. 201). Nevertheless, *what it means* and *what it meant* are not as easily or justifiably distinguished as most people assume.

The German philosopher, Martin Heidegger, proposed that we focus our attention not on the text and the author, but on the much overlooked third element in this relationship – the *reader*. Heidegger was most insistent that readers are not blank slates, passively waiting to be written on by the text they read. On his account, readers are important in their own right, as *active* participants in the hermeneutical task. They always have a view or a framework of understanding, and they bring this *pre*-understanding to all their encounters with the world – including their encounters with written or spoken words. According to Hans-

Georg Gadamer, we can only understand at all *through* the employment of these 'legitimate prejudices' (literally 'pre-judgements', that is pre-understandings). There is no other way of accessing and understanding a text, except through the irremovable spectacles of our own concepts. 'To interpret means precisely to bring one's own preconceptions into play so that the text's meaning can really be made to speak for us' (Gadamer, 1993, p. 358). So we understand the past through our present reflections. (But the more we are conscious of and critically scrutinize our own views, the better.)

The model for this encounter with the text is the one we looked at earlier: the idea of an implicit dialogue or conversation between two people. In our own case, of course, we are less concerned with the scholarly activity of interpreting the meaning of a Paul, Irenaeus, Zwingli or Küng in their own historical context. This sort of technical scholarship *already* involves a dialogue with the scholarly reader. Our main task starts rather further down the line, however, as we attempt to shape our own theology in conversation with what scholars take these theologians to mean. But the same sort of process is in play, although now through *our conversations as present-day Christians with the teachings of the Church*, as they are reported by scholars from their conversations with the original texts. So we find ourselves – with *our own* prejudgements – confronted by and addressed by the other that is 'Christian doctrine'. This hermeneutical interaction is no soliloquy, in which the doctrines speak and we silently record what they say; but nor is it a monologue in which we bang on about our own point of view, without ever hearing it challenged or criticized by the tradition. Either the past or the present may be dominant, but if this is a real (if metaphorical) *discussion*, then 'the Church speaks' but so do we.

In studying another – and especially in studying doctrine – we put at risk our own 'horizon of meaning': that is, our world-view, our cultural and theological assumptions, and the limits of our range of vision. In this encounter we are 'being transformed into a communion in which we do not remain what we were' (Gadamer, 1993, p. 379). As long as the text's horizon does not 'swamp', 'erase' or otherwise replace our own, what takes place is what Gadamer has called a merging or *fusion of horizons*. This is a powerful interaction that creates in us a new understanding that takes us beyond what we already think, but towards something that wasn't just 'contained in' the past text either. This is truly an active (*inter*-active) construction or creation of meaning, which is a particular meaning for this particular reader. And the process never stops. Because after the reader's beliefs are reshaped by reading a text, she brings this revised framework of understanding back to the text. So the conversation continues in a *hermeneutical circle* (or, better, *spiral*) of continuous, repeated revision of her understanding.

In reading doctrine, therefore, as in reading any 'text' that has any sort of relation to or resonance with our own ideas and concerns, there is always:

a meeting between the intended or received meaning of the text in its original context and the different mind-set of its contemporary readers. That process can be a creative one. At its best a new vision of truth may emerge – larger than anything seen by the original author and at the same time correcting and deepening the understanding of the reader. (Wiles, 1999, p. 21)

This meeting is an inevitable consequence of *any* reader's reading of Christian doctrine. But in the case of *Christian* readers, this 'new vision of truth' will become part of their own Christian theology, their own 'reflective God-talk'. Studying doctrine is *that* important.

Variety and Authority

These reflections give rise to two important questions:

- What are we to make of the idea of authority in doctrine?
- How much variety is permitted in doctrinal understanding?

The range of views that exist on doctrinal topics very often reflects the variety of ways in which people understand the authority of Scripture or Christian tradition. We shall consider these topics in more detail in the next chapter, but certain points are relevant here. The balance of importance within the triad author–text–reader is understood very differently in different ways of doing theology. Conservatives and fundamentalists officially place most authority on *the text and its author* (for example Mark the Evangelist or Paul, the authors of the Nicene Creed, even 'God himself'). Liberal theologians are likely to place as much, if not more, significance on the *readers* both of Scripture and of the doctrinal tradition.

While it has been customary for biblical scholarship to infer the intentions of a writer such as Mark from their literary products, in recent years some have turned to consider how the biblical writing operates – particularly as narrative texts – so as to produce a range of responses in their interpreter-readers, arguing that it is 'the interests or aims of the interpreters that are decisive, not the claims of the text as such' (Morgan with Barton, 1989, p. 7). This second approach can sometimes license a great variety of new interpretations of Scripture, adopting a radical relativism that refuses to say that some interpretations are better than others. But most scholars have resisted this move, believing that texts cannot just mean *anything*.

A parallel to this debate may be found in the way people read the inherited theological traditions of the Church. The existence of a hermeneutical conversation in this situation is, I believe, unavoidable. All that is left for debate – but this is a very great amount! – is the balance in the conversation between our voices, as individuals *and* as a contemporary Church community, and those of Scripture and the Church down the ages. There is always *some* conversation going on, if we are being affected by the Church's doctrine at all. *We* shall always have a contribution to make, even if we disagree about the extent to which our thoughts ought to be influenced by, and how far they should change, the tradition we inherit.

Gadamer argues that, historically speaking, our current presuppositions have already been (partly) given to us by the tradition we are now interpreting 'for ourselves'. We thus question, criticize and understand a tradition only by employing tools of interpretation that we inherit from generations of conversations between that tradition and its readers. *Christian* readers stand 'within' the Christian tradition, to a very large extent; so its 'history does not belong to us; we belong to it' (Gadamer, 1993, p. 276).

I use these qualifications ('partly', 'to a very large extent') because we have to admit that today we inherit a range of other traditions, in addition to those that originate in Christian teaching. This wider cultural conversation is bound to affect our preconceptions and preunderstandings. For example, we believe things about physical and biological nature, history, philosophy, psychology and other faiths that many previous theologians did not believe. And though the cultural 'horizon' of their own time might have been a very widely shared, and therefore unifying thing – ours certainly is not. 'It is characteristic of modernity that our horizon exists for us precisely as a question, as a conflict or debate between rival representations. . . . The question then is just what our own horizon really is' (Pattison, 2001, p. 118). In interpreting Christian theology, we are not absolved from confronting this issue either.

EXERCISE

From what you already know about Christian beliefs, try to identify *those features of your own thinking* that are likely to conflict with:

(a) beliefs about God's relationship to the natural world;
(b) beliefs about Jesus Christ;
(c) beliefs about Christian salvation.

Doctrinal Development?

In what sense is Christian doctrine today the same as, or 'identical to', any of its earlier formulations? Claims of identity are often compatible with evidence of change, of course, as witness the gross changes in the bodily and mental characteristics of 'the same person' throughout their lifetime. But the history of Christian doctrine is rife with mutual recriminations over questions about the sameness of doctrine, as theologians and Church leaders charge others with 'betrayal', 'novelty' or 'corruption' – even 'apostasy' – in departing from 'the faith that was once for all entrusted to the saints' (Jude 3).

In 1845, John Henry Newman, newly converted to Roman Catholicism, published his *Essay on the Development of Christian Doctrine*. It defended the notion of doctrinal development against all-or-nothing notions of doctrinal immutability (unchangeableness). He argued that doctrine grows as a plant does from a seed, unfolding new parts that were already implicit in its origin. Others prefer to speak of doctrinal 'enrichment' rather than development (Gunton, 1996,

p. 48). For David Brown, the long process of response and imaginative appropriation of the biblical message should not be seen as a discovery of something already latent in scriptural revelation, but as God's inspiration and revelation continuing *beyond* Scripture, with God always 'taking seriously our historical situatedness . . . rather than attempting to override it' (Brown, 1999, p. 8). This includes God generating 'creative insight that enables the original events or words to be read in a new way' (Brown, 1994, p. 128).

Liberal and Conservative Theology

One marked difference in doctrine is between 'liberals' and 'conservatives'. The adjective *liberal* comes from the Latin word for 'free'. It is used to describe a theology and way of theologizing that thinks of itself as more open to new ideas, and less willing to be bound by tradition (while still claiming to value it). In particular, the term describes a willingness to evaluate or judge (to 'criticize') received opinions, especially on the basis of principles of rationality and morality – but not to do so in an anarchic, 'anything goes', fashion. Liberal theology strongly emphasizes the human element in the creation of Christian doctrine, and vigorously opposes any suggestion that Christian teaching has been transmitted or received in ways that have bypassed the risky, flawed intermediaries of human reflection and experience.

Keith Ward argues that the Christian faith is *essentially liberal* because from its New Testament origins onwards it has been 'rooted in freedom from written rules', in an encounter with God in Christ and 'not primarily acceptance of a set of beliefs'; and has constantly been revising itself. The manifesto of liberal Christianity is that 'Christian faith is essentially revisable in terms of new knowledge or historical circumstances' (Ward, 2007, pp. 200–1).

Conservative theologians, by contrast, place much more emphasis on the importance of protecting Christian teaching from change or loss, preserving or *conserving* it.[2] They are especially hostile to rapid and radical changes in the content of Christian doctrine. When liberals argue that the Christian tradition must accommodate new knowledge and ways of thinking, conservatives fear that this can only lead to an indiscriminate baptizing of human thinking and

---

2 People can be conservative in their theological or moral beliefs, while being open to (say) new forms of Christian expression in worship and mission.

culture, which will forfeit Christianity's ability to challenge and critique the wisdom of the world.[3]

Both conservatives and liberals have existed in every period of the Church's life, and both emphases are to be found across mainstream Christian denominations today. The differences between liberals and conservatives are also a matter of degree; they don't represent two distinct types of Christianity.

In this book I often refer to this general phenomenon using the metaphor of a *spectrum*. In the real, 'visible spectrum', colours don't exist as completely separate bands of uniform and easily distinguishable kinds. Instead, they occupy a progressive series of different wavelengths that bleed into one another, so that colour differences become questions of degree rather than differences of kind. Those at the ends of this spectrum are more obviously different from one another than are the intermediate hues.

EXERCISE

- What do you regard as the strengths and the weaknesses of liberal and conservative versions of Christian belief?
- Where would you place yourself along the liberal–conservative spectrum, and on what grounds?

Embracing Variety

Most new students are rather taken aback by the kaleidoscope of Christianity, not least in the area of Christian belief. The liberal Catholic theologian, Hans Küng, even allowed that 'everything can be called Christian which in theory and practice has an explicit, positive reference to Jesus Christ' (Küng, 1977, p. 125). And Ninian Smart exclaimed (from a Religious Studies perspective):

What a variety Christianity presents, and one is often tempted to drop the singular and speak only of Christianities ... It is not possible to define an

---

3 Fundamentalism is only one, very extreme, species of conservative Christianity. Most conservative Christians take the Bible and/or the Church's teaching very seriously, but they don't think that these sources are wholly without error (see Chapter 2).

essence of Christianity, beyond saying that the faith relates to Christ, either in historical continuity or through religious experience or both. (Smart, 1979, pp. 11, 128)

Most serious scholarship accepts the view that the Bible contains a wide spectrum of different theologies. The history of Christian theology is also primarily an account of internal variety, as is the story of the formulation of Church dogma. There is no doubt that plurality of both belief and practice has always existed across and within the Christian churches. 'If there is such a thing as Christian unity, it will necessarily be in the form of a containment of diversity within bounds' (Sykes, 1984, p. 240).

I attempt in this volume to show a little of this variety, by sampling the beliefs of Orthodox, Catholic, Protestant and Anglican Churches; and quoting authors of a range of theological views across the liberal–conservative spectrum. I hope that portraying Christian doctrine in this way will help to broaden this conversation between your own theology and that of the Church's teachings. I trust it won't seem too flippant to say, in this context, that there is 'something for everyone' in the Church's vast treasure-house of doctrine.

Of course, I do hold views of my own about what is true and valuable in Christian doctrine; and it shouldn't be too hard for you to discover what those beliefs are, as you labour through this book. It would be a great pity, however, for you to let me get in the way of your own theology *too* often.

Living Doctrine

It is important to put doctrine in its proper place. This is a very important place, but it should not sideline other aspects of Christianity. There is much more to Christianity than its beliefs. To learn to be Christian involves learning to behave and experience, worship and pray, value and feel as Christians do; as well as learning to believe and think in a Christian fashion. To uproot the belief component from all of this, as both defenders and critics of Christianity tend to do, is to separate a part – albeit an integral part – from a greater and richer whole. In religious matters, it is especially dangerous to detach cognition (knowing, thinking) from *affection* (feeling) and *action*:

We entirely fail to capture what is involved in someone's adoption or rejection of a religious worldview if we suppose we can extract a pure cognitive juice from the mush of emotional or figurative coloration, and then establish whether or not the subject is prepared to swallow it. (Cottingham, 2005, p. 80)

Christians are called ... to *live* and not just to think obediently, ... worshipfully and appreciatively ... I simply don't think that we can say that the essence of Christian education lies in the imparting of a view. (Wolterstorff, 2002, p. 108)

Religion ... was not primarily something that people thought but something they did. ... Religion is a practical discipline that teaches us to discover new capacities of mind and heart ... It is no use magisterially weighing up the teachings of religion to judge their truth or falsehood, before embarking on a religious way of life. You will only discover their truth – or lack of it – if you translate these doctrines into ritual or ethical action. (Armstrong, 2009, p. 4)

If *doctrine* is understood as teaching or communication, it is *also* something we do. According to Terrence Tilley, religious traditions are best understood 'as communicative practices, in which the communication of the "how to" is as important as, or more important than, much of the "what" communicated'. He writes, 'How to love God with one's whole mind, whole heart, and whole self is primary; doctrines about God, mind, heart and self are derivative.' For many Christian theologians, historical and contemporary, *Christian practice comes first.* 'One learns the meaning of the *tradita* [the content – that is the doctrines, attitudes, skills, practices etc. that are being passed on] as one is inaugurated into participating in the practices of the tradition' (Tilley, 2000, pp. 79–80).

As a student you can learn about these practices, and even perhaps how to engage in them, without *actually* participating in them. Such an understanding will only be an observer's understanding, however, and therefore rather restricted compared with the understanding of a full participant. Not everyone reading this book will commit themselves that far. But both the Christian 'outsider' and the 'insider', both the 'mere student' and the 'committed believer', need to recognize that doctrine only matters – because it only *works* – when it is grounded in activity, belonging and experiencing. So a 'textbook on doctrine' is bound to seem a bit odd, and rather disappointing, by comparison with the riches of Christian living, lauding and loving.

That's my excuse, anyway.

Suggestions for Further Reading

Introductory

Astley, J., 2004, *Exploring God-Talk: Using Language in Religion*, London: Darton, Longman & Todd, chs 1, 9 and 10.

Pattison, G., 2001, *A Short Course in the Philosophy of Religion*, London: SCM Press, ch. 6.

Pattison, G., 2005, *A Short Course in Christian Doctrine*, London: SCM Press, ch. 1.

Advanced

Astley, J., 2002, *Ordinary Theology: Looking, Listening and Learning in Theology*, Aldershot: Ashgate.

Hodgson, P. C., 1994, *Winds of the Spirit: A Constructive Christian Theology*, London: SCM Press, part 1.

Pattison, G., 1998, *The End of Theology – And the Task of Thinking about God*, London: SCM Press.

2

Discipleship Doctrine: Its Roots, Influences and Forms

Christian Discipleship and Spirituality

Christianity is many-sided, 'multidimensional'. Newman wrote of the dogmatical or philosophical, the devotional or properly religious, and the practical or political aspects of Christianity (*Via Media*, p. i). Ninian Smart distinguished (within all religions) the dimensions of the ritual or practical, doctrinal or philosophical, mythic or narrative, experiential or emotional, ethical or legal, organizational or social, material or artistic, political and economic ('the order is rather random': Smart, 1996, p. 10). Religious experience, however, is 'an essential aspect of each of the other dimensions' – as the internal intentions and sentiments that give them meaning (Sykes, 1984, p. 31). We may think of this non-public, religious 'inside' as *spirituality*.

Many argue that we should not understand Christianity primarily in terms of *any* list of 'Christian' beliefs, attitudes and affections, or religious and moral actions. First and foremost, they claim, Christians are called to be *disciples*. Certainly, the twelve did not first sign up to a credal statement, a philosophical theology or a form of worship; nor even to a set of virtues, principles or practices of religious morality. They simply responded to Jesus' open-ended call to follow him (Mark 1.17).

Later they came to learn what was involved in this response through a form of apprenticeship- or discipleship-learning, learning from their master and teacher as they followed him on the road that eventually led to Jerusalem – their final, definitive, 'learning experience'. Some of this learning on the road was cognitive learning, although it was very unlike the sort of dispassionate and distanced education that marks out learning a subject at a traditional school or university. Much of it involved learning a *practice*: a discipline for living expressed in their master's way of acting, which revealed his character and the inner life of his vocation. This sort of Christian education is more about formation than it is about information, and the 'communication' involved in it is not just the communication of ideas (see Chapter 1).

A vital element in any apprenticeship is learning how to see things in a certain way, as the master sees them. Spiritual learning is 'essentially ophthalmic; it is a correction of vision' (Astley, 2007, p. 11). To learn Christianity, I would argue, is primarily a matter of learning *a new way of seeing* – seeing through the eyes of Jesus. Everything else, including our Christian believing, should be understood in the context of the Christian journey of discipleship, which is a pilgrimage in which we learn to see as he sees. 'In the light of this man's story do you not see the vision?' (Wiles, 1982, p. 53).

Spirituality and Belief

The word 'spirituality' is easy to use, but harder to define. Spirituality represents the fundamental human response that lies at the heart and soul of all religion. It is, if you like, what makes religion *religious*; it is the point of it. It is therefore also the heart, soul and point of Christian doctrine. While spirituality is more basic than belief, it is not alien to it. At its best, belief flows from – and is undergirded by – an authentic religious spirituality.

Thinking and acting are two of the more obvious aspects of religion, in that we can see people's religious and moral activity, and we can hear and read the religious thoughts they express. Spirituality lies behind them both. Christian spirituality comprises those deep attitudes, dispositions and life orientation that support, motivate and give depth to Christian doctrine and Christian action. As such, it represents what Christians are really like in their depths, and it intimately connects with the things that really matter to them. Spirituality is about what we value, what we take seriously; it labels what we live for and what we might be willing to die for. It is therefore bound to affect how we lean into our life. The object of faith – and of theology – is what is 'a matter of ultimate concern for us' (Tillich, 1968, vol. I, p. 15).

According to one definition, spirituality describes 'those attitudes, beliefs and practices which animate people's lives and help them to reach out towards super-sensible realities' (Wakefield, 1983, p. 549). I think that the spiritual *attitudes* (which include spiritual values and virtues) are fundamental here. They are the deep structures of our being that direct our lives and enable us to cope with and triumph over adversity. They form part of our inner stance, our spiritual *character*. Spiritual attitudes such as trustful, responsible concern for nature and other people, and humble, hopeful openness to God in contemplation and worship keep us in harmony with the world, keep us facing up to our true selves and to one another, and keep us oriented towards our God. Such fundamental 'attitude-virtues' – as Donald Evans labelled them (Evans, 1979, pp. 4–16) – are intrinsically valuable states and orientations of human life whose strength determines our human fulfilment, and which give rise to beliefs and behaviour in both morality and religion.

Our spiritual stance or character affects our spiritual vision of ourselves and our lives, other people and the natural world, and God. Who we are, and where and how we stand, determine how and what we see. As the eighteenth-century visionary, William Blake, put it, 'As a man is, so he sees. As the eye is formed, such are its powers.'

So we must never divorce Christian beliefs from their spiritual foundation, framework and perception.

Theological Formation

Where else does Christian belief and theology come from? What else has shaped it? Theologians sometimes refer to a 'three-legged stool' of Scripture, reason and tradition; or the 'Wesleyan Quadrilateral', which adds experience. Anglican theologian, John Macquarrie, listed the 'formative factors' in Christian theology under six headings (Macquarrie, 1977, pp. 4–18). He acknowledged that there are 'genuine tensions among the factors that go into the making of theology'. There are also several overlaps and complementarities between them.

- *Experience* ('of the life of faith') is listed first, but with a cautionary note about the problems caused by too exaggerated an emphasis on this element. The category covers not only explicitly religious experiences, but also the (more common) religious dimension of everyday experience.
- *Revelation* is listed second, but described as 'the primary source of theology'. It refers to a gift of God mediated through nature, history and other people; but pre-eminently through Jesus Christ. The Christian Church traces its origin to this classic or 'primordial' (that is, original) instance of revelation. For Macquarrie, 'revelation is a mode of religious experience'.
- *Scripture* is described as 'a kind of memory'. Macquarrie insists that it is 'not itself revelation, but it is one important way . . . by which the community of faith keeps open its access' to its primordial revelation.
- *Tradition* (the teaching and practice of the Church) is then added to the list, to be regarded as 'no rival to scripture but . . . its necessary complement'. Like Scripture, it is a bulwark against individualism.
- *Culture* is shorthand for a group's beliefs, values, experiences, expressions and activities, including its deep-rooted and often unquestioned assumptions. 'If theology is to be intelligible', Macquarrie argues, 'it has to use the language of the culture within which it is undertaken.' Culture is bound to mould our theology. Most theologians adopt the 'double movement' of the (Roman Catholic) Second Vatican Council (1962–5), by both going back to the sources and bringing the Church up-to-date.
- *Reason* is defined by the dictionary as 'the power of the mind to think, understand, and form judgements logically'. While theology often rejects speculative reason as a source or foundation for a 'rational religion', it uses human reason's ability to construct and systematize its ideas ('architectonic reason'), and to elucidate and correct them. Only with such help can Christianity claim to express a 'reasonable' system of beliefs.

EXERCISE

- How far have these six elements helped to create and give 'form' to your own religious beliefs? Why are some elements more important than others for *you*? For those who are raw recruits to academic theology, this may be a difficult exercise, even if you hold strong and clear Christian beliefs. This is because the categories are artificial and abstract, by contrast with the more personal influences of home, family, Church and significant life events. But please persevere! One of the purposes of the exercise is for you to uncover what *you* understand by these six factors.

- Try to score each element on a scale of 1 to 5, where 1 = 'no influence' and 5 = 'considerable influence'.
- Reflect on – and, if possible, discuss – your responses. If you can, compare your own ratings for each item against the range and average of the scores of a wider group.

As Macquarrie warned us, some of these formative factors are in tension with others. Indeed, the validity of certain members of his list has sometimes been denied.

Revelation versus Reason

Historically, the strongest opposition to reason has been directed at those who have identified 'pure reason' – that is, human reason without the benefit of God's help through revelation – as a *source* of religious truth. The medieval philosopher and theologian, Thomas Aquinas, distinguished between:

- those truths that are naturally knowable (provable) by human reason, often called truths 'according to reason'; and
- those that can only be known because God has disclosed them, truths that are 'above reason'.

The two categories overlap (area B in the diagram below). *Natural theology* is the label given to those religious truths – for example God's existence and the soul's immortality – that Aquinas claimed could be discovered by human reasoning, but which God had *also* revealed (for the sake of those who couldn't quite follow the arguments).

Truths revealed by God

A	B	C
e.g. doctrine of the Trinity ('Christian mysteries')	e.g. the existence of God	e.g. scientific truths

Truths 'above reason'   *Truths 'according to reason'*
                                        (can be proved by human reason alone)

In 1690, the English philosopher John Locke argued that even the 'Christian mysteries' (category A), which cannot be proved by reason, should only be accepted if we have *good reasons* to believe God has revealed them. (He thought that the evidence of miracles and fulfilled prophecy could give us such reasons, but not for the doctrine of the Trinity.) Thus reason judges revelation, and must be 'our last judge and guide in everything' (*Essay Concerning Human Understanding*, bk. 4, ch. xix). The Deists later ditched all these mysteries as 'superstitions', and treated revelation as superfluous to their 'religion of reason'.

While some theologians still support a version of a natural theology or 'general revelation',[1] many have followed Karl Barth, the Swiss Protestant theologian, in rejecting any hint that we can know God through our own efforts. According to Barth, only God's gracious gift of a unique revelation in Christ can provide this knowledge. This cannot be established or explained from any other source. Such a negative view of human reason, usually blamed on our human 'fallenness', tends to undermine any independent status for human rationality within theology. Reason will then be limited to the elucidation and illustration of the gospel, forbidding it any role in critically challenging religious knowledge from a non-revelational standpoint. On this view, the content of the gospel 'should not be measured by any other standards of what is possible than its own' (Barth, 1962, p. 849).

Criticizing Doctrine

Yet the adjective 'critical' is frequently used to describe the theological thinking of the academy. As a result, universities are often seen as enemies of Christian

---

1 Even Calvin did – though he thought it gave only enough truth to damn, and not to save.

belief. This is unfair. A 'critic' is simply one who makes a judgement (from the Greek *krites*, 'a judge'), which may be either positive or negative. A 'critical frame of mind' that results in a 'critique' involves nothing more than evaluating arguments, weighing evidence and making distinctions between concepts. The result is not always 'critical' in the sense of finding fault. But when critical reason does find fault it is usually justified in doing so – at least if we can trust human reason in this area. And, as human beings, it is hard *not* to trust our own reason.

Even so, criticism is never the final destination of theology. Paul Ricoeur suggests that we should not get 'stuck in the desert of criticism' (Ricoeur, 1967, p. 349). While our first encounter with a text is often naive and uncritical, it is frequently also a significant and 'holistic' (whole person) response. In reflective people, it naturally leads to the – sometimes painful – 'taking apart' of critical analysis and explanation. But we need eventually to *move on*, and to *return*. Critique and conviction must be combined, by revisiting the text and integrating it again (*appropriating* it) into our whole life. Only then will it be truly understood, not just as a truth 'one knows about, but something which one possesses and is possessed by' (McGrath, 1997, p. 78). This is the completion of the task of hermeneutics, 'as interpretation actualizes the meaning of the text for the present reader' – making what was previously 'foreign' to be 'one's own' again (Ricoeur, 1976, pp. 44, 74, 91–2).

Criticism, as 'corrective reason', is not restricted to an intellectual elite. I argued in the first chapter that ordinary (non-academic) theology must also have a reflective, critical dimension if it is to count as a type of theology. Reflection at this level already involves cognitive skills, processes and dispositions, even if they are not always as sharp or thoroughgoing as academic theology thinks they should be. Even to describe a belief or action as 'Christian' involves the exercise of critical theological judgement. Academic study of theology builds on this basic, reflective evaluation and thinking-for-oneself.

Nor is criticism solely limited to the cognitive domain. In ordinary theology, 'reflection' also involves imaginative skills and dispositions. Systematic theology, too, requires 'qualities of imagination and judgement in spiritual matters', in addition to the tools of the philosopher (Mitchell, 1991, p. 19). Good theological judgement, wherever it is found, thus goes beyond skills in logical argument and conceptual analysis.

Revelation versus Religious Experience

In addition to spurning natural theology, Barth also rejected liberal approaches to religious knowledge that located it in our natural capacity for religious experience. Friedrich Schleiermacher identified the individual's experience of God as the primary datum of religion, describing it as a 'sense and taste for the infinite', a 'feeling of absolute dependence' and 'God-consciousness'. Although he believed religious experience was shaped by belief and practice, doctrine was something secondary to and derivative from this experience: Christian doctrines were 'accounts of the Christian religious affections set forth in speech' (Schleiermacher, 1928, p. 76). This 'subjective' theology progresses 'from below up'; moving in quite the opposite direction from Barth's downward theological method, in which knowledge of God is objectively revealed 'from above'.

It is important to say that Schleiermacher understood religious experience mainly as a direct experience *of* God, as in prophetic and mystical encounters with the divine, rather than as a set of 'subjective experiences' or feelings (confidence, acceptance, joy) from which the existence and action of God may be inferred. Understood in the first way, revelation and religious experience are correlates – the one implies the other. God's activity can only function as a revelation, an 'unveiling', if and when someone experiences this – either by 'hearing' a divinely authenticated *truth about God* (a 'propositional revelation'), or by 'seeing' *God's activity* in nature or in human affairs (as a 'non-propositional revelation' that is only later expressed in truths). Revelation is 'nothing apart from human apprehension of it' (Tanner, 1997, p. 266).

Of course, the independent role of human religious experience is lost if God wholly takes over the cognitive and interpretative faculties of human beings. This is the position taken by those fundamentalists who picture the biblical authors as inerrantly recording God's truths (*inerrant* means 'incapable of error'; see below). But there is no need to view matters in this way. Biblical authors may be seen as human, and therefore fallible and sinful, recipients of God's message, activity or encounter. Scripture will then include human theological interpretation in response to God's revelation.

Barth was no fundamentalist, incidentally. For him, the Bible is not in itself the Word of God, a 'deposit' of 'truths of revelation'. It is a hidden revelation that can only be seen with the eyes of faith. The fallible, uncertain Bible – 'a human document like any other' (Barth, 1928, p. 60) – only *becomes* the Word of God as and when God allows people to hear him in these Scriptures. 'The miracle which has to take place if the Bible is to rise up and speak to us as the Word of God has always to consist in an awakening and strengthening of our faith' (Barth, 1956a, p. 512). Everything is all still God's work, rather than the active product of human experience or human reason alone. This is Barth's slant on the famous principle, 'through God alone can God be known'.

The category of experience may be understood in a wider sense, however, as something 'lived through for oneself'. And on that interpretation, it is hard to disagree with Luther's claim that 'only experience makes a theologian'; and tempting to extend the category to include the experience of any 'inner witness' of the Holy Spirit that authenticates Scripture.

Scripture and Tradition

Roman Catholic and Orthodox thinking allows great authority to tradition (from the Latin *tradere*, 'to hand on'). This is the publicly transmitted (and, therefore, not secret) teaching and practice of the Christian faith that their churches have passed down the generations. Alongside Scripture – but normally not exalted above it – tradition is here regarded as another medium of God's revelation, since the Church's thinking is itself understood to be permeated and led by the Holy Spirit.[2] Tradition has been described as that faith 'which has been believed everywhere, always and by all' (Vincent of Lérins); and, more modestly, as the 'persistent, public expressions of the faith through which that faith is not merely preserved but actively transmitted' (Norris, 1979, p. 8).

However, the Reformation claimed that God's revelation is to be found in 'Scripture alone', which is therefore 'the sole rule and norm of all doctrine' (*Formula of Concord*). This is taken by extreme Protestants as grounds for criticizing more mainstream Protestant denominations for not jettisoning the entire 'Catholic baggage' of non-biblical liturgies, practices and formularies. 'The Bible is not only supreme but *sufficient*. Add to what is complete and you take from it.' Arthur Wallis's preference is therefore for a 'pure Christianity' that rejects all Church traditions, on the grounds that they 'tend to obscure or nullify the

---

2 In the sixteenth century, however, the Catholic Council of Trent defined tradition as Jesus' unwritten teaching passed on by the apostles. (Scholars also speak more generally of a 'religious tradition' as *anything* that is passed on, including Scriptures.)

word of God', by restricting the flow of the Holy Spirit and preventing Christian maturity (Wallis, 1981, pp. 109, 119).

It is, of course, true that Luther's churches retained much of the Catholic Mass, and that both Luther and Calvin took over the creeds and accepted many dogmatic decisions of the ancient Church – while rejecting the infallibility of its councils. Anglicanism, too, hung on to those parts of tradition that it regarded as 'agreeable to Scripture', and venerated the writings of the Fathers.

But 'restorationist' critics of tradition are wrong to think that there is *any* Christian worshipping fellowship with a lasting identity that is without some tradition. 'Even those who have attempted to exist without tradition have only succeeded in establishing a tradition of dispensing with tradition' (Hanson, 1983, p. 574). In many ways, tradition is *prior to* Scripture.

1 'Oral tradition' (stories passed on by word of mouth) pre-dates written tradition. It is like a chemical 'solution', out of which our biblical books later 'crystallized' or 'precipitated'.

2 The Bible is the Church's book in the sense that it is the Church that decides, and then passes on, the list of authoritative writings ('canon') that constitute the Scriptures.

3 Doctrines about the authority of Scripture exist as a part of tradition. The inerrancy of Scripture cannot just be 'found' in such (late) biblical texts as 2 Timothy 3.16 or 2 Peter 1.21. The fundamentalist must already have a tradition that encourages him or her both to trust these texts, and to interpret them in a particular way.[3] Alister McGrath asserts that the Reformers had no problem with the medieval notion of tradition, because it was not then viewed as a source of revelation in addition to Scripture, but as a 'manner of *interpreting* scripture and transmitting the *kerygma* [gospel proclamation] which it contains' (McGrath, 1997, p. 173).

4 Tradition also provides the necessary 'spectacles' for reading Scripture more generally – including the tools for selecting from it, explaining and interpreting it, interrogating it, relating one part to another, relating it to other knowledge and applying it to life. Logically, no book can contain within itself its own interpretation. It is *people* who read and interpret what a book says, and it is the Church that interprets Scripture. 'Every reading of the Bible

---

3 'Many central biblical passages do not mean what the tradition of fundamentalist interpretation has taken them to mean' (Barr, 1984, p. 174).

is an *ecclesial* reading, in which the reader is never a solitary individual but is formed in particular virtues and animated by the life of the reading community' (Cunningham, 1998, p. 140). And this community is the community of the Holy Spirit, in which Scripture can be read 'through the same Spirit whereby it was written' (Thomas à Kempis, John Wesley). In Eastern Orthodoxy, priority is given to finding the meaning of Scripture within the framework of worship, 'understanding words as summons, and as icons that open us up to reality' (Zizioulas, 2008, p. 159).

When the Church decided which Christian writings it considered sacred enough to read and expound in public worship, some texts didn't make the list. Although the limits of the canon remained fluid until the fourth century, most of the books we have in our present Bibles were regarded as 'inspired' by the middle of the second century. This is in marked contrast to the view of Marcion (died 160), who discarded all of the Old Testament and much of the New, arguing that the Old Testament God had nothing to do with the God of Jesus Christ.

Throughout the period of early, medieval and early Reformation Christianity, inspiration (Latin *in* + *spirare*, 'to breathe') was understood as an extra supernatural gift of the divine Spirit to the authors of Scripture. But it was not thought to have suppressed human error or interpretation. Many valued figurative (allegorical) and typological, as well as literal-historical, interpretations; or allowed that God 'accommodates' his revelation to the limitations of human understanding. The view of *verbal inspiration*, that divine inspiration has determined the exact wording of the text (usually regarded as inerrant), only arose in the late nineteenth century among Protestants, becoming dominant in Catholicism even later.

Today, while the 'inspiration' of Scripture is accepted by most Christians, it is understood in a wide variety of different ways: from the 'mechanical dictation' model at one extreme, to an 'inspired-because-it-is-inspiring' understanding at the other (with God 'illuminating' the writers' minds). In between lie interpretations of inspiration that allow the biblical authors different degrees of influence.

God speaks to us in a manner congruous with the Incarnation itself, through human words and human minds conditioned by the circumstances of place and time, subject to our ordinary limitations. They are human minds peculiarly able, as our experience and the collective experience of the Church can testify, to discern the true spiritual significance of history, which is to say that they are inspired: but they are none the less liable to error and ignorance. There is no mechanical inspiration of the words they use. (Lampe, 1963, p. 142)

This metaphor of incarnation ('enfleshing') resonates with the wide theological theme that we hold all our divine treasure 'in clay jars' (2 Cor. 4.7). Liberal understandings of inspiration accept that God was in contact with people in the formation of the biblical tradition, but often claim that 'the mode of this contact was not different from the mode in which God has continued to make himself known' (Barr, 1973, p. 18). Scripture is special; but it is not totally different in kind from any other medium of revelation.

Doctrine and the Bible

When Christians sometimes try to use the Bible as a doctrinal textbook, academic theologians respond that belief cannot be simply 'read off' Scripture.

- Biblical material is made up of many different traditions woven together. One of the difficulties in deriving 'a doctrine' from the Bible is that these different strands give rise to different doctrinal positions.
- The Bible is more a practical book of religious poetry than it is a theoretical textbook of theological prose. Hence the confessions, stories, hymns and parables of the Bible – with their riotous mixture of images – have to be sifted, qualified, sharpened, interpreted and ordered to produce consistent, systematic doctrine (Chapter 3).
- The hermeneutical principle implies that most Christians come to the Bible wearing doctrinal spectacles of some form or another, which lead them to view it in particular ways. These spectacles will have been manufactured using material drawn from the Bible itself. But other factors must also have contributed, including the Christians' own religious experiences, the tradition of their Church, the culture they live in, and their reasoning processes and beliefs.

The Church has always been engaged in a dance with the Bible, sometimes holding her very close while at other times they hardly touch. Although the Bible is certainly one very important source of theology, it is *not* a basic introduction to Christian theology. 'Christianity is a process to which parts of the Bible contributed, but is not itself the product of the Bible' (Carroll, 1997, p. 72). (And we need to be cautious of appeals to a doctrinally selective 'biblical Christianity', which never existed.) Although this Studyguide contains many references to Scripture (which you should find and read!), these are not intended as premises in an argument. Scripture will always form *part* of theology's raw material, even if only as 'a supplier of images, metaphors and a pool of insightful phrases' (Carroll, 1997, p. 62) – and of striking narratives too. But for many Christians, Scripture is more normative than that. They will want somehow to test all doctrine against the (many and varied) criteria implicit in Scripture.

EXERCISE

In reality, how *do* you understand the 'authority of Scripture'? How does your view affect your approach to Christian doctrine, and to the other 'formative factors' of your theology?

The Scripture Spectrum

If we were to draw a spectrum of attitudes to the Bible, *fundamentalism* would appear at the extreme ('right wing'?) end. For fundamentalists, as the Bible is inspired by God it can contain no errors – or at least its original 'autograph' manuscripts cannot. Most critical historical study of the Bible is therefore rejected. (Fundamentalists do not hold that all parts of the Bible are *literally* true, which is an impossible view to take of references to the 'hand' of God or Jesus as a 'vine'.)

Fundamentalism is the limiting case of the much broader *conservative* position, which also takes a high view of the authority and trustworthiness of the Bible,[4] but refuses to describe it as 'inerrant' – particularly in its science.

---

4 In moral and theological matters certainly, but often when it makes claims about history too.

Liberals appear to the left of conservatives in the spectrum. They are less sure of the trustworthiness of the Bible across a wider range of topics, while accepting its general authority – and often its centrality – for Christian believers. Beyond the liberals lie *radicals* (sometimes called 'modernists'), who adopt a highly relativist view of the meaning and truth of Scripture, and are willing to dispense with large parts of both Old and New Testaments in constructing their doctrinal systems. Dennis Nineham did not go quite that far, arguing that 'we can never dispense with, or replace, the New Testament story'; but he maintained that 'there is nothing properly described as "*the* meaning" of the Bible, no fixed quantum of truth which it contains, and which we have only to take over as it stands' (Nineham, 1976, pp. 223, 262).

David Kelsey (Kelsey, 1975, 1999) offers us a more detailed analysis of how many modern theologians have used Scripture. (You might try to plot your own view of Scripture on this spectrum.)

1 Scripture as containing inspired, inerrant *doctrine*. (Fundamentalism, for example, Benjamin Warfield.)
2 Scripture as containing inspired, authoritative *concepts*: one variant of 'biblical theology'.
3 Scripture as the recital of *salvation history*. This is the view of those biblical theologians for whom the Bible is the book of the 'acts of God in history'.

These three ('conservative') uses of Scripture treat it as authoritative by virtue of its *content*, although only (1) focuses on the actual words of Scripture. The other two categories direct our attention to something 'critically reconstructed from the writings, namely, a system of technical concepts or a set of distinctive events' (Farley and Hodgson, 2008, p. 78). Positions (2) and (3) are therefore more open to critical historical study. All three positions assume that the role of theology is that of *translating and citing the content* of Scripture.

4 A 'mediating' position regards Scripture as the (human, fallible) *medium through which God may disclose himself in his Word.* Here the text is not authoritative by virtue of its content, but only because of the way it functions as the medium for a new encounter with Christ. This is Karl Barth's view – Scripture is 'inspired' in that it can become the occasion of a new revelation.

The next three ('liberal') interpretations treat Scripture as authoritative because of its power to express past revelatory events, and give rise to new occasions of revelation and salvation. For types (5) to (7), theology has the task of *redescribing in contemporary thought-forms* (not directly translating) what was expressed in the Bible in its own language. (All insist that the Bible should be studied critically.)

5 Scripture as expressing past revelation and occasioning a present revelation through *poetic images* (as in Austin Farrer).
6 Scripture as expressing past revelation and occasioning a present revelation through *religious symbols* (as in Paul Tillich).
7 Scripture as expressing past revelation and occasioning a present revelation through *kerygmatic statements* of the proclamation of faith, such as 'Christ is risen' (as in Rudolf Bultmann).

Kelsey argues that a great variety of theologians (including Barth) adopt a *functional* view of Scripture. 'Biblical texts are taken as "scripture" in virtue of their *doing* something'. In particular, they so transform people's identities that they are:

'redeemed' by being drawn into salvation-history or by being placed in the presence of the redeeming agent; by personally appropriating beliefs, or concepts, or images in such a way that they are made new [people]; or by being brought to 'authenticity' or 'new being'. (Kelsey, 1975, pp. 90–1)

Treating the Bible in terms of how it works is illuminating. If taken to extremes, however, Scripture can become merely a medium or catalyst for our contemporary discernment, inspiration or understanding. The particular nature or original meaning of the Bible may then be treated as a matter of no real significance. For many Christians, such a view is too relativistic and not sufficiently authoritative.

Even liberal theologians admit that we can still find great value in the 'scripture principle' (treating the Bible *as* authoritative Scripture). Not only does it create in us a respect for antiquity and a focus for the community, it also offers us an escape from our subjectivity and a witness to the 'over-against-ness' of God (Maurice Wiles). While supporting the 'necessity and centrality of scripture', however, many will insist on a *distinction between scriptural traditions and revelation itself.*

The Creeds

Christians have for a very long time used summaries of their beliefs. But creeds (from the Latin *credo*, 'I believe') have never been merely statements of doctrine. The *Apostles' Creed* is the common creed of Western Christianity. Certainly not composed by the apostles (as later legend claimed), it probably originated in second-century Rome. It was used within the baptism service when candidates actively committed themselves to God in faith, and as a basis for their previous instruction. Its present form dates back to the eighth century. The more universal *Nicene Creed* was also originally based on a baptismal creed, this time from Jerusalem, and therefore originates from the Eastern branch of the Church. It was adapted by the great councils of the Church at Nicaea (325) and Constantinople (381) as a test of the orthodoxy of Church leaders. After the fifth century, the Nicene Creed began to be used as a medium for praising God in eucharistic worship in the East, a practice that eventually spread to the medieval Western Church.

The wording of the creeds, particularly the 'conciliar' (from 'council') Nicene Creed, distinguished *orthodoxy* from *heresy* (from the Greek word for 'choice'). The orthodox (with a small 'o', literally those 'right in opinion') were the winners in the debates. As the Nicene Creed also met the concerns of Christian emperors who desired a united Church for political reasons, the creeds were inevitably 'the children of their age'. Nevertheless:

> Important as ecclesiastical and political pressures were, the credal forms adopted were not simply imposed from above. They grew out of the church's continuing attempt to articulate the faith more clearly for its work of teaching and preaching. Despite the outside pressures and internal rivalries that influenced the councils at which they were formally adopted, they were also the fruit of devoted study, reflection and prayer. (Wiles, 1999, p. 28)

Two Creeds

Nicene Creed

We believe in one God,
the Father, the Almighty,
maker of heaven and earth,
of all that is,
seen and unseen.

We believe in one Lord, Jesus
    Christ,
the only Son of God,
eternally begotten of the Father,
God from God, Light from Light,
true God from true God,
begotten, not made,
of one Being with the Father;
through him all things were made.
For us and for our salvation he
    came down from heaven,
was incarnate from the Holy Spirit
    and the Virgin Mary
and was made man.
For our sake he was crucified under
    Pontius Pilate;
he suffered death and was buried.
On the third day he rose again
in accordance with the Scriptures;
he ascended into heaven
and is seated at the right hand of
    the Father.
He will come again in glory to judge
    the living and the dead,
and his kingdom will have no end.

Apostles' Creed

I believe in God, the Father almighty,
creator of heaven and earth.

I believe in Jesus Christ, his only Son,
    our Lord,
who was conceived by the Holy Spirit,
born of the Virgin Mary,
suffered under Pontius Pilate,
was crucified, died, and was buried;
he descended to the dead.
On the third day he rose again;
he ascended into heaven,
he is seated at the right hand of the
    Father,
and he will come to judge the living
    and the dead.

I believe in the Holy Spirit,
the holy catholic Church,
the communion of saints,
the forgiveness of sins,
the resurrection of the body,
and the life everlasting.
Amen.

We believe in the Holy Spirit,
the Lord, the giver of life,
who proceeds from the Father and
 the Son,
who with the Father and the Son is
 worshipped and glorified,
who has spoken through the
 prophets.
We believe in one holy catholic and
 apostolic Church.
We acknowledge one baptism for
 the forgiveness of sins.
We look for the resurrection of the
 dead,
and the life of the world to come.
Amen.

Translation: *English Language Liturgical Consultation* © ELLC 1988

EXERCISE

- What main *differences* do you detect between the two creeds, and what is their likely significance?
- Note any elements that (a) you think were never intended to be understood literally; (b) that were intended literally but you don't take that way; and (c) you find difficult to believe without considerable reinterpretation.

The Apostles' Creed seems much the more straightforward text (it was originally much briefer, perhaps only three lines long), and reads as an individual testimony; whereas the Nicene Creed looks more like a corporate confession, but written by a committee.

They are both highly selective. Practically nothing is said, for example, about the content of Jesus' ministry and message;[5] and while the Eastern creed articu-

---

5 The tendency to take Jesus' life and teaching for granted, and concentrate on the gospel *about him*,

lates in detail the pre-existent divine status of Jesus Christ, the Western creed only refers to his virgin birth. Nothing is said about the doctrines of justification, the Eucharist or ministry. But many summaries of religions concentrate on what is distinctive and 'orthodox' about their beliefs, rather than other features that may feel more important to many religious adherents.

Culture Wars?

Theology has always had an uneasy partnership with society's habitual ways of thinking and seeing, and the values of the changing cultures that have served as Christian faith's living context down the ages. Inevitably, many of the dominant ideas and values of a society, its period and place, are incorporated into its theology. But others are resisted as representing a world-view opposed to the current understanding of the 'culture of Christianity'. In our own day, Christians sometimes see themselves as in a state of siege against a secular ('worldly', 'not sacred') culture, marked by attitudes to religion ranging from indifferent to militantly atheistic.

Richard Niebuhr (1952, pp. 53–7) distinguished five different attitudes towards culture.

1 *Christ against culture* marks a sense of opposition between the claims of Christ and the dominant culture. Tertullian (*c.*160–225), one of the founding fathers of Latin theology, countered the ridicule with which his philosophical contemporaries treated Christianity with the question: 'What has Athens to do with Jerusalem?'
2 The *Christ of culture* perspective takes a diametrically opposite stance, wholly embracing culture and treating Christianity as its fulfilment. It is exemplified by Abelard in the Middle Ages, and by Schleiermacher and liberal theology in general in the nineteenth and twentieth centuries.
3 *Christ above culture* distinguishes the spirit of Christ from the spirit of the age, but regards them as complementary and seeks some form of synthesis between them, for 'streams flow from all sides' into the 'perennial river' of

---

may be traced back to our earliest versions of Christian theology in the letters of Paul and the speech of Peter at Pentecost (Acts 2.22–36).

truth (Clement of Alexandria). Thomas Aquinas adopted this position, as did the Anglicans Richard Hooker and Joseph Butler.

4 Proponents of a view of *Christ and culture in paradox*, while sympathetic to position (1), tend to be more realistic in accepting their inescapable involvement in human culture *as well as* Christian faith. The two realms are held in an uneasy tension. Paul, Luther and Søren Kierkegaard are exemplars.

5 Augustine and Calvin share the 'conversionist' view of *Christ as the transformer of culture*, believing that culture can be and must be radically reformed or regenerated.

EXERCISE

Which of these positions are you most likely to adopt? How would you justify it?

Faith and Belief

What do you understand by the word 'faith'? The phrase '*the* Christian faith' refers to the Christian religion or (more often) its teachings, especially its beliefs and values. It may be thought of as the *object or content of faith*, where 'faith' is now understood as a *human activity* – part of our relationship with God and Christ. In this second sense, faith consists of a human orientation, assent and commitment. It is what is meant by the credal phrase, 'I/We believe in'.

Belief-in and Belief-that

Although we often use the two terms synonymously, 'belief-in' involves much more than 'believing-that' something (God or Christ) exists, or that some other doctrine is a fact. The key additional elements are:

- a positive evaluation (we are 'for' God, regarding God as possessing supreme worth);

- an attitude of trust; and
- commitment to God and active obedience to the will of God.

Believing *that* God exists is quite compatible with possessing none of the above. Believing-in is believing-that with attitude, and consequent actions. It involves forging a relationship with God. Unfortunately, believing-that is often the state of mind tested by surveys that ask the general public whether they 'believe in God' or not. (We use the phrase in this way when we talk about believing 'in' ghosts.) This important distinction is not always obvious from the language used in the New Testament either. Yet if faith is belief-in, then *faith is much more than factual belief.*

Although 'even the demons believe' that there is one God (James 2.19), this is not enough to make them believers *in* God. They do not deny God's existence; but they will not go so far as to worship him or to engage in the works of faith. Similar distinctions apply to other objects of faith. (Hence, in the old joke, the grumpy interviewee asks rhetorically, 'Do I believe in baptism? Dammit, I've seen it done.' See also pp. 88, 94–5 and Chapter 8.)

All the same, many Christians have used the word 'faith' as if it *were* identical to belief-that. Aquinas did so, treating faith as the intellectual conviction of believing *what* God has revealed – a willed assent to theological truths. When Luther insisted on the Pauline concept of faith, as personal commitment to and trust in God himself, Catholics and Protestants had something to argue about (see Chapter 6). But it was mainly a semantic argument, a dispute over the meaning of words. The Protestant conception of faith certainly involves or implies the conviction that God exists, and has a particular nature. And Catholic theology does not deny the importance of our relating to God in a loving and trusting, worshipful and adoring manner: for Aquinas, assent was completed and formed by love. In both traditions, then, faith is at base the most complete form of 'saying "amen" to what God speaks' (Immink, 2005, p. 245), and to whom God is.

Other Interpretations

Faith as an activity or process has also been interpreted in more radical ways, so that faith as 'belief-in' does *not* imply a 'belief-that' claim about God's existence.

For those who interpret religion *non-cognitively* (that is, as not asserting truths about God or an afterlife), faith takes the place of God – since on this view, God is no more than a symbol representing a human orientation and commitment. This is usually described as a *non-realist* view of God, in which 'God is the role God plays in developing our self-understanding, focussing our aspirations, and shaping the course of our lives' (Cupitt, 1986, p. 103; see Chapter 3).

John Hick has a very different understanding of faith, using the word to label the interpretative element within religious experience – by which we experience the world *as* God's world, 'life as divinely created and ourselves as living in the unseen presence of God' (Hick, 1983, p. 47). Faith construed in this way is a perspective on the world, an interpretative vision that enables some to discern *the deeper meaning* of what everyone can plainly see before their face. This disposition to interpret life with the eyes and ideas of faith is an additional attitude-component of faith (see above).

Fleshing out Faith

Both Catholic and Protestant theology hold that the assistance of God's grace is essential to the believer's faith; faith is therefore a 'supernatural act'. But faith is also a *free* human response. Theology often has to balance human and divine activity in this way. As *belief-in* is partly under our control, many argue that 'unfaith' may be regarded as sinful. If intellectual assent (*belief-that*) is *not* under our direct control, however, 'honest doubt' cannot be blameworthy. (If you think I am reliable, you *should* trust me. But you can't directly control your belief about my reliability.)

The idea that believers must rely on faith quite apart from *reason* is called 'fideism'. This is faith that is wholly beyond reason. The term has been wrongly applied to many thinkers who are simply rejecting *narrow* understandings of reason. Faith goes 'beyond reason' only in the sense that it builds on, but does not contradict, what we otherwise know to be true. It goes beyond what is known (or 'seen' – cf. 2 Cor. 5.7; Heb. 11.1), and beyond what we can prove or what can be proved. But most theologians think it does not do so in blind trust, ignoring evidence and argument. Faith is never exactly a 'leap in the dark', then, but a leap across to somewhere that isn't as brightly lit as the jumping-off point.

Such 'going beyond' what is known is something that happens daily, whenever we trust the promises of a friend or a lover, a train driver or airline pilot; or any 'authority' whose knowledge, skill and insight exceed our own.

Suggestions for Further Reading

Introductory

McGrath, A. E., 2007, *Christian Theology: An Introduction*, Oxford: Blackwell, part II.

Pattison, G., 2005, *A Short Course on Christian Doctrine*, London: SCM Press, chs 5 and 6.

Strange, W., 2000, *The Authority of the Bible*, London: Darton, Longman & Todd.

Advanced

Avis, P. (ed.), 1997, *Divine Revelation*, London: Darton, Longman & Todd.

McGrath, A. E., 1990, *The Origin of Doctrine: A Study in the Foundations of Doctrinal Criticism*, Grand Rapids, MI: Eerdmans.

Pinnock, C. H. with Callen, B. L., 2006, *The Scripture Principle: Reclaiming the Full Authority of the Bible,* Grand Rapids, MI: Baker Academic.

3

Attempting God-Talk: Exploring Divine Discourse

The Spectrum of Religious Language

We won't progress very far in our study of doctrine if we do not first explore the nature and purposes of religious language. I am using 'religious language' here in a very wide sense, to include *both* the language of prayer, worship, Scripture and ordinary religious expression; *and* the more conceptually developed and often technical discourse of academic theology, and of many forms of official ecclesiastical theology. People sometimes distinguish these two categories by labelling them *religious language* and *theological language*. But in exploring doctrine, I think we must always think of scholarly theology within the wider context of religion.

It is also important to acknowledge a broad spectrum or continuum of language that allows the possibility of intermediate forms, rather than two discrete and separate species. In the case of such a spectrum, it would be natural to place at one end examples of direct expressions of religious experience and devotion. These represent the *primary* language of living faith. It includes believers' talk to God in prayer, as well as the 'celebratory theology' of much preaching, hymnody and choruses (Williams, 2000, pp. xiii–xiv). 'Communion with God, symbolically focused in liturgy, is the primary focus of religious language for the Christian' (Wainwright, 1980, pp. 20–1). Hans Urs von Balthasar has described this broad area as 'theology at prayer', in distinction from the 'theology at the desk' of the academic theologian (von Balthasar, 1989, p. 208). That second type of theology would be located at the other extreme of the continuum or end of the spectrum – and may be thought of as *second-order* talk about God. Although less personal than the primary language of faith, it has the advantage of being more conceptually precise, consistent and critically reflective. I would place what I called 'ordinary theology' (Chapter 1) nearer to primary religious discourse, for it lies closer to its religious roots than does academic theology. (Ordinary theology is an especially spiritual species of theology.) So this spectrum stretches between (a) the poetic and story language of Scripture, piety and worship, with the autobiographical, anecdotal and figurative discourse of ordinary theology, at one end; and (b) the 'more prosaic' academic theology, whose language is systematic and consistent, and employs carefully defined concepts, at the other.

Many churchgoers distrust the language of doctrine, particularly the abstract, theologically enhanced God-talk of academic theology. They sense that it will take them away from the concrete experiences of prayer, worship and the life of faith. They are often right. But some real advantages come from creating a more conceptual theology, with its greater clarity of ideas and argument. It is important, however, to keep tracing the connections between the primary and secondary forms of religious discourse, as well as recognizing the underlying spectrum on which *both* are located.

Ludwig Wittgenstein insisted that language is best – perhaps only – understood as 'part of an activity, or of a form of life' (Wittgenstein, 1968, §23), by which he probably meant a natural, almost instinctive way of *behaving*. Philosophers should not legislate in advance what the rules of any particular type of language, or 'language game', should be. Rather, they should explore the real world and discover *how language is actually used*, and therefore what it really means; for it is our acting that 'lies at the bottom of our language-game' (Wittgenstein, 1974, p. 204).

This is evidently true in the field or practice of religion. The different religious language games are sometimes played according to rules – their deep 'grammar' – that are different from those we find in science, history or philosophy. If the meaning of religious belief is grounded in religious behaviour, 'we actually have to *look* at how our language about God works, how it is used, if we are to get any real understanding of what it is [for example] for God to be a person, an agent' (Moore, 1988, p. 102). And this includes looking closely, seriously and intelligently at the religious life *in which* this language is spoken.

At its root, then, all religious language is earthed in the expression of religious faith. It therefore needs to retain some connection to, and must at the last be interpreted in terms of, that context. A major danger for doctrinal theology is that of losing touch with its spiritual and practical religious roots, so that it becomes only a 'theoretical understanding of the nature of God'. For then doctrines turn into 'speculative exercises . . . rather than ways of understanding the meaning and significance of our lives in relation to God'.

> What we need to say about God is therefore limited to the constitutive presuppositions of [the assumptions that underlie] our spirituality and our concrete life of fellowship with God. . . . The existential nature of our God-talk therefore excludes mere intellectual speculation about how God is apart from the way we relate to him in our spirituality and in the life of faith. (Brümmer, 2005, pp. 12, 17)[1]

When our doctrine becomes disconnected from the ways we relate to and respond to God in our attitudes and actions, *or* from the ways in which we believe God relates to us, we become unsure what existential relevance it any longer has for our lives. Without this link with our human faith and practice, theology becomes bad news: *irrelevant* (and, sometimes, spiritually misleading) speculation.

What Use is Religious Language?

In analysing religious words, then, what matters is 'the difference they make at various points in your life', as '*practice* gives the words their sense' (Wittgenstein, 1980, p. 85). So we find the meaning of religious language in the way it is used. But what use is religious language?

---

1 *Existential* here refers to real life. The word means something like 'relating to our human concerns and immediate lived experience', in the ever-changing circumstances of our free (but finite), individual and concrete human existence.

Making Statements about God

In the area of doctrine, of course, it is mainly used to talk *about* (or *of*) God, and God's activity. We shall explore this usage in some detail shortly (pp. 51–8). It is important to glance first, however, at the range of *other things* that religious language can do, *in addition to* describing God.

Providing Rules for God-talk

Religious language that appears to be making direct statements about God may sometimes be working at a different level, by *providing rules* for making statements about God – 'rules for consistent and adequate discourse' (Ramsey, 1963, p. 38). This analysis of *talk about* talk about God has been applied to the doctrines of the person of Christ (where the rule might be, 'use both human and divine language when talking of Jesus Christ') and the Holy Trinity ('in speaking of God, use Father-language, Son-language and Spirit-language'). George Lindbeck argued that we should always interpret doctrine, *when it is functioning as doctrine*, as doing no more than providing the rules or 'grammar' for regulating Christian discourse. Its function is 'to recommend and exclude certain ranges of [beliefs]' (Lindbeck, 1984, pp. 19, 80).

While this can be a useful way of analysing certain doctrines, it is hard to see how these rules could be justified, except by claiming that the theology they sanction adequately *represents* the nature and activity of God. At some stage we must attempt a description of God.

But religious language, like all language, has other functions – to ask questions, issue commands, make requests or express feelings. These are also *non-cognitive* uses: they do not directly assert or deny facts, as do statements or assertions (*cognitive* language). In its cognitive uses, language may be judged either true or false; but that distinction doesn't apply to its non-cognitive functions. I list below more religious 'speech-acts' that do things other than making statements.

Expressing Attitudes, Feelings or Beliefs about God

When I say, 'I feel bored' or 'My soul thirsts for God', I am not engaged in auto-biographical self-description. Rather, I am *giving voice* to my 'affects' – my feelings, emotions or desires. In prayer and worship, Christians speak to God by expressing their adoration, thankfulness, penitence, concern for others (and themselves), and many other spiritual and psychological states of their hearts and minds.

Sometimes the language of worship can be 'expressive' in this way, even though the worshippers utter words or phrases that make no sense in their own language. This is the case with 'speaking with tongues' (*glossolalia*) in Pentecostal and charismatic worship. At other times, the words may sound like descriptions (of God, heaven, or the worshippers' sinfulness), but their main force is to express the believer's attitudes towards the 'holy God' whose glory fills 'heaven and earth', or towards their own sins (about which, presumably, God does not need to be informed). This sort of 'expressive force' is also carried by many of the examples characterized below under other forms of linguistic action. (The same words often do more than one thing.)

Committing Oneself to God and Others

'I believe in God', 'I turn to Christ', 'I bind unto myself today the strong name of the Trinity', 'I take you to be my husband/wife' are all *acts of commission* performed by using words. In speaking the words of the creed, we enter into a relationship with God, Father, Son and Spirit. '"I believe in God …" both says this connection and makes it' (Norris, 1979, p. 19). Other examples in this category include making a religious vow to God, or a promise to another person. In all such examples we are not just expressing a view or a feeling; we are entering into a connection, an exchange, a relationship. Old Testament theology is largely concerned with God's covenant agreement with his people, a commitment into which they had freely entered but which they repeatedly broke (Gen. 17.1–8; Ex. 34.10, 27–28; Deut. 4.31, 29.10–15; Josh. 24.14–28; Hos. 8.1–3; 11.1–9).

Making Requests to God or Commands to Others

'Forgive us our trespasses', 'O Lord, have mercy on us' and even 'O Come, O Come Emmanuel' are all *prayerful requests* to God. They ask that God might behave in a particular way and/or adopt a particular attitude towards us. Much of our confession, petition (prayer for ourselves) and intercession (prayer for others) is like this. Liturgical and moral *imperatives* ('orders' or 'biddings') include 'Let us pray', 'Go in peace to love and serve the Lord', 'Be imitators of me as I am of Christ', 'Love your enemies and pray for those who persecute you' and 'Let the same mind be in you that was in Christ Jesus'. This category also includes the *commandments and ordinances* that form part of God's covenant.

Evoking an Experience/Revelation of God

According to Ian Ramsey, many forms of religious language have the power to evoke a religious experience (what he called a 'discernment') and revelation (a 'disclosure') of the divine mystery. That mystery can then be represented by these same words. Much language of prayer and worship seems to operate in this way, as religious language takes us into 'a moment of vision, a moment of silence where God discloses himself' (Ramsey, 1971, p. 21). According to Ramsey, however, the process also works for the narratives, poetry and reflections of Scripture, for Christian hymnody – and even for doctrinal theology. All theology is anchored in 'a characteristically religious situation – one of worship, wonder, awe' (Ramsey, 1957, p. 89).

This might happen when language is brought alongside our experience: when we think of 'fathers' (or 'mothers') as we witness the world's gratuitous bounty, or see our own life as a 'gift'. Another way is when the little words of theology, such as 'infinitely', 'heavenly' or 'eternal' (Ramsey calls them *qualifiers*) are placed before 'good', 'Father' or 'rock', so as to form phrases like 'heavenly Father' or 'infinitely good'. This alters the meaning of these 'models' (see pp. 55–6), 'qualifying the analogy' in a particular direction. However, Ramsey believed that qualifiers also generate in our imagination a series of (for example) people of increasing degrees of goodness, or fathers of various kinds. Through this process we may come not only to an intuitive grasp of the meaning of 'infinite goodness' or 'heavenly Father', but also have an experience of the divine object which this language can now (partially) represent. Our God-talk will then have evoked a disclosure of the creator, revealed not as the last term of any series but as a different sort of good Father altogether.

Significance for Doctrine

You may wonder what relevance many of these non-cognitive uses of religious language have for *doctrine*; especially as I have limited it to propositional talk about God, together with rules for regulating such theological statements.

First, these other forms of religious discourse are important components of the larger whole of Christian existence, which is the *context in which doctrinal statements are set*. It is a profound mistake to ignore this practical and existential context of doctrine, for that would be to deny the heart in it. 'Receiving the gospel is not a matter of having brains but of free personal response where imagination, thought and emotion are integrated' (Tinsley, 1996, p. 94). We must acknowledge again that doctrine is no more than a part – the cognitive, conceptual part – of the more richly variegated, affect-laden and affect-driven whole that represents the concrete, individual and corporate expression of Christianity (see Chapter 1).

> It is because people exult and lament, sing for joy, bewail their sins and so on, that they are able, eventually, to have thoughts about God. Worship is not the result but the precondition for believing in God. (Kerr, 1986, p. 183)

Second, some radical theologians argue that religious language never imparts information about reality (about 'what is true or false'); it *only* serves to arouse, deepen and express emotions, attitudes and commitments, and to stir people to religious and moral activity. On that interpretation, doctrine is never a type of factual belief, but solely an expression of religious feelings and attitudes to life, and of commitment to certain ways of behaving. For Don Cupitt, for example, God is a symbol for our spiritual values: a powerful ideal that corresponds to no reality outside ourselves. So he writes that belief in the God of Christian faith is solely 'an expression of allegiance to a particular set of values' (1980, p. 69). Faith is 'something like morale'; it does *not* presuppose 'the real existence of something that calls for faith' (Cupitt, 2006, pp. 80–1). A non-cognitive interpretation is being applied here to *all forms* of religious language, including doctrine. The resulting view of God is *non-realist*, since its God does not exist as an objective reality outside human discourse and experience.

Third, however, we can allow the non-cognitive functions of much religious language, while arguing that it is *ultimately grounded* in a factual belief. After all, when we express certain attitudes and emotions we normally *assume* or *imply* that their objects or 'targets' really exist, so that other factual claims may be made about them. Most believers would maintain that you can't express your own trust in or thanksgiving to God 'without presupposing that this God exists in fact' (Brümmer, 1981, p. 268). And the same goes for praising, admiring or loving God, making requests and committing ourselves to God and so on. On a *realistic* interpretation, some 'statements about God' – as actually existing, and not just an idea – are implied by practically all the other forms that religious language can take. Hence doctrine undergirds our other religious discourse.

EXERCISE

Copy down a favourite (a) Bible passage, (b) prayer and (c) hymn or religious song. In each example, note as many different uses of religious language as you can find; and any words or phrases that you take to be literal descriptions of God.

Ways of Talking about God

We can now look more closely at the ways in which Christians 'describe', 'portray' or 'represent' God's nature and activity in human language. *Human* is the main issue here. In talking about God like this, we are applying human language to a realm that 'transcends' human nature, life and activity. The word 'transcend' is from the Latin words *trans + scandere*, meaning 'to climb across' or 'beyond'. In talking of God, we are taking language beyond *any* finite (limited) reality or event of our universe of space and time. As human language developed to describe *this* world, there are bound to be problems when we seek to use it of its infinite, mysterious creator.

This problem is often hardest to resolve where people insist that our ordinary nouns, adjectives, verbs and adverbs should be applied to God *directly*, in their usual or primary sense. At first sight, this is the natural thing to do. After all, we would then know exactly what is meant by calling God a father, rock or king; Jesus a shepherd or vine, or the one who 'came down at Christmas'; the Church a bride or a temple; or the wine at communion 'the blood of Christ'. Unfortunately, we might also have made our faith a stumbling block – even a laughing stock – to others; and eroded it of all meaning for ourselves. Frequently, this is because 'anthropomorphic' talk describes God in the exact form (Greek *morphe*) of a human being (*anthropos*), depicting God as a human being identical to us. And that makes Christian teaching foolish to the point of senselessness. It would seem, then, that we cannot speak of God *literally*.

Literal Theology

But there are exceptions to this rule. The first covers certain *technical theological concepts* that apply *only* to God. Examples include (i) philosophical terms such as aseity ('self-existence', see Chapter 9) and (ii) negative terms – I have already used the term 'in-finite' (= not finite); another example would be 'immortal' (= not subject to death).

Some philosophers of religion, however, argue that many human terms have a core abstract meaning in terms of *function* that we *can* apply to God without stretching its sense. For example, the adjective 'wise' basically means 'knows many things'; and the verb 'wills' basically means 'intends and brings about'. Understood in that way, these words can be applied *univocally* ('with one voice' – with the same meaning) to both God and us, even though there remains a great deal of difference between the ways that God and human beings perform these functions.

> What it is for God to *make something* is radically different from what it is for a human being to make something; but that does not rule out an abstract feature in common, for example, that *by the exercise of agency something comes into existence*. (Alston, 1987, p. 24)

Analogical Theology

A great deal of theology is based on analogy. An analogy is a *partial similarity*, a 'likeness with a difference'. Such language is stretched. God is *like* a 'living' thing, but God is not 'alive' in the way that created animals and plants are alive.

Many theologians argue that, even when we apply human analogies to God, we are still engaged in *literal* God-talk. For God *really is* wise; whereas he isn't 'really' a rock or a father. Aquinas took this line, as do his present-day followers ('Thomists'). They argue that when a word or phrase is applied to God analogically, its sense is extended (so that it is *not* used univocally of God and human beings) but not stretched *beyond* the normal range of its literal meaning. Hence, words like 'wise', 'lives' or 'good' are *not* being used figuratively – even though God is good and lives 'in God's own way', which is certainly different from how *we* are good or alive.

Others, however, prefer to think of analogy and metaphor as different only in degree from one another. For them, analogy *is* a non-literal use of language.

Coming to Terms with Theology: *Analogy*

Analogy of being (*analogia entis*) – the similarity between humans and God that stems from their having been created in his image (Gen. 1.26); we can therefore learn about God by studying ourselves.

Analogy of faith (*analogia fidei*) **or revelation** – Karl Barth denies the analogy of being, arguing that we only know what words apply to God because God has graciously revealed this information.

Types of Analogy

Analogy of proportionality – God is 'wise' in God's own way, as we are wise in ways appropriate to our (different, human) nature. The shift in the meaning of the term relates to the difference that being God makes.

Analogy of attribution – Aquinas thought that all effects resemble their causes, so we can also say that God is 'wise' because God is the *cause of wisdom* in us. (It is hard to maintain that there is any such general analogy between causes and effects.)

Metaphorical or Symbolic Theology

At last we can begin to explore the use of figures of speech in Christian theology. We should get two things clear from the start.

1 We must avoid disparaging references to 'mere metaphors', as if metaphorical language was some sort of poetic frippery that offers no insight into the truth of things. On the contrary, it serves an essential role in all human understanding – even in the sciences. Figurative language is *serious* talk. In order to take theology seriously, we *must* take a great deal of it figuratively.

2 The other misapprehension is that metaphors are rather 'up-market', 'classy' talk. But metaphors are fundamental to the way we *ordinarily* think and speak. Listen to any conversation and you will hear lots of metaphors. One reason for this is that there are more things and events in the world than we have words to describe them.

When we can no longer stretch the meaning of a word without breaking it, we are forced to search for a 'figure of speech'. We then refer to something using the name of something else, speaking about 'one thing in terms which are seen to be suggestive of another' (Soskice, 1985, p. 15). And we alight on particular words or phrases as appropriate metaphors for something else through our *imagination*. We spot some underlying analogy or resemblance between (a) whatever the language normally refers to, and (b) the thing that we want to describe. There is a 'common quality' that includes both of them.[2]

What is happening here is that two sets of associations, or worlds of meaning, are being brought together so that they interact. This helps us to see our subject-matter with new insight, 'in a new light'. So 'the Church' is illuminated by ideas associated with 'a body'; or 'God' is seen in the light of activities associated with shepherds. And this is a two-way revelation. We now think differently about God – *and* about shepherds.

We may think that the word *victory* applies literally and primarily to a process of military action, but the transformation of meaning in which we are involved will teach us that we are wrong. A real victory is the kind of thing that happens when Jesus goes to the cross. In this a metaphor may enable

---

2 Metaphors are contracted forms of *similes*: 'the Church *is* a temple' is a metaphor, 'the kingdom of God *is like* a mustard seed' is a simile.

us to change our way of thinking, *and therefore our world*. (Gunton, 1988, pp. 78–9)

We need figurative speech most when we have to explain something that is unfamiliar or hard to understand. This is the case with the things of God, and particularly with God himself. So we grab at words whose reference and meaning are *already* familiar. But God is the ultimate mystery, above and beyond any pictorial representation (which has often been castigated as 'idolatry') – *and any human words and concepts*. So we must be cautious, and *treat metaphors as metaphors*. Otherwise we shall reduce the creator to the level of a creature. 'Because God is ultimate, . . . he falls outside the categories which are used to classify things and events in the world . . . When we use words to talk about God, we are not describing but pointing; not grasping but intimating' (Norris, 1979, pp. 51–2).

EXERCISE

- List as many metaphors as you can that are applied to God in Scripture, with a biblical reference for each (a Bible concordance will be helpful – an online version is available at http://www. biblestudytools.com/). Share your list around, and compare it with others (for example, Caird, 1980, pp. 154, 174–6; Astley, 2004a, pp. 40–1).
- Try to organize the metaphors under the headings 'impersonal' (for example, rock, light) and 'personal' (for example, potter, judge), further subdividing each category into different groups.
- Reflect on this multidimensional picture of God. What implications do you draw from it for your own theology? Which of these metaphors are most important to you, and which least important?

Models

Theologians often talk about using different *models* in doctrine. Although 'model' is sometimes used interchangeably with metaphor, models are really 'sustained and systematic metaphors' (Black, 1962, p. 236). They are less literary and poetic than metaphors, and more conceptual, systematically developed, stable and long-lasting. Sallie McFague treats them as a 'further step along the route from metaphorical to conceptual language' (McFague, 1983, p. 23). They are widely used in science, for example, in accounts of electrons that employ the models of particles (like billiard balls) and waves (as in the sea). Although models are more concise and disciplined – and less ambiguous – than metaphors, in the end their richness and power still come from their underlying images.

We shall explore a range of metaphors and models in this book. Doctrine uses them in speaking of the sacraments (for example as acted prayers), the death of Christ (for example as a legal transaction), the person of Christ (for example as the 'Son' and 'Word' of God), creation (for example as the relationship between a writer and her characters), and the nature of God (for example as one 'person' or three). Sometimes the models we inherit from the tradition are best understood more figuratively, as metaphors, and sometimes as more abstract and conceptual – and therefore as more technical and literal. But even in this second form, we should be wary of treating models as simple and straightforward, plain and simple, literal language. The view that theological models apply to a real God is often described as 'realism'; more accurately it is a form of *critical realism*, for which God is 'nonpicturable but real' (McFague, 1983, p. 97). Models aren't pictures.

Story Theology

We are all inveterate storytellers, shaping our own lives as stories. 'It is not possible to read or hear a story without it impinging on our own story, or even becoming our story' (Drane, 2000, p. 140). According to Lindbeck, becoming and being Christian is like learning and speaking a language. Specifically, it is a matter of 'learning the story of Israel and of Jesus well enough to interpret and experience one's self in its terms'. And we do this best by immersing ourselves in strong communities who speak this language well, and who are faithful to the Christian narrative and its performance (Lindbeck, 1984, pp. 33, 132–4).

Christian thinking often asserts that 'story is the non-doctrinal basis upon which doctrine rests' (Loughlin, 1997, p. 53). Narrative comes first; only later do the beliefs implied by and embodied in narrative give rise to doctrines. And just as we should not forget the metaphorical basis of our theological concepts, neither should we overlook the original theological stories that lie behind so much doctrinal theology.

These stories include the great *historical narratives* of Israel's exodus from Egypt and conquest of the land that God promised, and the nation's own later defeat by the empires of Assyria and Babylon; followed by the story of her exile and her subsequent (partial) return. They also include the drama of Jesus' ministry, miracles, passion and resurrection, and of the creation and expansion of the Church. Together, these represent 'the narration of the saving events' (Sauter and Barton, 2000, p. 3).

Beyond many of these historical (and sometimes legendary) narratives lie the great *cosmic stories* that scholars refer to as *myths*. As used here, the word 'myth' does *not* imply that these stories are false; only that they are story-metaphors. They present a 'moving picture of the sacred' (Ninian Smart), in which God is not portrayed statically like a king on a throne, but *dynamically* – making Adam out of the dust, catching him out in the Garden of Eden, shutting the door of Noah's Ark, or 'coming down' at Christmas to be born in a manger. Like all metaphors, these story-metaphors cannot be literally true; nevertheless, many believe that they express and give rise to deep truths (basically doctrines) about the nature of the universe, and about who we are and who God is.

Stephen Sykes has argued that some of these stories, especially the incarnation and atonement, are 'irreplaceable and necessarily temporal and sequential'. They cannot be rewritten in any non-story form without real loss, not even by replacing them with conceptual models; and they are not *necessarily* metaphorical. These stories have 'doctrinal implications', but their meaning 'cannot be rendered otherwise than by the narration', because they uniquely (and truthfully) identify the nature of God's love (Sykes, 1979, pp. 116, 122). (See Chapter 6.)

EXERCISE

- What are the advantages and disadvantages of expressing Christian beliefs in stories?
- Would it matter if you came to believe that many historical accounts in the Old and New Testaments were 'just stories'?

Jesus' teaching contains another type of story. *Parables* work as metaphors with plots – story-metaphors or similes that tell a truth about God through the medium of *fiction*. For these stories are not literally or historically true; there presumably never was a Good Samaritan or a Prodigal Son. The parables were frequently designed to shock people out of their theological complacency, by running counter to their normal expectations about Pharisees and tax collectors, the owners of vineyards and so on. The Bible contains other 'shocking' stories that are probably also literary fictions, but serve as the vehicle of religious truth. Is this how we should see the Books of Jonah and Ruth, even Job?

Enriching and Sharpening God-Talk

As theologians, what do we *do* with all this material? We should, first of all, welcome the great variety of metaphors, models and stories contained within religious language, for three reasons.

1 It provides a rich and varied resource for our theological thinking, helping Christians of different perspectives, backgrounds and needs to respond to one and the same faith tradition (cf. Chapter 1).
2 It allows us to combine two or more complementary models, generating a deeper understanding than any one model could on its own. Endorsing and favouring one model does not necessarily mean wholly dispensing with others. Ramsey even argued that orthodoxy 'aimed at having every possible model', whereas heretics often fasten on *one* understanding – and run it to death (Ramsey, 1957, p. 170).
3 A plurality of models prevents the naive equation of any one theological model with reality, and permits the mutual qualification or 'balancing' of one model by another. If Jesus is not only 'shepherd' but also 'king', not only 'prophet' but also 'brother', then each of these words must shift in meaning so as to accommodate its fellows.[3]

All this implies that we should *mix our metaphors* and models, recognizing the diverse 'mix' that we actually inherit from the Christian tradition. However, despite the advantages of multiple metaphors, models, analogies and stories,

---

3 As in John Newton's hymn, 'How sweet the name of Jesus sounds'.

critical reflection often needs to find the right balance between them. And theology does sometimes need to be selective, when there are too many poetic images pulling in different directions. Theology often *begins* with the 'selection of certain preferred images'. But we should recognize that it cannot *then* provide a wholly 'exhaustive account of biblical language' (Carroll, 1997, p. 27).

We also need to *sharpen our religious language*. If we don't, we shall find it difficult to draw *any* inferences in our theology, or we shall draw the *wrong* inferences. So we must ask ourselves what we *really mean* when we employ this human language to speak of God. We find out what people mean by discovering the implications that *they* draw and don't draw from what they are saying. What follows from our describing God metaphorically as a 'rock', and what doesn't? What is and is not implied when we say that God 'loves' us, in a way that is analogous to human love? If God is 'our father', is God male? How do you answer these questions?

Aquinas recognized that analogical terms have both *an affirmative (positive) and a negative component*. The first consists of those features that the analogy has in common with that for which it stands, and the second those features that are dissimilar. Theologians need to be aware of both elements, emphasizing the former and playing down the latter. This enables us to go beyond the analogy (or metaphor, model or story) by *specifying* our *God-talk*.

Doing theology involves a great deal of this sort of qualification-by-specification. So we say that God's life is *not* like biological life in some respects (God does not reproduce, for example); and we acknowledge that God's knowledge is *not* acquired as human knowledge is acquired (by learning and experience), and is *not* restricted as ours is. We need not fear that this process will replace all this evocative figurative, analogical and narrative language, exchanging it completely for concepts that literally apply to God. This can – and should – sometimes happen (see p. 52). But often our God-talk will *remain* as analogy, metaphor or myth, since ultimately God is a mystery that cannot be encapsulated or captured in our human terms. 'Even our theological language is figurative all the way down' (Stiver, 2009, p. 155). In theology, our language will always be inadequate for representing the reality to which it points. Nevertheless, this sort of reflection can help us sort out which of the associations and implications of our metaphors can – and which cannot – be transferred to God. This illuminates the meaning of the underlying resemblances between God and his creation, 'by determining the limits between "it is" and "it is not"' (Brümmer, 2005, p. 7).

Our theology can be sharpened at another level, by *ordering our models*. Some will seem more reliable than others, perhaps because they are 'dominant models' that can *include* the insights of the other models (Ramsey, 1965, p. 20). (Ramsey argued that 'protector' should come higher in our hierarchy of models than 'laundress', 'king' or 'power'; and 'love' even higher.)

But, finally, we must also note the considerable change involved in the transition from biblical, mainly Hebraic, imagery and narrative, to the more abstract and systematic philosophical language of the Greek and Latin Fathers. Luther said that philosophical concepts need to be baptized before being used in theology. This is perhaps *the* task of Christian theology; but we should not underestimate its difficulties.

> The figurative nature of much of the language of the Bible makes it highly unsuitable for theologizing . . . When philosophically-minded theologians get their hands on Bibles there is a terrible tendency for the metaphoric to be turned into the substantive and for the figurative to become abstracted into theology . . . Pulling and tugging biblical metaphors kicking and screaming into a theological system can be the death of the biblical imagery. (Carroll, 1997, pp. 51, 53, 145)

We have been warned!

Talking at the Edge of Mystery

Using analogies, metaphors and stories, religious people can 'articulate' their faith, at least to some approximation. Language has to be drawn from the world to make theology intelligible; but its meaning must be qualified and stretched in order to allow it to apply to what lies beyond. Therefore theology is never more than what Ramsey called a 'significant stuttering', or 'theological stammering', about a great mystery that is linguistically beyond us. It is *always* going to be a struggle to speak about mystery. 'Whatever we say of God in such human concepts can never be more than an indication of Him' (Barth, 1966, p. 46).

Negative Theology

I want us to think finally about another spectrum of religious language, this one running from the univocal application of language to God, at one end, through the increasing stretching of meaning shown in analogical and metaphorical theology. The natural limit of this stretching – the other end of the spectrum – might seem to be reached with what is technically called an *equivocal* (literally 'double voiced') usage.

Here words and phrases are applied to God *with a completely different meaning* from the meaning they have when applied to human beings. (Some words in the dictionary are equivocal in this way, having more than one *wholly unrelated* meaning – for example 'bank', 'tap', 'rape'.) Is equivocal God-talk the proper way of safeguarding the otherness and mystery of God? The trouble is that employing religious language equivocally implies our complete ignorance of what this language now means – and why we are using *these* words to speak of God at all. 'God is our father, rock and king' now actually says nothing.

Can we ever win at this game? Only by keeping our balance on the tightrope. When describing God, we are always at risk of falling over – in one direction or another:

- *either* by using language univocally when this makes theology *anthropomorphic* – picturing God as 'a big daddy in the sky';
- *or* by slipping into *agnosticism*, employing theological language with a completely different (equivocal) – and therefore wholly *unknown* – meaning.

Beyond even equivocation, however, there lies the ancient method of doing theology often employed by mystics. This is an extreme version of the 'negative way' (*via negativa*) or *apophatic* way (in Eastern Christian theology). It occupies the *real end* of the spectrum of religious language. God is now said to be 'ineffable', for we are reduced to stripping away all positive images whatever from the divine mystery. As a result, we can only say that God is 'not this' and 'not that' (which does say *something*, of course). We might even insist that God is beyond all categories of thought and language. God is not any of the things we call him; he cannot be conceptualized at all, but belongs 'in the divine darkness which lies beyond concept' (Bondi, 1983). Here, presumably, God-talk grinds to a halt and wholly dissolves in an enigma. As Wittgenstein once avowed, 'Whereof one cannot speak, thereof one must be silent.' It is surely proper to confess that, *in the end*, humans are bound to be baffled and tongue-tied by God's mystery.

But *first*, we must attempt some doctrine . . .

Suggestions for Further Reading

Introductory

Astley, J., 2004, *Exploring God-talk: Using Language in Religion*, London: Darton, Longman & Todd, chs 3, 4, 5 and 8.

Caird, G. B., 1980, *The Language and Imagery of the Bible*, London: Duckworth, chs 8–10, 13.

McFague, S., 1983, *Metaphorical Theology: Models of God in Religious Language*, London: SCM Press.

Advanced

Avis, P., 1999, *God and the Creative Imagination: Metaphor, Symbol and Myth in Religion and Theology*, London: Routledge.

Brümmer, V., 1981, *Theology and Philosophical Inquiry: An Introduction*, London: Macmillan, ch. 2.

Stiver, D. R., 1996, *The Philosophy of Religious Language: Sign, Symbol and Story*, Oxford: Blackwell.

4

Christian Activity: Worship, Ministry and Mission

Moving On

We now move from these general issues to explore the substantive content of Christian teaching, beginning with the Church. We shall look at the doctrine of the Church more closely in the next chapter, starting here with the Church in action.

Worship

Theologians maintain that worship should have a central role in our thinking about the Church. 'Every act of worship that is in the Spirit is a constituting of the Church' (Gunton, 1996, p. 202). It has even been described as an integral part of evangelism: 'praise is the primary form of the communication of the gospel ... All other communication is an overflow of this' (Hardy and Ford, 1984, p. 149). Fundamentally, 'worship' (from the Old English *weorthscipe*, 'acknowledgement of worth') involves recognizing the dignity, merit or honour of another. It is therefore the proper word for paying respect or reverence to God. As we saw in Chapter 2, those who believe *in* God do not just affirm God's existence. They must also *esteem* God. This attitude lies at the core of worship, and it explains why we must be discriminating in the worship we offer. This also matters because we inevitably come to model ourselves on what we worship. Worship cannot be expected by and should not be offered to an alien overlord; only the divine lover who makes us whole is worthy of supreme honour (see Chapter 9).

Christianity is sometimes denigrated for a spirituality that turns away from contact with the perceptible world – a matter of 'hands together, eyes closed'. In fact, it is a religion that you can touch, hear and see; take, hold and eat; walk through and feel. Other faiths have similar concrete dimensions, of course, but Christianity has been described as 'the most avowedly materialist of all religions' (Temple, 1934, p. 478). 'I worship the God of matter', said John of Damascus (*c.*655–750). God 'likes matter', C. S. Lewis proclaimed, 'He invented it' (Lewis, 1952, p. 51).

It is in its worship, and particularly in its sacraments, that Christianity is at its most material. That claim does not, of course, signify a preference for material possessions (although Christians are often guilty of that vice), nor any metaphysical viewpoint. It simply expresses a commitment in Christian theology and practice to the view that God acts and is known *primarily through the physical*. God works through the material world, including human bodies and their physical actions (with their speech) – and especially in the actions of Jesus, but also those of his followers (see 2 Cor. 4.7).

The Nature of Sacraments

'Sacrament' comes from the Latin *sacramentum* (a 'sacred pledge'); the word translates the Greek *musterion*, 'mystery'. Sacraments are physical objects or human acts that are thought of as bestowing God's grace. They are ordinary enough to be sure: bread, water and wine; washing, eating and drinking. But Christians set them apart and give them a special significance in rituals that symbolize and convey grace. Sacraments are therefore described, in the traditional language of the Church of England, as 'effectual signs' of God's goodwill, and 'outward and visible' signs of 'an inward and spiritual grace' (Articles of Religion, Catechism, Book of Common Prayer).

Although the word is not itself used by Orthodox Christians (who prefer to speak of 'Holy Mysteries'), the Orthodox and Roman Catholic Churches normally identify seven sacraments, including marriage and ordination. Most Protestants restrict the list to the two dominical sacraments of baptism and the Eucharist.[1] Salvationists and the Society of Friends ('Quakers') dispense even with these two, although their worship employs powerful symbols, such as flags, the 'mercy seat' – or silence.

Broadly speaking, Catholic and Orthodox Christians lay greater emphasis on the *objective status* of sacramental objects and actions, as God's instruments of grace; while Protestants tend to focus on the importance of the *subjective* (and 'worthy') *appropriation* of that grace by the worshipper, sometimes even interpreting the role of the sacrament itself in purely psychological terms. Most accept, however, that sacraments are acts of *God*, not just human acts.

Catholics speak of sacraments working *ex opere operato*, 'through the performance of the work' in and of itself, not by any work of the priest. As a consequence, worshippers don't need to worry about seeking out uncorrupted clergy from whom to receive Holy Communion. However, the *fruits* of the sacrament remain dependent on the recipient being in the right relationship to God, not obstructing his grace.

How do sacraments 'work'? There are several theories about the operation of a sacrament, listed below from the most objective to the least:

1 *an instrument in God's hands*, conveying grace to the worshipper directly;
2 *a means to a new status*, which then itself opens the worshipper to receive God's grace;
3 *an 'acted prayer' to God*, who may then decide to respond by bestowing grace on the worshipper;
4 *a symbol evoking ideas and feelings* that enable the worshipper to receive God's grace.

In each case, God's grace can only be effectively received if the worshipper is worthy to receive it – that is, if she or he approaches the sacrament with faith, love and penitence. This claim is intended to outlaw any 'mechanical' or 'magical' transaction involving grace as a sort of holy fluid – an influential view in parts of the Church during the Middle Ages.

---

1 'Dominical' here means associated with Jesus.

EXERCISE

Which of these theories best fits your understanding of sacraments? What are its strengths and its weaknesses?

It is important to say something more about *symbols*. In normal usage, the word is quite neutral with respect both to the way the symbol works, and the status of what it signifies. A symbol is something that represents – or 'stands for' – something else that may be present or absent, real or unreal. Interpretation (4) implies that the sacrament is 'merely' or 'only' a symbol – in other words, that its effects are wholly psychological or 'subjective', rather than 'objective'. But among those who say that the bread and wine at the Eucharist symbolize the body and blood of Christ, many hold that these symbols *also* somehow 'participate' in what they symbolize, or 'communicate' it. That is, the symbols stand for something that is *present* – like the Royal Standard flown over Buckingham Palace when the monarch is in residence. They don't stand for something that is *absent*, as would be the case when someone 'stands in' for the monarch at some function. 'In classic sacramental teaching a sacramental sign both is related to and is that which it signifies' (Jenson, 1997, p. 212).

We may also distinguish intrinsic and conventional symbols. Intrinsic symbols seem, at least in a particular culture, to symbolize something quite naturally. Thus ritual washing symbolizes some sort of cleansing, and light symbolizes life and safety. With ('merely') conventional symbols, however, such as the majority of flags and some road signs, the connection to what is symbolized is artificial and has to be learned and explained. In the case of the sacraments, we are ultimately dealing with potent – and still 'live' – intrinsic symbols, such as washing and eating, bread and water.

Word and Sacrament

The Protestant Reformers quickly came to speak of the Church as the place 'where the word of God is rightly preached', as well as where 'the sacraments are duly administered'. One of the traditional differences in emphasis between Protestants and Catholics (plus the Orthodox) is that the worship and theology of Protestants is dominated by the word, while the second group is more sacramental. A glance into their respective places of worship – even when empty – will quickly confirm this difference. Where the buildings of the so-called 'liturgical churches' are normally dominated by an altar (even though it may be hidden by the screen or iconostasis in Orthodox church buildings), Protestant places of worship are traditionally constructed as 'preaching boxes' in which the pulpit occupies a prominent position, and the 'Lord's table' or 'communion table' is frequently rather insignificant in both size and location.

This difference is unsurprising. Services of the word seek to communicate God to the worshipper through the medium of sound and the sense of hearing, with words conveying intelligible concepts to the minds of the worshippers. Sacramental services use words as well, of course, but they also utilize other media and other senses (sight, smell, touch and taste), offering a broad range of additional, non-verbal 'messages'. Sacraments *say* something; Augustine called the sacrament 'a kind of visible word'. Protestants have routinely worried about worshippers being distracted by the non-verbal communication arising from these actions and objects; and have insisted that we should *understand*, and not just respond to, what is being offered. By contrast, until relatively recently the language of most Catholic and Orthodox liturgies was very different from that used outside the church building, and was often understood only by a small minority of worshippers.

We shouldn't make too much of these differences, however, especially as in recent years many Christian traditions have become more open to a greater variety of ways of worship – through liturgical reform, and the ecumenical and charismatic movements. In any case, even such a 'wordy' activity as preaching can itself serve a sort of sacramental function, by providing 'a way of God becoming present to the believing community' that exceeds its purely intellectual effect on the worshippers' minds. Preaching, in common with the reading of Scripture, is more of a *performance*, and has a more holistic ('whole person') effect on people than many recognize. The living Word is 'itself physically handed over in the speaking, embodied action of preaching' (Pattison, 2005, pp. 108, 112). 'We can say that preaching, teaching, and so forth are "audible sacraments" as well as we can say that baptism, anointing and so on are "visible words"' (Jenson, 1984b, p. 303).

Furthermore, word and sacraments alike are channels of God's grace, or modes of divine communication, that are under the control of the Church. This 'limitation' is not restricted to the sacraments. Naturally, God may speak, act, heal and forgive through other means, but God has placed these particular channels in human hands. If the Church messes up here, she can truly get in the way of God's work; 'both Word and altar can become symbols of the human attempt to enclose God within safe and manageable boundaries' (Gorringe, 1989, p. 162). But handing over responsibility for grace in this manner, and accepting limits on the exercise of divine power, is surely part and parcel of the way God works in the world. God 'has no hands but our hands', as the poem puts it. In the pious legend, the ascended Christ explains to the angels, in response to their questioning, that he has left behind him on earth no book or other religious artefact, only a motley band of disciples. 'But what if they fail?', they ask. 'I have no other plan' is the only reply.

Connecting Doctrines

Systematic theology seeks to relate together the various aspects of Christian teaching into a self-consistent whole. It is second nature, therefore, for the systematic theologian to trace connections between different doctrines. We must attempt a little of this ourselves.

Many connect sacraments with Christianity's most distinctive doctrine, that of the *incarnation* ('enfleshing') of God in Christ (see Chapter 7). The incarnation shows that matter is capable of being the vehicle of God's truth and grace. We sometimes even read that sacraments, like the Church that administers them, are 'an extension of the incarnation': a continued embodiment of God's Word, and an earthly medium through which God's life can continue to be expressed. If the Church is the body of Christ (see Chapter 5), then these sacramental acts are his acts as well as ours.

Others, however, criticize such sentiments as impugning the unique, once-for-all character of Christ's incarnation. They might prefer to make their theological connections between the sacraments and the doctrine of *creation*, in terms of the expression, manifestation and mediation of God's presence and love through the world of matter and energy he continually holds in existence (see Chapter 8). The Roman Catholic geologist-priest, Teilhard de Chardin, thought that God is 'incarnate in the world', and prayed that the creation should repeat to itself, 'This is my body' (King, 1997, pp. 31, 65). Such interpretations readily lead to the notion of a *sacramental world*. The whole of nature is now viewed as a cosmic sacrament, within which the sacraments recognized by the Church can find their place. Each of them represents only a small element, set apart so that people may be helped to focus on it as *one* channel of God's wider grace: a particular thing or action that can help us understand, and respond to, a presence and power that is far more universal. As is sometimes said, 'one meal is called holy so that all meals may become holy.' This theme is well captured in the (Orthodox and Catholic) notion of *sacramentality*: the view that all reality, potentially or in fact, is 'the bearer of God's presence and the instrument of God's saving activity' (Richard McBrien). But where for the Orthodox the Church's sacraments are primarily a revelation of the sacramentality of creation itself, most Catholics – along with many Protestants – distinguish them from a general sacramental view of the world grounded in creation.

Instead, they link these explicit sacraments with the doctrine of redemption (Chapter 6), pointing to their specific 'institution' (establishment) as effective symbols of God's historic salvation in and through Jesus Christ. Donald Baillie found a mediating view in Calvin's theology, by recognizing that because God is the creator of nature, God can use – and we can see – the things of nature as 'sacramental expressions of His mercy and faithfulness'. 'It is only when God speaks and awakens human faith that the natural object becomes sacramental. But this can happen to material things only because this is a sacramental universe' (Baillie, 1957, pp. 46–7).

Baptism

Most readers will have witnessed a baptism (from the Greek *baptizein*, 'to immerse'); and most will have been baptized themselves. These are likely to have been infant baptisms, and were perhaps not understood as matters of much significance.

But both the New Testament and Christian theology take the rite of baptism very seriously. The Synoptic Gospels (Matthew, Mark and Luke) all begin their account of Jesus' ministry with references to John the Baptizer, Jesus' baptism at his hands and the experience of God that accompanied it. Although John's Gospel avoids saying that Jesus was baptized, it clearly draws on a similar tradition (see John 1.6–9, 19–36). According to this Gospel, Jesus' disciples practised baptism as well (4.2). Baptism also forms part of the 'Great Commission' from the risen Christ (Matt. 28.18–20).

In the rest of the New Testament, baptism is clearly an integral aspect of joining the Christian community (Acts 2.37–42; 8.12; 1 Cor. 12.13; Gal. 3.27). The ritual is particularly freighted with meaning in Paul's theology, and interpreted as a baptism 'into' Christ's own death and resurrection (Rom. 6.3–4; Col. 2.12). This emphasis makes most sense in the case of adult converts, although it is likely that children would also have been baptized as part of an adult's 'household' (Acts 16.14–15; 1 Cor. 1.16).

This act of *Christian initiation* soon became a very big deal indeed. In the third and fourth centuries of Christianity it was preceded by months or years of instruction, prayer, fasting, testing of the candidates' attitudes and conduct, blessings and exorcisms. In the baptism itself, after stripping naked and entering the baptismal bath, candidates renounced Satan and – turning east – confessed their Christian beliefs. Then followed a threefold immersion in the water and the invocation of the threefold God. Clothed in new garments, they next submitted to the bishop's laying on of hands or anointing, as he prayed for the gift of the Spirit and grace. Finally, they joined the faithful for the first time at a full celebration of the Eucharist.

In time, however, the Church almost inevitably came to baptize mainly infants (*paedobaptism*), who had sponsors ('godparents' in England) who spoke for them and gave the requisite confession of faith, including the commitment to 'turn to Christ'. Unfortunately, the great increase in infant baptism in the West after the fifth century – as the Church became more established, and most people entered it through birth – resulted in the separation of the one initiation rite into two. Baptism occurred in infancy (normally administered by priests), followed by a later rite (often by a bishop) of *confirmation* of the pledges given for them when the children were old enough to 'answer for themselves'. The Orthodox still retain a unitary rite, however, normally administered by a priest and directed to babies, who receive the bread and wine on a spoon after their initiation – as Orthodox adults still do, and most other Christians did until the twelfth century. Adult converts in Catholic, Anglican and many Protestant churches can experience a similar unbroken rite. But for these churches the usual pathway is still infant baptism followed by confirmation in late childhood/early adolescence.[2]

---

2 This rite (or the desire for it) is often required for admission to Holy Communion in Anglican Churches.

Baptists – who originated in seventeenth-century England, partly influenced by the sixteenth-century Anabaptists ('re-baptizers') on the Continent – only practise 'believer's baptism', as do many new Protestant Churches. These Churches also retain the practice of total immersion.

The Effects of Baptism

What does baptism do? Of the four consequences of baptism listed below, the first two resound with theological meaning. They also relate closely to the 'matter' of the sacrament of baptism, which is water. Water is a powerful natural symbol of both washing and drowning. Regrettably, in a culture where water is literally 'on tap' and most of us are well protected from the dangers of the sea, these symbols have rather died on us.

1   *Spiritual washing* or 'cleansing' from sin is a very ancient idea, widespread across religions. The 'proselyte baptism' of Gentiles who wished to become Jews was practised by some at the time of Jesus, and John the Baptist's ministry continued and deepened this motif. The stripping of candidates in early accounts of Christian baptismal ceremonies, and their being afterwards clothed in clean white garments, constituted a sign of their 'taking off' their old ways and 'putting on' the new life in Christ. In 1439, the Council of Florence decreed that baptism remitted 'all original and actual guilt' and 'all penalty' (see Chapter 6). (See Acts 2.38; Gal. 3.27; Eph. 4.17–32; Col. 3.1–17; Titus 3.5.)

2   Paul's linking of the Christian's baptism with the *dying and rising* of Christ made symbolic sense when people were baptized by total immersion in rivers or lakes, which involved being pushed under the water before coming up, gasping for air, in a psychologically potent, drowning-saving movement – a vividly felt, 'new birth'. There are hints in the Bible of water representing the chaos that only God can tame; it served as his agent of destruction in the flood. But water is also associated with salvation in the Israelites' escape across the Red Sea (or 'Sea of Reeds') during their exodus from slavery in Egypt. (See Gen. 1.2, 6–7, 9–10; 7.11—8.4; Ex. 14.15–31; Ps. 33.7; 77.16; Isa. 43.16; Rom. 6.3–4; 1 Cor. 10.1–2; 1 Peter 3.21.)

3   *Initiation into membership* of the Church has been described as the socio-logical effect of baptism, the 'rite of lay ministry', and the beginning of grace. It is a baptism 'into one body' (1 Cor. 12.13) because Christ is the sacramental agent of baptism and the Church is his body (Chapter 5). In the early Church, this emphasis would have been symbolized by the fact that the non-baptized were excluded from the most sacred part of the Eucharist, and only permitted to join other Christians to receive the bread and wine after their baptism. This theme lies behind the Catholic notion of the 'permanent character' of baptism, which implies that it should not be repeated.

4   *Gift of the Spirit.* From the New Testament onwards, Christians have claimed a 'special dispensation' of the Holy Spirit for the members of the Church. The baptized were said to be 'marked with a seal' by the Holy Spirit 'for the day of redemption' (Eph. 4.30). Traditionally, the driving away of evil spirits prior to baptism became a preliminary to this special gift of God.

It is plausible to interpret these four effects in terms of God's grace being truly offered in this sacrament, bestowing (1) forgiveness, (2) renewal, (3) mutual acceptance and (4) the Spirit.

EXERCISE

- From your own theological perspective, rank these four effects in order of significance. How would you justify your evaluation?
- How might baptism bestow God's grace?

Those who fear an over-objective interpretation of baptism may prefer to prioritize effect (3), treating the other effects as flowing from the impact of their new fellowship with other believers on the new Christians' spiritual life. For the free, forgiving love, renewal and empowerment of the Spirit may be received – at least in an ideal Church – at the hands of their brothers and sisters in Christ. On this account, it is possible to distinguish between (a) baptism as a 'rite of passage', that is, a ritual used to mark a change in a person's status – in this case becoming a member of the Christian community; and (b) the *actual effect* of joining and living within this community. Many would argue that, if the rite of baptism is separated from its context of actual Church membership, the high-sounding theology that surrounds this sacrament becomes empty of real meaning. But the corollary of this is that baptism itself is only of second-ary significance, compared with the truly important factor of belonging to and worshipping with the Church.

Others are uneasy with any account that emphasizes the importance of human activity. They would prefer a more objective account, with God work-ing to bestow unique supernatural actions and gifts that can come in no other way – and certainly in no natural way – albeit *through* the ministers of baptism. (Some have argued that the practice of infant baptism can be defended as expressing the claim that God acts for our good *before* we can ever be worthy of, or even capable of seeking, God's grace.) But most theologians also want to avoid any hint that baptism is a mechanical process – as it presumably was for the legendary religious zealot who used to throw water over bystanders while invoking the name of the Trinity, in an attempt to baptize as many as possible. An explicit confession of faith, which those who are baptized as infants should later take on themselves, is regarded as an important safeguard against such extreme sacramental behaviour.

Yet one may still argue that God's grace is *objectively* given through a par-ticular sacrament, while insisting that the gift can be wilfully resisted, or may simply fail to be received and appropriated, by the person to whom it is offered. If so, God's grace is always a matter of gift and invitation; it is never a violent assault on a human being's freedom – never, in other words, a form of rape. Here, as elsewhere, 'God is not coercive, God woos rather than forces' (Stiver, 2009, p. 395).

Eucharist

Many Christians regard the communal re-enactment of Jesus' Last Supper with his disciples as the most important form of Christian worship. It is 'the centre of the Church ... Here the Church is truly itself' (Küng, 1971, p. 223). The sacrament is known by a variety of names: Holy Communion, Mass, the Lord's Supper, the Supper, the Holy Meal, the Breaking of the Bread, the Divine Liturgy or the Holy Mystery. Most theologians prefer the title 'Eucharist' – from the Greek *eucharistia*, 'thanksgiving'.

The tradition of Jesus' 'institution' of this sacrament is found in its earliest form in Paul's account in 1 Cor. 11.23–6. The (later) Synoptic Gospels record slightly variant accounts (see Matt. 26.26–9; Mark 14.22–5; Luke 22.15–20). John's narrative of Jesus' last meal omits this tradition, substituting the story of the washing of the disciples' feet (John 13.1–20).

Blessing God for his gifts was normal Jewish practice at meals (cf. Acts 27.35), and interpreting the symbolism of the food was a feature of the Passover supper celebrating the exodus and the destroying angel 'passing over' the homes of the Hebrew slaves.[3] It is likely that the Last Supper was a Passover meal, and that Jesus' words built on its symbolism. (See Ex. 12.1–27; Mark 14.12–16; Luke 22.15; 1 Cor. 5.7–8.)

The story of the gift of the Holy Spirit at Pentecost, sometimes described as the 'birthday of the Church', concludes with the new converts being baptized and devoting themselves 'to the apostles' teaching and fellowship, to the breaking of bread and the prayers' (Acts 2.42; cf. 2.46; 20.7). The Eucharist was often set in the context of an 'Agape' or 'love feast', a proper meal that itself served as a ritual of fellowship. This real meal slowly disappeared, possibly because of abuses like those criticized by Paul in 1 Corinthians 11.17–22. The Orthodox churches retain an echo of it in their practice of distributing blessed (but non-consecrated) bread, the *antidoron*, after the Liturgy.

The Theology of the Eucharist

A number of theological themes are associated with eucharistic worship.

1   *Thanksgiving.* The Jewish notion of blessing involved thanking *God* over something. In later eucharistic rituals, Jesus' words over the bread and wine were set within a prayer of thanksgiving for all the great acts of God in creation, redemption and sanctification.

2   *Eschatological Meal.* The adjective 'eschatological' signifies a concern for a future in which God will act decisively to make his reign real, in this world or the next (see Chapter 10). The Passover became a festival of messianic hope, and the Last Supper is sometimes said to have deliberately pre-figured the eschatological

---

3 *Pasach* is Hebrew for 'to pass' – from which we derive the adjective 'paschal'.

or messianic 'banquet' that would mark the coming in power of God's kingdom (see Mark 14.25; Luke 22.16, 18, 28–30). Paul's teaching about the Eucharist includes the claim that 'as often as you eat this bread and drink the cup, you proclaim the Lord's death until he comes' (1 Cor. 11.26). The second-century theologian, Irenaeus, described the sacrament as an anticipation of 'the mystery of the final harvest' (*Against Heresies* 4.17–18). Some scholars have interpreted the hard-to-translate petition in the Lord's prayer, 'Give us this day our daily bread' (Matt. 6.11; cf. Luke 11.3), as 'Give us today our bread for [the eschatological] tomorrow', and have linked it with the Eucharist.

3   *Communion with Others.* In the East, eating with another person is a serious matter. It creates a commitment and community solidarity, perhaps even to death. Jesus' practice of eating with prostitutes, tax collectors and others considered to be outside the Jewish law was highly contentious (Mark 2.15–17). The importance of table fellowship also underscores the heinous character of the betrayal of Jesus by 'one who is dipping bread into the bowl with me' (Mark 14.18–21). In Christian theology, the fellowship of the Church is not only symbolized, but also partly created by, its eucharistic common meal. For many Christians, it is also a sharing with the Church in heaven.

4   *Sacrifice.* We explore the concept of sacrifice further in Chapter 6. It is sufficient at this point to note that in biblical thinking sacrifice – literally a 'making sacred' – focused on the offering of a life back to God, rather than (as later) on the death of the victim. It was essentially a *gift*, symbolized in the spilling of blood. Jesus' consecration of himself to his death at the Last Supper included reference to the wine as 'my blood of the covenant [promise, agreement], which is poured out for many' (Mark 14.24). Descriptions of the Eucharist in the epistles sometimes draw on connotations of sacrifice as a shared meal with God (1 Cor. 10.18–22). However, no New Testament author *directly* calls the Eucharist a sacrifice.

After the destruction of the Jewish Temple in 70 CE, animal sacrifice became no more than a memory for Judaism. Christianity never attempted to take it over. For Augustine, 'true sacrifice is designed to unite us to God in a holy fellowship' (*City of God* x, ch. 6), perpetuating the memory of Christ's sacrifice. Later Orthodox and Catholic theology thought of the Eucharist as somehow *re-presenting* the sacrifice of Christ. Protestantism recoiled from the late medieval degeneration of this theme into a *repetition* of Christ's sacrifice on the altar, severed from the communion of the people. All now agree, however, that the Eucharist is primarily *our* sacrifice 'of praise and thanksgiving'. It is an offering of the Church as the body of Christ (cf. Rom. 12.1), in union with Christ's once-for-all sacrifice: 'a universal sacrifice to God ... so that we might be the body of so great a head' (Augustine, *City of God* x, ch. 6) – and in which 'we are strengthened by grace to make his sacrifice our own' (Burnaby, 1959, p. 175).

5 *Consecration.* To 'consecrate' is to 'make sacred'; although the act is often understood as setting something apart not so much to *make* it holy, as to allow us to perceive its holiness. The original *blessing over* the bread and wine has in many traditions become a *blessing of* these elements, and the thanksgiving prayer a 'prayer of consecration'. Liturgists now urge a wider understanding of consecration that involves the four so-called actions of the Eucharist. These are often further interpreted by those who speak of the *taking, blessing, breaking* and *sharing* not just of bread and wine but of the Church itself, as an expression of its unity and solidarity with its Lord.

6   *Anamnesis of Christ's Passion. Anamnesis* is Greek for 'remembrance'. In celebrating the Eucharist, Christians follow Jesus' instruction, 'Do this in remembrance of me' (1 Cor. 11.24–5). Some understand this in a wholly psychological way, as a mental act. For others, anamnesis involves an actual re-calling of the past into the present, so as to fully enter into its meaning. On this latter perspective, the risen Christ and God's action in Christ are truly present, essentially through their effects. There is a parallel here with Jewish remembrance of the exodus, which is celebrated by the descendants of those who experienced that deliverance as if it were *their* own story (see Deut. 5.3; 26.8–10).

The Eastern Orthodox Liturgy also 'remembers' the *future* second coming of Christ: 'What we experience ... is the end times making itself present to us now ... the penetration of the future into time' (Zizioulas, 2008, p. 155). Compare (2) above.

7   *Celebration of Christ's Presence.* Like all Christian worship, the Eucharist is seen as a communion ('sharing') with God in and through the risen Christ, and therefore as a truly 'holy communion', as well – and *therefore* – as a communion with fellow worshippers.

But further dimensions of Christ's presence are often associated with eucharistic worship: both as the real host at the table and in the eucharistic elements of bread and wine, if Christ is present in a special way as a form of spiritual sustenance (or 'spiritual food'). This last factor is often described as the *real presence* of Christ:

> The mode of Christ's presence under the Eucharistic species is unique. . . . In the most blessed sacrament of the Eucharist 'the body and blood, together with the soul and divinity, of our Lord Jesus Christ and, therefore, *the whole Christ is truly, really, and substantially contained*' [Thomas Aquinas]. 'This presence is called "real" – by which is not intended to exclude the other types of presence as if they could not be "real" too, but because it is presence in the fullest sense: that is to say, it is a *substantial* presence by which Christ, God and man, makes himself wholly and entirely present' [Pope Paul VI]. (*Catechism of the Catholic Church*, 2000, p. 309)

The focus here is on the bread and wine, which Jesus spoke of as his 'body' and his 'blood'. Most New Testament scholars reason that these words were intended to be understood neither literally or metaphysically, but represent Hebraic imagery (cf. John 6.54–8; 1 Cor. 10.16–17). Jesus applies the language of sacrifice to himself, making 'the broken bread a simile of the fate of his body, the blood of the grapes a simile of his outpoured blood' (Jeremias, 1966, p. 224).

In the developing Church, the rite of consecration of the eucharistic gifts included an *epiclesis* ('calling down') of the Holy Spirit. In the Eastern churches this was retained as the occasion of God's transformative change of the elements into the body and blood of Christ. The Western Church, however, came to associate this event particularly with the 'words of institution' ('This is my body'/'This is my blood'), although more recent theology has tended to reconnect it with the whole prayer of thanksgiving.

It is Western theology that has the most divergent accounts of the nature of this particular presence of Christ at the Eucharist. (Although many Christians in both West and East, while affirming the real presence of Christ, refuse to define it further.)

(a) *Transubstantiation.* According to this traditional Roman Catholic doctrine, the 'substance' of the bread and wine (its inner, essential nature) is miraculously changed into the substance of the body and blood of Christ, while their 'accidents' (their outward properties, such as how they look or taste) remain unchanged. As with the other views considered below, this still claims to be a spiritual rather than a material change in the matter of the sacrament.

(b) *Consubstantiation.* This word is often used of the view, adopted by the Lutheran Church, that involves a 'sacramental union' but no miraculous change in the substance of the consecrated elements. In this union the substance *both* of the bread *and* of the body of Christ are present together – as both iron and heat are present in a red-hot poker. Again, the outward appearance remains the same, but Christ is truly present 'in, with and under' the bread and wine – even for the unworthy recipient. More fundamentally for Luther, *whatever* makes a person 'available to and intendable by other people *is* that person's body' (Jenson, 1984b, p. 359). So Christ, even in his human nature, may be said to be *ubiquitous*: 'present' or 'found' everywhere, including the bread and cup.

(c) *Trans-signification.* Catholics today often say that transubstantiation affirms the fact of Christ's presence through a change in the elements, without specifying how this change takes place. The Belgian theologian, Edward Schillebeeckx, used the term trans-signification (together with 'transfinalization') to indicate 'a new establishment of meaning'. The *meaning and purpose* of the bread and wine are changed, not by human beings but by 'the living Lord *in* the Church, through which they become the *sign* of the real presence of Christ giving himself to us' (Schillebeeckx, 1968, p.137). The focus is now on an act of discernment in which the Church engages, on the authority of Christ.

(d) *Virtualism.* On this account, classically formulated by John Calvin and later supported by the Anglican Archbishop Thomas Cranmer, faithful communicants receive (together with the elements) the spiritual 'power, virtue and effect' – but not the substance – of the body and blood of Christ, by being truly joined with him in heaven through the mediation of the Holy Spirit. Understanding Christ's spiritual presence in terms of the *effect* of the sacrament is characteristic of many Protestants.

(e) *Receptionism*. According to the Anglican Richard Hooker, the body and blood of Christ are really received at the Eucharist in the hearts of the communicant, at the same time as – but separately from – the (unchanged) bread and wine: 'the real presence . . . is not therefore to be sought for in the sacrament, but in the worthy receiver' (*Laws of Ecclesiastical Polity* 5, 67). As in (d), Christ is not really present, and thus not really offered, to the *unbelieving* communicant. The Anglican William Temple objects, 'The receiver finds, and does not make, this Presence. By means of the elements Christ is present, that is, accessible . . . [although] Christ is only actually present to the soul of those who make right use of the means of access offered' (Temple, 1924, pp. 240–1).

(f) *Memorialism*. The Swiss Reformer, Ulrich Zwingli, thought that sacraments were mere symbols or signs; they were not also *causes*. He interpreted the 'is' in 'This is my body' as equivalent to 'signifies', making the real presence a figure of speech.

> The words 'This is my body' should be received not literally but figuratively, as is true of the words 'This is the Passover.' For the lamb that was eaten every year with the celebration of that festival was not the Passover but signified what had taken place. (*Final Statement on the Eucharist*)

Since Christ is now located in heaven, in the Eucharist he is simply being remembered in his 'real absence'. Clearly, no change in the nature of the elements is to be expected, and Christ is only present in the spiritual apprehension of the worshipper. Christ's future presence (at the second coming) is also affirmed in this symbolic memorial and act of faith. Rather surprisingly, one researcher has claimed that 'the majority of [US] Catholic weekly church-attenders . . . believe that the consecrated host is only a symbolic representation of Christ, rather than Christ himself' (Morris, 1997, p. 393).

EXERCISE

In your own theology of the Eucharist, which themes do you stress most and which least? And why?

Ministry

The Latin word for a servant is *minister*, and those who aspire to (or have already been granted) this title must never forget its humble origins. Theologically, all Christian ministry is to be regarded as a continuation of Christ's ministry, not only of teaching and healing but also of reconciling the world to God. As such, ministry is first and foremost the vocation of baptism: a calling that is shared by *all* members of the Church, with their enormous variety of gifts, roles and contexts. Much is made today of the role of *leadership* in the Church, but Jesus taught about ministry in terms of servanthood rather than the power of 'being in charge' (Matt. 20.25–8; John 13.1–17).

The Priesthood of all Believers

1 Peter 2.9 – 'But you are a chosen race, a royal priesthood, a holy nation, God's own people' – was taken up by Luther in his attempt to reform a Church suffering from the failings of many of its recognized ministers, and a decline into institutionalism. For Luther every Christian was a priest, but not everyone was called to the 'office and work' of a priest.

The text itself does not mean, however, that every Christian is his or her *own* priest; but that *the whole Church* is the appointed 'priest-nation' to the world, to 'proclaim the mighty acts' of God (v. 9). The Church as 'royal priesthood' in the New Testament is equivalent to Israel's election in the Old Testament to service to its outside world, the Gentiles (cf. Ex. 19.6). This role is therefore a priesthood of the *laos* (Greek for 'people'), the whole 'people of God', rather than a priesthood of the *laity* (the unordained). It is a real calling, 'ordination' to which is through baptism. The Second Vatican Council of the Roman Catholic Church also emphasized this calling of the laity, and their sharing in the priesthood of Christ.

New Testament ministry may be regarded as the work of the whole Church; but there are also some who exercise particular 'ministries'. Although the Bible never calls individual ministers 'priests', it recognizes people with special gifts and ministries – apostles, prophets, evangelists, pastors, teachers and so on – whose task is 'to equip the saints [that is all Christians] for the work of ministry' (Eph. 4.12; cf. Rev. 1.6; see also Rom. 12.6–8; 1 Cor. 12.8–11, 28–30).

Separate Ministries

This rather chaotic, ad hoc and intensely localized state of affairs provided no clear pattern for later ages; nor were the Protestant Reformers agreed about how a Church based on New Testament principles should be constituted. Both 'bishops' (overseers or inspectors) and 'deacons' (assistants, helpers) are mentioned in the New Testament (for example Phil. 1.1); as are 'presbyters' ('elders') at Acts 14.23 and elsewhere. But these are all likely to have represented local, unofficial arrangements. The term 'apostles' was used not only of Jesus' closest disciples, but also of others to whom the risen Christ had appeared, or who had planted churches (see 1 Cor. 4.6, 9; 15.7–9). There is no real evidence that they had official 'successors', apart from some allusions in the late 'pastoral epistles' (to Timothy and Titus).

'Ministry in our modern sense of it ... is a development. There were no ministers, as we rate ministers, in the beginning' (Hanson and Hanson, 1981, p. 252). But these authors do not disparage the gradual development of a uniform, permanent 'ministry' of bishops, presbyters and deacons; nor the even later emergence of the idea of a Christian priest – a term originally applied mainly to bishops – who came to be thought of as having the role of forgiving sins and serving in some sense as a representative figure. He represents Christ to his people and them to him, and was therefore for some an 'icon' of Christ. In the middle of the third century, Bishop Cyprian of Carthage likened bishops to the sacrificing priests of the Old Testament, offering Christ's sacrifice at the Eucharist (the *sacerdotal* conception of priesthood). Later still, presbyters become regular presidents at the Eucharist, and not just the bishop's deputies. We should recall, however, that 'the purpose of the special ministry is to enable the Church to carry out its ministry, which is in fact Christ's ministry' (Hanson, 1975, p. 87).

The historic threefold ministry.   The threefold ministry of deacon, presbyter and bishop ('holy orders') became the standard conception of ministry in Orthodox, Roman Catholic and Anglican Churches ('episcopal Churches').

The *deacon* originally had an administrative and charitable role, with some pastoral and minor liturgical functions. In the Middle Ages his duties became essentially liturgical, while today the diaconate is mainly a step on the way to the priesthood – although there are 'permanent deacons' in some churches. *Presbyters* or *priests* could 'do' everything except ordain.[4] On this model, the presbyter/priest is the main minister of word and sacraments, and in traditional Catholic circles offers the sacrifice of the Mass. *Bishops* are the symbol of the apostolic mission and authority of the Church, but their 'overseeing' is for service – not an excuse for autocratic governance. The bishop is now usually regarded as the chief pastor and teacher of the faith, imaging the work of the apostles. He (or she in some churches) represents the whole Church to the diocese and the diocese to the whole Church. The bishops continue the apostolic mission through their power of ordaining both priests and bishops. Yet – at least in principle – the work of a bishop has to be 'received' by the Church community saying their 'Amen' to it.

The *apostolic succession* is the doctrine of the bishops' continuous succession from the apostles. Roman Catholics, Eastern Orthodox and many Anglicans understand this as a statement of an actual historical continuity of bishops down the ages from the first apostles: a 'lineal authentication'. But the concept also reflects the importance given to a doctrinal continuity – which Protestants also stress, whether they have bishops or not – as well as a felt need for continuity of office or function within the ministry. The Swedish (Lutheran) Church's bishops retain this historical continuity, whereas Methodist bishops do not.

Protestant ministry.   At the Reformation Protestants rejected this threefold ministry as unbiblical, along with much of the traditional Catholic theology of priesthood. But they retained the notion of a separate ministry. In what is sometimes called a *Presbyterian order of ministry*, no claims are made about a 'holy

---

4 Hence the scandal when Methodism's founder, the Anglican priest John Wesley, ordained clergy for the British colonies.

order'. Rather, the minister is seen as occupying a removable *office* (of preacher, pastor, leader, etc.) delegated from the laity.[5]

Where the threefold ministry exists it is often thought of as part of the very structure of the Church; but this later view is more utilitarian and organic, treating ministry as a matter of convenience and often adapting it to varying conditions. In both patterns of ministry, authority is (at least partly) independent of the particular qualities of the minister. Among some Protestants, however, more stress is placed on the minister's recognized calling and gifts (*charismata*) from God, than on the notion of an office.

There is a related shift in Protestantism away from an *ontological* concept of ministry, common among Catholics, Orthodoxy and Anglicans, in which ordination is viewed as a change wrought by God in their 'being' or 'nature' – and is traditionally held to be 'indelible' (cannot be lost). (According to the Council of Trent, this character was the power to offer absolution and the sacrifice of the Mass.) Protestants are far more likely to regard ministry in a *functional* way: a minister is what a minister does, and what he or she does is 'to minister' (serve) – which is an activity, a function. Hence the 'ministry of preaching the gospel and providing the sacraments' of classical Protestantism. In recent decades, a more functional account of ministry has also appealed to many in more traditional Churches.

Mission

Christianity is essentially a missionary religion. 'A Christianity with no mission to all would not be Christianity' (Barth, 1961, p. 304). The root meaning of the word is sending (Latin *mittere*, 'to send'). Like ministry, mission is essentially an activity of God. It is God who sends prophets, evangelists and apostles (Greek *apostellein*, 'to send forth') – and supremely his Son – in order to communicate and express, in their lives as well as their teaching, the good news about God's intentions towards his creation.

The Mission of the Church is always to proclaim the Gospel of salvation in Jesus Christ, in word and deed. It is to witness to the forgiveness and new

---

5 An 'office' is defined as a 'position of authority or service'.

life which God offers to all ... It is also to witness in intelligent and faithful action to His compassion, His reconciling love and His righteousness among all people. It is to bear witness to the grace and power of the new creation in every aspect of daily life. (From Evans and Wright, 1991, p. 451)

A *broad understanding of mission* includes three elements that 'go necessarily together ... [and] constitute an indivisible unity' (Hastings, 1975, p. 968):

1 to proclaim God's words (*kerygma*, 'proclamation');
2 to inaugurate God's salvation, by enacting God's works through a ministry (*diakonia*, 'service') that is continuous with God's compassion (pastoral ministry) and justice (pastoral and prophetic ministry); and
3 to create God's community (*koinonia*, 'fellowship'), by means of activities (1) and (2).

Many argue that (3) should not be narrowly understood, as the Church is merely God's agent in the mission of salvation. 'Where evangelization wins new members of the church, the aim of that work is not to increase the church's size but to enable it to penetrate the world more successfully with the message and actuality of God's own ministry to the world' (Hefner, 1984b, p. 235). The true end of God's mission – and therefore of the Church's calling – is not the Church, but *the kingdom of God* (see next chapter). On this view, evangelism forms only a part of a larger and wider whole. The Indian Orthodox priest, G. M. Osthathios writes, 'Evangelism is the spreading of the good news by proclamation, whereas mission is the outflow of the love of God in and through our life, word and deed' (cited in Abraham, 1989, p. 42).

However, Church pronouncements and popular theology often distinguish a *narrower conception of mission.* This concentrates on the proclamation of good news, as in (1) above, and the consequent expansion ('planting', 'growth') of the Christian Church, which is a particular, limited interpretation of element (3). It therefore clearly distinguishes mission from the diaconal, service or 'ministry' dimension of the Church's work contained in element (2).

So the narrower conception of mission restricts it to the explicit proclamation of the gospel through words (evangelization or 'explicit mission'); whereas the broader conception includes other activities under the heading of mission ('implicit mission'?) – especially service, prophecy, the enabling of fellowship and even perhaps worship. On the latter view, 'the words "ministry" and "mission" point to the same phenomenon, though they draw attention to different aspects of it' (Macquarrie, 1977, p. 420). This interpretation emphasizes that 'evangelism should not be separated from holistic care for the other' (Stiver, 2009, p. 396). Both the World Council of Churches and the Second Vatican Council have described the *Missio Dei* ('Mission of God') in terms of the 'humanization' of the world, 'the nurture and maintenance of the dignity of the image of God in human beings', which includes work for social justice as an integral part (Koyama, 1992, p. 314).

EXERCISE

- How do you react to these different understandings of mission?
- Who are the 'ministers of mission' in your theology?

Suggestions for Further Reading

Introductory

Hanson, A. T., 1975, *Church, Sacraments and Ministry*, London: Mowbrays.
Macquarrie, J., 1997, *A Guide to the Sacraments*, London: SCM Press.
Thompson, R., 2006, *SCM Studyguide to the Sacraments*, London: SCM Press.

Advanced

Dulles, A., 1997, *The Priestly Office: A Theological Reflection*, Mahwah, NJ: Paulist.
Jenson, R. W., 1978, *Visible Words: The Interpretation and Practice of Christian Sacraments*, Philadelphia: Fortress.
Newbigin, L., 1995, *The Open Secret: An Introduction to the Theology of Mission*, Grand Rapids, MI: Eerdmans.

5

Christian Belonging: The Church's Self-Understanding

Church-Talk

In this chapter we explore 'ecclesiology', the doctrine of the Church. The social unit of Christianity may be traced back to Jewish origins. In the Hebrew Old Testament, *kahal* meant the 'congregation', the nation of Israel assembled before God (see Ps. 111.1). The word used for this in the Greek New Testament, as in the Septuagint,[1] was *ekklesia* – literally those who are 'called out'. This term mainly denotes the local assembly, but on occasions it also refers to the whole Christian community (Matt. 16.18; Rom. 16.5; Col. 1.18).

The continuity of language between the two Testaments is another reminder that Christians see themselves as the New Israel; Jesus himself chose twelve followers to symbolize the twelve tribes of Israel. Like Israel, the Church is called to be the *people of God* (Lev. 26.12; Rom. 9.25–6; 1 Peter 2.9), a *vine* (Ps. 80.8–15; Isa. 5.1–7; Hos. 10.1; John 15.5) and a *flock* of sheep of whom God is the 'shepherd', although he sometimes operates through human shepherds (Ps. 77.20; Jer. 31.10; John 21.15–17; Acts 20.28–9; 1 Peter 5.1–4). Various other images and metaphors are used of the Church:

- an *ark* (1 Peter 3.18–21);
- a *tree* (Rom. 11.17–24);

---

1 The Greek translation of the Old Testament.

- a *temple*: a building in which Christ or the Spirit dwells, which has the apostles as its foundation and Christ as the 'cornerstone'; this building is still being 'built up' (1 Cor. 3.16–17; Eph. 2.19–22);
- a lowly, virgin *bride* who is given status and purpose, and is loved and made fecund, by Christ her Bridegroom (Eph. 5.25–32);
- a *family* (Gal. 6.10);
- a *body* made up of different 'members' (our language of 'membership' comes from this image of limbs and organs). The *body of Christ* (Rom. 7.4) is already somehow 'there' for Christians to enter and fill up, rather than being constituted by Christians (1 Cor. 12.12–27; cf. Eph. 4.12). In Colossians and Ephesians, Christ is the head and the Church the rest of his body (Eph. 1.22–3; Col. 1.18; 2.19). Later Christians sometimes developed this image in speaking of the Church as a *continuation of the incarnation*: that is, another material, 'enfleshed' form that expresses and enacts, and thus makes available, the loving will of Christ. It is therefore also a body constituted by Christ 'like a sacrament – a sign and instrument ... of communion with God and of unity among all' (*Lumen gentium* 1) – the 'sacramental gathering of believers' (Jenson, 1997, p. 211).

Later Christian tradition has spoken of the Church using the figures of 'the city of God' (Augustine) or 'an outpost of Heaven' (Barry Harvey). The Catholic theologian, Avery Dulles, discerns in the Christian tradition five basic models for the Church: institution, mystical communion, sacrament, herald and servant (Dulles, 2002, pp. 7–94).

Behind all these metaphors and models lies the claim of Christian experience that the Church is the place where the Christ-like God may particularly be found. It is pre-eminently a place of revelation and presence, and of response to and participation in Christ.

EXERCISE

Choose two New Testament images of the Church that you find illuminating, and two that you think might be problematic. How would you justify your choice?

Unity and Diversity

The metaphor of the body has a special significance in underscoring the idea of the Church as a *diversity-in-unity*. 'For just as the body is one and has many members . . . so it is with Christ' (1 Cor. 12.12). This unity cannot be a uniformity. So Archbishop Rowan Williams writes:

> The slogan of the Church's life is 'not without the other'; no I without a you, no I without a we. Yet that doesn't mean that the identity of the Church is a 'herd' identity, with everyone's individuality submerged in the collective. . . . So believing in the Church is really believing in the unique gift of the *other* that God has given you to live with. (Williams, 2007, p. 106)

The *diversity* of the Church is natural and inevitable; it is also – as Williams implies – highly valuable. It is sometimes a nuisance as well: especially for those Church leaders and others who want to iron out or ignore differences, so as to make their congregations and denominations more manageable and appear more unified. Human nature will usually resist such moves – as does the essential thrust of Christian doctrine.

A Common Unity?

While this is not quite the meaning of *community*, the etymology of that word indicates the condition or quality of an 'equal' – or at least a general – 'belonging' (Latin *communis*). Membership of the Church is one form of 'holy communion', fellowship or sharing (see 1 Cor. 10.16–17). Such language bears the connotation of unity, expressed in the idea of a group of individuals belonging *together* in a *single* club, neighbourhood, nation or other group.

It is partly because of our 'intercommunication with others throughout all of the dimensions of human existence' that the Christian religion is 'an ecclesial religion' (Rahner, 1978, p. 323). As social animals, it is our instinct to belong to one another, at least to some degree – to be 'in communion'. As social men and women we recognize our kin and support our hometown's sports clubs, viewing ourselves as connected with *these* others. But the dark side of this perception generates an equally natural urge to draw limits to our belonging, and to seek out and police the boundaries of the concept of 'neighbour' (see Luke 10.29). And that can result in our fighting *those* others represented by neighbouring fans, packs, tribes or nations. So Christians, too, quarrel among and between their ecclesial selves.

As we shall see, this belonging – and the unity that it promotes – is understood theologically as flowing from God in Christ. Like Israel, the Church is created to receive and proclaim God's love. It has therefore been called 'the beloved community' (by Martin Luther King, Jr). The English word 'Church' ultimately derives from the Greek *kyriakon*, which means 'the Lord's belonging'.

One might expect this emphasis on God as the one who intends and creates the Church to shift our attention away from ourselves, our status and our rights as members of the Church. This has never been easy; jostling for position has sullied Christian belonging from the beginning – even among Jesus' closest disciples. Jesus' response to the spoken or unspoken question, 'Which of us is the greatest?', was to confront the questioners with a little child as the model for adult discipleship – presumably because children had *no status* in the society of the time (Mark 9.33–7; 10.13–16, 35–45). Many believe that we need to hear this acted parable of censure in our own social world, where 'status anxiety' – our anxiety about our place in society – still corrodes, psychologically and spiritually. It is also the cause of many deep fault-lines within the Church. As called by God, however, the Church is *intended* as 'a community in which all are equal because everyone is equally an undeserving and surprising guest' (Williams, 2007, p. 120). It is therefore good to know that when the Church falls to its knees, its members are all close to the same height.

Theology regularly stresses the Church's communal status, in conscious opposition to the idea of a religious response and commitment that is purely personal and individual. Many see the very idea of the Church as a defence against an *individualism* that leads to selfishness and perverted notions of self-reliance. Michael Ramsey, later Archbishop of Canterbury, wrote that such individualism 'has no place in Christianity', but added that it is through the death of individualism that 'the individual finds himself' (Ramsey, 1936, p. 38). The Reformed theologian, Jürgen Moltmann, contends, 'We are no longer individualists but a congregation in which the one accepts the other . . . *Christian* (and this means liberating) community . . . no longer means only to sit next to those with whom I agree' (Moltmann, 1978, pp. 32–3).

The idea of a Church connects closely with the biblical theme that *salvation itself is a social concept*, which meshes with the Old Testament understanding of the communal or corporate nature of human beings and their sin (see Chapter 6). This claims that our humanity is always a shared humanity, and that our wrongdoing is never merely an individual thing but affects society as a whole. God's dealings with individuals are therefore always set within God's choice of, hope for and criticism of a *people*. Adopting these theological perspectives, the 'new creation' of which the New Testament speaks was inevitably perceived as more than an individual matter. So Paul writes, 'as all die in Adam, so all will be made alive in Christ' (1 Cor. 15.22). Here both Adam and Christ are individuals, each of whom 'embodies or represents a whole race of people' (Dunn, 2003, p. 200); and '*in Adam*' (a Hebrew word that denotes 'man', humankind) means 'as members of the human race which has departed from its original vocation in God's intention' (Barrett, 1971, p. 352).

This corporate theme is sometimes presented in different terms, with talk of the Church as an *organic* rather than a *contractual* society. On an organic view, society is regarded as prior to its individual members, both historically and in terms of status. This is the case with a family or nation; we are literally 'born into' such societies. A contractual society, on the other hand, is created when certain *individuals* decide to come together so as to share their common interests, and bind themselves together by some form of contract. This second understanding suggests the much more self-conscious and freely willed unity of a club. The organic interpretation is sometimes thought of as the more Catholic idea, although it developed first among the Greek Fathers of the undivided Church. The influential theologian Origen (*c*.186–255) even wrote of a *pre-existent* Church, a mystical society of all who are in communion with the Logos (the divine Word, manifested in Christ).

A History of Disunity

Clement of Alexandria argued in the second century that heresy represented 'spurious innovations of the oldest and truest Church', which was marked by unity. The Western Latin Fathers, such as Cyprian (*c*.200–58) and Augustine (354–430), were much concerned with the question of schism (Greek *schisma*, 'rent') – separation from the main body of the Church. They had to face the practical problem of whether groups that split away from the majority should be considered 'truly Church' or not. They ruled it out: 'there cannot be a Church among the heretics' (Cyprian, *Letters* lxxiv, 4); 'whoever is outside the Church has not the Holy Spirit' (Augustine, *Sermons* 268, 2). Eventually the papacy became the focus and test of the unity of the Church in the West; whereas Eastern churches looked more to a unity centred on the consensus of bishops, and a Church law increasingly overseen by the Byzantine emperor. For these and many other reasons, these two great folds of the fabric of Christendom themselves slowly pulled apart and finally separated in 1054, creating a rent in the Church that has yet to be repaired.[2]

Shifting the metaphor, we may now think in terms of two great flowing rivers of Christian practice and theology. The current of the Western Catholic Church suffered a second major division across the watershed of the sixteenth-century Protestant Reformation. New *denominations* (autonomous branches of the one Church) then arose as Martin Luther, John Calvin and others, with their sympathizers and followers, split – often reluctantly – from Rome's authority, and from many of the practices and doctrines of the Catholic Church. As we saw in the last chapter, these 'Churches' (as they are also routinely called) often claimed to be returning to the faith and practice of apostolic times, which represented for them a period before the waters of Christianity had lost touch with their source, and become polluted. Further downstream, however, many other Protestant groups later separated from the main streams of the Reformation, producing a confusing geography of multiple tributaries. Some see this 'fissiparous' tendency (to undergo splitting) as a reflection of Protestantism's shift to a more contractual conception of the Church, which tends to place greater stress on the status and responsibilities of the individual believer by comparison with those of the wider ecclesiastical society.

---

2 An earlier, permanent split in the Eastern Church had taken place in the fifth century over the definition of the nature of Christ.

Individualism Revisited

It is a great mistake, however, to think that the classical Reformers, or many of the later Protestant leaders, took either a low view of the Church or an individualistic notion of Christianity. They did not advocate allowing individuals to interpret the Bible wholly in 'their own way'. There is no doubt, however, that making the Bible and the liturgy more accessible to Christians, by translating them out of Latin into the 'vulgar tongue' of Church members, encouraged a move in that direction. This accelerated when printing became so cheap that large numbers could own Bibles and prayer books, and read them on their own – away from the authorities of the Church and its 'common worship'.

There is a tension here, which reflects our theme of individuals responding to Christian teachings in their own individual ways. I argued in Chapter 1 that this is never simply reproductive or repetitive, but always (to some degree) a 're-creation' or 'new creation' of religious meaning. The more we do our religious reading and reflection on our own, losing sight of the Bible as *the Church's* Bible and Christian tradition as what *the Church* passes on, the more 'on our own' we shall feel about our faith. Sometimes this is a good – perhaps essential – thing; but not always. For that which the Church 'passes on' (including, of course, its Scriptures) represents what the Church as a whole has taken to be the best and most authentic expression of its own response and witness to God. It is the Church's testimony. Individual Christians would be equally misguided in ignoring this wider wisdom, as in refusing to criticize any part of it. It has been said that the Church is like a great junk shop. Those who never enter its doors miss the chance of rooting out some pearl of great price, hidden under the dross on its dusty shelves. But 'it is as foolish to pass it by as to buy up its entire contents' (Drury, 1972, pp. 40–1).

In reality, people only ever take up that part of a tradition that evokes in them their own positive response. It is then that doctrine really engages Christians in a real conversation that changes them – as individuals, yet *within* a community of other Christian learners.

The quotations from Ramsey and Moltmann (pp. 89–90) offer a critique of what we might call 'hyperindividualism'. It should not swamp the authentic 'individuality' or individual character of Christians. 'There must be an essential particularity about the call to discipleship, because there is an essential particularity about people. God calls us by name' (Astley, 2007, p. 32). The real challenge that faces the Church is to find the proper balance between individual and community.

Can You See It Yet?

Theologians sometimes refer to two understandings of the Church.

- A doctrine of *the visible Church* teaches that its membership is known and that people (and whole 'Churches') may be said to fall from membership.
- A doctrine of *the invisible Church* claims that *we* cannot see who belongs to the true Church; God alone knows the membership roll of the company of God's elect.

Augustine, Luther and Calvin all saw the need to recognize *both* a visible fellowship *and* a hidden community of true believers. Others, however, have tended to emphasize one option at the expense of the other.

Some strange bedfellows have come together under the roof of the concept of an invisible Church, as extreme Protestant sects and liberal Christians can both endorse the idea that the Church's true membership is unknown to us; although the liberals are more likely to allow that 'true Christians' can exist without showing any *explicitly* Christian behaviour, and can therefore exist outside the visible Church.

John Calvin avoided distinguishing two Churches by arguing that the invisible Church of the elect, the Church 'as it really is before God', cannot for practical purposes be separated from the visible, mixed, 'external Church'. In any case, the former will not come into being before the final judgement. Until then, he recommended loyalty to the Church we *can* see, despite its defects. 'As it is necessary to believe the invisible Church, which is apparent only to the eye of God, so we are also commanded to respect that Church which is so called on the human plane, and cultivate its communion' (*Institutes of the Christian Religion* iv, ch. 1, 7). Calvin also saw that such loyalty requires humility, in making us 'willing to be washed in the same fountain as the most impure' (*Commentary on Matthew* 9.12). As Barth argues, applying the idea of invisibility to the Church can devalue it as a 'visible coming together' (1966, p. 142).

The idea of schism only makes sense within the doctrine of a visible Church, although even then people will dispute whether the separating Christians are still *part* of the Church after such a division: that is, that there has been a schism '*within* the Church'. On this view, the Church is clearly capable of sub-division. The alternative standpoint would argue that schism is always '*from* the Church' when one group rejects the 'faith and order' (doctrines and visible structures) of the other, or ceases to recognize their sacraments.

EXERCISE

How does your own experience and theology of the Church respond to these distinctions between:

(1) individual and collective,
(2) organic and contractual,
(3) visible and invisible Church,
(4) one Church or many Churches?

The Marks of the Church

Protestants are sometimes surprised when they are expected to voice belief in 'the holy catholic Church' (Apostles' Creed) or 'one holy catholic and apostolic Church' (Nicene Creed). 'Catholic' is the usual issue, and for this reason the Reformers substituted 'Christian'. But all four of these adjectives – generally, but not universally, labelled 'marks' or 'notes' of the Church – can seem problematic to the thoughtful Christian. This is not least because the epithets make such high claims for the Church. As Temple (allegedly) put it, 'I believe in the Church, One Holy, Catholic and Apostolic, and I regret that it nowhere exists.' Precisely!

But if we are to respond to this paradox, we shall need to stress that the Church is one, and also holy, catholic and apostolic, only in God's (eternal?) *intention*; not as an empirical (observable) fact. Biblical thinking is more interested than we are in God's intentions. Where we are content to rest our gaze and minds on things as they are, the Bible sees beyond to a vision of things as God calls them to be. The marks of the Church are not just ideals, however, for God's election is the deepest reality of things. Rather, they are *divine givens* that it is the responsibility of human Church members to 'realize', in two senses of that word: to understand and to make real. The Church *must become* what in God's call it *already is*, striving after the marks of that calling. The Church's attributes therefore have both an imperative and an indicative force.

Yet can we believe *in* the Church, bearing in mind our analysis in Chapter 2? Some have appealed to the Latin of the Apostles' Creed to argue that, though we rightly believe in God, Jesus and the Spirit, 'we do not believe *in* the Church' – believing only *that* it exists 'in spite of its faults and deficiencies . . . as the field of activity of the Spirit of Christ' (Barth, 1966, p. 143; Pannenberg, 1972, p. 145). 'To say that we do not believe *in* the Church means that the Church is not God' (Küng, 1971, p. 32). However, the Nicene Creed does have we 'believe *in*' the Church, so the argument cannot be resolved solely on linguistic grounds.

Unity

Doctrinally, the unity of the Church – its calling to be one – is grounded in the unity of God. The Church is God's, and therefore one; it is not ours, for then it would be many.

> The unity of the Church is a spiritual entity. It is not chiefly a unity of the members among themselves, it depends finally not on itself but on the unity of God . . . It is one and the same God who gathers the scattered from all places and all ages and makes them into one people of God. It is one and the same Christ who through his word and his Spirit unites all together in the same bond of fellowship. (Küng, 1971, p. 273)

As we have seen, the unity of the Church is always a unity-with-diversity. The Church is not called to be a colony of cloned individuals, or identically pro-grammed robots. According to Paul, it is to be a complex, co-ordinated organ-ism made up of many specialized elements, each engaged in different tasks for the good of the whole. As an organic entity, its unity is therefore compatible with any amount of what biologists call 'specialization' and 'division of labour'.

'Unity is strength' is an old trade union slogan, as well as the motto of a number of nations. But another of Temple's reputed *bons mots* was his claim that the Church is the only organization that exists for those who are not its members. The strength that the Church needs is strength for a ministry and mission of love to those who are outside its walls (see Chapter 4 and pp. 103–5 below). So we should perhaps expect from the Church a *wider unity*, beyond the obvious unity of those who confess the same Lord. The unity of the 'called' – whether Israel or the Church – should never be at the expense of too sharp a division from those outside, whether they are the 'Gentiles', the 'non-Church' or 'the world'. The Church can recognize, and may even perhaps 'shade into', a unity that marks the whole of humanity – and the whole of creation (cf. Eph. 1.10). Such a wider unity is reflected in Paul's sermon in Athens (Acts 17.24–8) and the Genesis account of God's covenant with all creation through Noah (Gen. 8.21—9.17). To find Christ's Spirit in the Church is to find the one who is *also* Lord of the world, the one through whom all things were made and will be redeemed. Therefore the Church's unity may itself serve as a symbol or sacrament of a wider unity, by helping us acknowledge this broader unity-in-diversity of Church and non-Church *together*.

The traditional 'sign' of the unity of the Church is said to be the possession of a common Bible, and therefore of a common story. It is a story that is most often heard as a challenge by the world. But the prophets often suggest a different relationship between God's people at home and those beyond its borders. 'Did I not bring Israel up from the land of Egypt, *and* the Philistines from Caphtor, *and* the Arameans from Kir?' (Amos 9.7). 'Many nations shall come and say: "Come, let us go up to the mountain of the Lord . . . that he may teach us his ways and that we may walk in his paths"' (Micah 4.2). 'It is too light a thing that you should be my servant . . . to restore the survivors of Israel; I will give you as a light to the nations, that my salvation may reach to the end of the earth' (Isa. 49.6).

Communion of Saints

Properly interpreted, unity implies the next two marks of the Church, catholicity and apostolicity, as the Church is called to be one across both space (geography) and time (history). But it is under the mark of unity that theologians have most often laid claim to a union that transcends both space and time: a unity between the Church as it now is on earth, and as it is now in heaven. In more traditional language, this is the unity of the Church 'militant' (engaged in spiritual warfare) 'here on earth', and the Church 'expectant' in purgatory or 'triumphant' in heavenly/paradisal rest (see Chapter 10).

As a consequence, the phrase 'communion of saints' from the Apostles' Creed can be used to refer *both* to all Christians currently alive, since Scripture applies the word 'saints' to all Christians (Rom. 1.7; 1 Cor. 1.2; 2 Cor. 1.1; Phil 1.1), *and* to the earthly Church's fellowship with those Christians who have 'gone before' (Col. 1.12).[3] While for some this second form of human fellowship is a purely passive relationship, others believe that the 'heavenly saints' can assist those on earth (cf. Rev. 6.9–10), and that the prayers of the living faithful can sometimes help the dead who have yet to appear before God in judgement. Invoking the saints (particularly Mary) is a traditional Orthodox and Catholic practice, shared by some Anglicans and others. But many in these denominations, and practically all other Protestants, reject this idea. A much less controverted notion is that we join our prayers *with* those of the saints in heaven (a process sometimes called 'comprecation'), so that the whole Church together may be regarded as praying to God *for* the whole Church.

Holiness

From the first, then, the Church was regarded as holy, with the Greek New Testament describing fellow Christians as *hoi hagioi*, 'the holy ones' or 'the saints'. Unfortunately, this particular mark of the Church seems to be a very bad joke – not only to most people outside the Church but also to many who belong to it. For it appears to ignore the sinfulness of the Church, while allowing it hypocritically to be 'removed away into a sanctimonious distance' (Edward Irving).

An honest theology must acknowledge what has been described as the Church's 'Jekyll-and-Hyde character'. This paradox has also been there from the beginning: Jesus' twelve disciples received the highest calling but repeatedly failed to live up to it. Nevertheless, the tradition remembers that the one rebuked by Jesus, and who later denied him, was characterized as the Rock of the Church by its Lord (Matt. 16.17–19; cf. 16.22–3). But the problem did not end with these failed friends, and neither does the paradox. Paul is forever criticizing the early Christian communities for their sin, quarrels and lack of love, while at the same time using the highest language to describe their status.

---

3 By the eleventh century, the phrase was also taken to refer to participation in the sacraments, as 'holy things'.

In the Bible, however, holiness is pre-eminently the mark of *God*. It can therefore only be claimed of humans as a gift to a Church that belongs to God by divine grace. 'Holy people do not make the church holy' (Hefner, 1984b, p. 206); 'Christ is the head and the source of all [the] body's life and holiness' (Zizioulas, 2008, p. 152). There are obvious dangers in the Church taking on itself an adjective ('holy') that is almost equivalent to 'divine'; but after the gift has been given holiness surely comes with the territory, in the sense that the Church has become part of the calling of God: 'You shall be holy, for I the LORD your God am holy' (Lev. 11.45; 19.2). As these biblical references show, holiness – which literally means 'set apart-ness', and was in essence a unique quality of otherness experienced as both dread and blessing (see Chapter 9) – became associated with purity (see Isa. 6.1–7). The theme of imitating God, in the sense of living in accordance with the character of God, is prominent in Scripture (Eph. 4.1; 5.1; 1 Peter 1.14–16). In the New Testament it becomes almost a 'transitive relation' (one applying between successive members of a sequence) – so Paul can say, 'Be imitators of me, as I am of Christ' (1 Cor. 11.1).

However, 'purity' does not seem to be the right idea here at all. In the Bible it often means avoidance of ritually and religiously 'unclean' things or persons (as the text from Leviticus 11 confirms). This behaviour was practised by the Temple ministers and the lay Pharisees (from the Hebrew for 'separatists'). But Jesus resolutely puts it in its place (Matt. 23.23–8; Mark 2.15–17; 7.1–23; Luke 7.31–5; 10.29–37; 11.37–41). Where holiness had become exclusive isolation from what was 'common' and 'worldly', holiness in Jesus 'identifies itself . . . with the world of sinners'. And in the Church's expansion among the Gentiles, the work of the Holy Spirit becomes 'ever more *in*clusive, "common"' (Burnaby, 1959, pp. 139–40). In truth, this returns to the roots of the theology of holiness, for the Bible views God as set apart in order to be himself and accomplish his purposes – 'the Holy God shows himself holy by righteousness' (Isa. 5.16). So our second 'you shall be holy', from Leviticus (19.2), comes at the beginning of a chapter that speaks more of moral than cultic holiness, and includes love of neighbour (v. 18) and merciful care for the poor and the alien (vv. 10, 14, 33).

In the teaching of Jesus, the Leviticus combination of imperative and indicative is rendered, 'Be merciful, just as your Father is merciful' (Luke 6.36). But Matthew's version (5.48) has, 'Be perfect, therefore, as your heavenly Father is perfect.' 'Merciful' sounds like what we need; 'perfect' poses another problem. However, the Greek word for 'perfect' (*teleios*) probably means 'fully developed' or 'matured' (Borg, 2006, pp. 324–5). The *Scholars Version* of the Bible translates it 'unstinting'.

We may also note that 'holiness/holy' and 'whole' are related in their etymological roots. Wholeness is about completeness and entirety; it marks an undiminished state with no parts removed – the perfection of inclusion, not exclusion. Spiritually speaking, holiness is received by obedience, which is closely linked to the virtue of humility. Many Christians cherish the model of the humble Mary who allowed Christ to be formed within her (Luke 1.38) – and of others who have 'let it be' for the sake of God's kingdom. The Church, like Mary and all the saints, is *called as it is*, 'warts and all'. There is a comforting unsaintliness about the biblical accounts of saints: so different from the spruced-up, hagiographical half-truths often found in later Christian tradition. The biblical saints help us to see God working through the very ordinary. All that is required of them – as of Christians today – is an inevitably human, fallen and failing, and therefore humble response to God's call. Only by God's grace could the Church ever be *indefectible*, 'not liable to fail'.

Therefore the Church's holiness does not involve righteousness or moral purity as a species of self-concern. It is not a closed-off holiness of separation from the world, but a holiness or wholeness of embrace – a type of love. For 'the Church exists for the sake of the world' (Barth, 1966, p. 32).

> The Church can never be satisfied with what it can be and do as such. As His community it points beyond itself. At bottom it can never consider its own security, let alone its appearance. As His community it is always free from itself. In its deepest and most proper tendency it is not churchly, but worldly – the Church with open doors and great windows, behind which it does better not to close itself in upon itself again by putting in pious stained-glass windows. It is holy in its openness to the street and even the alley, in its turning to the profanity of all human life. (Barth, 1956b, pp. 724–5)

If Christians are secure in the Church's call and vision, and confident of God's continuing grace in this ramshackle home for habitual offenders, they can symbolize and convey their experience of the grace-given life to a wider constituency. So holiness, too, is part of the Church's vocation to exist for those who are not its members. 'The elect *are* set apart, but this separation is not for privilege but for service' (Burnaby, 1959, p. 140).

The traditional sign of the Church's holiness is its sacraments, or – more generally – its distinctive worship (see Chapter 4). Here Christ is portrayed, prayed to and present; and it is through this worship that the grace of the Christ-like God is given and received. The Church's worship also enables *Christian formation*, in so far as worshippers recognize the true Christ disclosed in worship and allow his character and vision to be formed within themselves. The Church preaches the gospel to itself so that it may be constantly 'turned about' ('converted') by being reoriented towards Christ, and thus ready to love and speak the gospel to the world. In Christian worship, we 'learn Christ' by being transformed as well as formed. No portrayal of the true 'image of Christ' is without this power to convert. When worship is truly *Christ*-ian, by presenting, praising and evoking the Christ-like God, Christians are remodelled in this image. And therefore 'made holy', as they too become open to others, in love. Even in the alley.

Any body of people that does *not* so reveal and proclaim the true Christ, in word, ritual and service, is not truly the holy Church – because they are not truly living or worshipping 'in Jesus' name' (cf. Kelsey, 1992, pp. 137–9).

Catholicity

The puzzled Protestants of p. 94 need to know that the word 'catholic' in the creeds – best spelled with a small 'c' – does not mean Roman Catholic, but 'all-embracing' or 'universal' (Greek *katholikos*). 'Catholic' is itself from the Greek *kata*, 'in respect of', and *holos*, '[the] whole' or 'totality' – which is now a familiar theme! Catholicity is the mark of the continuity of the body of Christ across geographical space, beyond the individual and local congregations. This calling of the Church to be 'for all' marks the Church out, not only as *supra-national* and culturally universal (Matt. 8.10–11), but also as *non-sectarian*. Sociologists distinguish between Church and 'sect': whereas the Church is inclusive of a population, 'sects are always somewhat exclusive bodies which impose some test of merit' on their members (Wilson, 1966, p. 180).

Who is to be included? Fellowship can be hard work, even among friends and in a family. In Charles M. Schultz's 'Peanuts' cartoon strip, Linus is criticized for wanting to be a doctor despite lacking the appropriate attitude to humankind. He retorts: 'I love humanity, it's people I can't stand.' In the case of the Church, our experience of particular congregations, churchgoers, clergy and other Church leaders can sometimes evoke a similar response: 'I love the Church, it's just the . . .' C. S. Lewis's 'senior devil' is advising his nephew how to tempt a new Christian:

> One of our great allies at the present is the Church itself. . . . When [your patient] gets to his pew and looks round him he sees just the selection of his neighbours whom he has hitherto avoided. You want to lean pretty heavily on those neighbours. Make his mind flit to and fro between an expression like 'the body of Christ' and the actual faces in the next pew. It matters very little, of course, what kind of people that next pew really contains. You may know one of them to be a great warrior on the Enemy's side. No matter. Your patient, thanks to Our Father below, is a fool. Provided that any of those neighbours sing out of tune, or have boots that squeak, or double chins, or odd clothes, the patient will quite easily believe that their religion must there-fore be somehow ridiculous. (Lewis, 1955, pp. 15–16)

One of the great dangers of theologizing about the Church is that of speak-ing pious abstractions. The claim that these marks of the Church are true only within God's intention can tempt us to move in this direction. The above pas-sage cuts through such language, and helps us get 'down and dirty' among the concrete realities of human relationships.

At one level, Christian *prejudice and discrimination* is a problem for individu-als. But when the Church corporately closes its doors against certain classes or groups of people, it can become a doctrinal issue. Such action is challenged by the teaching that the Church should be open to all whom God calls without dis-crimination, just as God's love is unconditionally offered even to the unlovely, and as the Church's mission should similarly express its 'catholic' universality.

> A Church founded on unmerited and unconstrained mercy may not at times be the Church we would like; but it is the only Church we have been given. It may fail to guarantee our proud entitlements or protect our vulnerabil-ities; but it is the only kind of Church that could make space for the new life, the rejected perceptions or the unexpected love on which our shared future depends. Above all, it is the kind of Church there would have to be if God really means to love the unwanted more than those whom human structures

of power would reward, the only kind of Church that could carry the life that comes from the Cross. (Selby, 1991, p. 78)

A recent book has argued that we should not see the demand for inclusivity in the Church as merely aping secular political correctness, but as a fundamental practical imperative that follows – as they all should – from theological claims about God's character and activity. 'The Church should be inclusive because God is inclusive' (Shakespeare and Rayment-Pickard, 2006, p. 1). Such theology-driven inclusivity, they continue, should extend not just to the ordination of women and the welcoming of people of all races and classes, but more controversially to welcoming gay men and lesbians fully into the life and organization of the Church. These are certainly contentious issues in today's Church. Is the Church truly 'open to all'? *Should* it be? Other voices would say that the correct measure is whether it is 'open to all those whom God has called', and that some have by their lifestyle deliberately refused God's word of invitation. It is not for human beings to try to be more inclusive than God. What do you think?

The Church claims to be universal not only geographically, but also doctrinally, in that it is said to preserve the complete, authentic, orthodox or real Christian faith. Traditionally, catholicity is symbolized by the Church's creeds: those common formulations of belief designed to protect the unique Christian claim that in Christ we find the true God. But it may be argued that orthodoxy, as 'right thinking' (as Western Christians came to emphasize) or 'correct worship' (the more characteristic Eastern emphasis), should be viewed as having no more than a subordinate, regulatory function. It is an instrument to keep the Church focused on the true Christ and *his* kingdom. In this area, in particular, catholicity overlaps with our final mark of ecclesial identity.

Apostolicity

Apostolicity refers to the Church's calling to an identity or continuity down the centuries of Christianity – its 'temporal universality'. It is claimed as a sign of authenticity, in so far as the Church continues in the basic teaching and practice of the apostles, who are pivotal as eyewitnesses and first guardians of its message. The Church is dependent on its past, but its norm is Christ. And 'whatever does not teach Christ is certainly not apostolic even though St. Peter or St. Paul teach it. Again, whatever preaches Christ is apostolic even though Judas . . . might say it' (Luther, cited in Schwarz, 1984, p. 260). But if *apostellein* is Greek for 'to send forth', the Church is also apostolic to the extent that it is part of the mission of God in Christ (see Chapter 4).

The apostolicity of the Church is certainly part of its calling, but here too, the extent to which it is truly apostolic will depend on whether in practice and experience it can be identified with God's mission to the world – as shown in Jesus' ministry, and carried forward by his first disciples. The Church's apostolicity is therefore symbolized by the Church's ministry, traditionally regarded both as the guarantor of its continuity with the Church's earliest tradition, and as the enabler of the whole Church's wider service to the world. But Küng writes that even 'apostolic succession' is the invitation to *all* Christians in the Church to become 'more apostolic', by striving to be loyal to the Church's origins (Küng, 1993, p. 136).

On Boundaries

Abstract ecclesiology can make identification of the Church a rather all-or-nothing thing, with a sharp distinction between what is Church and what is not. Aren't the boundaries between Church and non-Church more *blurred* than that?

Jean Bouteiller has described those at the edge of Church life as *threshold Christians*. He argues that the Church is still 'visited, frequented, questioned, explored, loved, criticized by a crowd of people who call themselves more or less Christians. ... Many encamped at the Church's doors are willing to be recognized as being of the Church and to be linked to it, but they are very hesitant about being recognized as being integrally *within* the Church.' Such people enable, encourage, demand and sometimes force the Church to be open. Bouteiller's account would also push us, then, towards an *open ecclesiology*.

When one speaks of threshold Christians, one pictures the Church as a building or as an open space, places arranged more or less for entering or leaving, coming and going. These are the building's entrances, the doors. One can easily imagine the many activities that can take place on these thresholds: meetings, movement, mixing of people, waiting, initiation, revelation, discussion, ceremonies, and so on. Moreover, the threshold is an integral part of the building; it is neither an accessory nor an appendix. (Bouteiller, 1979, pp. 67–8)

This account of ecclesiological *liminality* rather suggests that we should reject at least one of the ancient models of the Church – the Church as an ark of salvation, whose sailors pluck the saved from the turbulent currents of worldliness, in order to protect them on a journey away from this dangerous secular ocean to a safe haven far away. There are alternative, more attractive, metaphors for the Church.[4] But we might also consider some images that Jesus used in speaking to and of his disciples: the leaven in the lump, the salt in the stew and the candle on the candlestick (Matt. 5.13–16; 13.33). These do not only tell of a distinctive taste and power, they also image an ecclesiology that recognizes no impermeable, rigid and protective barriers between Christian disciples and those who do not follow 'the Way'. Christians are not safe in the ark, with the rest lost in the sea – for God has promised that 'never again shall all flesh be cut off by the waters' (Gen. 9.11).

The salt enhances the stew, the yeast leavens the dough, the light shines to the edges of the room, and beyond. None of them can do their stuff unless they are different from the environment in which they work; but nor can they function unless they are *released* into that environment, not hermetically sealed from it. Yeast and salt are stirred into the cooking; the candle flame blazes out openly into the alley. The Church can only succeed in being Church, as the disciples can only truly follow their master, when they are willing to 'mix it' with the world – even sometimes to die out or fade out into it.

Where the life of the Church is exhausted in self-serving, it smacks of death; the decisive thing has been forgotten, that this whole life is lived only in the exercise of . . . the Church's service as ambassador, proclamation, *kerygma*. . . . Christianity is not 'sacred'; . . . it is an out-and-out 'worldly' thing open to all humanity. (Barth, 1966, pp. 146–7)

Do *you* think this is how Church should work?

---

4 The missiologist, Paul Hiebert, prefers a third way to the alternatives of the sharp boundaries of a 'bounded set' view of the Church, and the liberal interpretation of a 'fuzzy set' of various degrees of inclusion. A more dynamic understanding of Church suggests the model of a 'centred set' defined by movement towards or away from its centre (Christ).

Church and Kingdom

The Church lives to proclaim, and proclaims so as to live, the Christian gospel. It is therefore secondary to the gospel. As we saw earlier, the Church is an interim, temporary, penultimate thing. The Church's vocation is to help to bring about, then to make way for, its goal of God's kingdom. (Not to get in the way of it.) 'The meaning of the Church does not reside in itself, in what it is, but in what it is moving towards. It is the reign of God which the Church hopes for, bears witness to, proclaims' (Küng, 1971, p. 96). The Church is 'primarily a foretaste of the eschatological assembly of the Lord, made present in the world' (Zizioulas, 2008, p. 127).

The kingdom is the reign or rule of Christ: 'what life would be like on earth if God were king' (Borg, 2003, p. 135) – and in whatever future consummation God brings. Theologically, the kingdom is God's final purpose for creation, and his last and greatest gift to it. As such, it is at the same time the fruition of the glorious liberty of the children of God, and the liberation of all humankind from all their oppression. (This is what makes it especially good news for the poor.) To open people's eyes to see the kingdom, and their lives to respond to it, is the greatest privilege and responsibility laid upon the Church. In so far as it does this, the Church *may* be called 'the effectual sign, the sacrament, of the Kingdom of God' (Burnaby, 1959, p. 152).

Spirit, Church and Grace

The Church was from the start the new creation of the Spirit. The Holy Spirit as wind or breath (Hebrew *ruach*, Greek *pneuma*) appears throughout the Old Testament as the 'living energy of a personal God' (Geoffrey Lampe). The Spirit is particularly active as a creative and re-creative power (Gen. 1.2; 2.7; Ps. 51.10–12; 104.29–30; Ezek. 36.26–8; 37.1–14), and as an unpredictable, mysterious, holy gift to God's servants and prophets – although 'the word of the Lord' is perhaps more significant for prophetic 'inspiration' (Judg. 6.34; 14.6; 1 Sam. 16.13; Isa. 11.1–2; 42.1; 61.1; Joel 2.28–9).

But there is a new outburst of the Spirit in the life and ministry of Jesus, 'the man of the Spirit' (James Dunn). The Spirit empowered, inspired and filled him;

and in his resurrection and exaltation he in turn bestows the Spirit (Luke 24.49; John 20.22; Acts 1.8; 2.1–36). The Church now becomes *the* location for the Spirit – not as a doctrine, but as an experienced reality. In particular, the Church expresses the 'sharing [fellowship] in the Spirit', as a corporate means of grace and a social reality where God as Spirit is best found and known (1 Cor. 12.13; 2 Cor. 13.13; Eph. 4.1–4; Phil. 2.1). Pentecost is the Spirit creating this community, and Jesus himself returning to his disciples.

From now on this 'Spirit of Christ' can no longer be seen as an impersonal power. It is this experience that eventually pushed the Church to a Trinitarian confession, which included the Holy Spirit as a 'person' equal to the Father and the Son (Chapter 9). No aspect of the Church's work and Christian self-identity is thought of as without the Spirit, which is essential to faith and grace, preaching and prayer, baptism and Eucharist, conversion and sanctification, mission and ministry, and Christian life and character in general.

In addition to all this, some parts of the Church point to the effects of a particular 'baptism in the Spirit', in *charismata* ('grace gifts') – especially the gifts of tongues and their interpretation, and prophecy, discernment and healings. Paul welcomes such gifts as authentic (if often ambiguous) marks of the presence of the Spirit, which should be used to promote Christian community. But, as all acknowledge, they are *special* graces. The more *fundamental* result of the Holy Spirit's work is the grace given to all Christians. God's love 'poured into our hearts' (Rom. 5.5) is the 'more excellent way', and the greatest of gifts (1 Cor. 12.31—13.13). Grace is what it means to be indwelt by the Spirit (Rom. 8.9–11; Gal. 4.4–7) and to be 'in Christ' (1 Cor. 1.4–9; 2 Cor. 5.17; Phil. 2.1–5). 'Grace is not something other than God . . . it is God himself dwelling within people as the Holy Spirit and working in them their identity in Christ' (Norris, 1979, p. 184). It is 'theological shorthand for God's continuing engagement with us' (Gorringe, 1989, p. 169).

EXERCISE

Which themes in this chapter most resonate with your understanding of the Church, and which do you find most strongly challenge it? And why?

Suggestions for Further Reading

Introductory

Avis, P. D. L., 1993, 'Ecclesiology', in A. E. McGrath (ed.), *The Blackwell Encyclopedia of Modern Christian Thought*, Oxford: Blackwell, pp. 127–34.

Hanson, A. T., 1975, *Church, Sacraments and Ministry*, London: Mowbrays.

McGrath, A. E., 2007, *Christian Theology: An Introduction*, Oxford: Blackwell, ch. 15.

Advanced

Dulles, A., 2002, *Models of the Church*, New York: Doubleday.

Jay, E. G., 1977, *The Church: Its Changing Image through Twenty Centuries*, two vols, London: SPCK.

Moltmann, J., 1977, *The Church in the Power of the Spirit: A Contribution to Messianic Ecclesiology*, London: SCM Press.

6

Christian Healing: Experiences and Images of Salvation

'Are You Saved?'

It is unfortunate that the fundamental claim of Christianity, that Christ is God's agent of salvation, has become a cause of such quarrels and divisions among Christians. For some it is delightful both to ask and to answer the question, 'Are you saved?' For others, the words are an embarrassment, even an insult, and represent the last thing they would say to their non-Christian friends or neighbours. I wonder which you are – and why?

The English words 'save', 'salvation' and 'saviour' are from the Latin *salvus*, 'safe' (hence our words 'salve' and 'salvage'). People used such language in quite secular contexts, speaking of situations of rescue, preservation or protection from danger or harm. In biblical and Christian terms, the idea of salvation has a similar range of meaning, and is associated with ideas of 'broadness' and 'wholeness' – being 'made whole'; the words *sozo* ('I save') and *soteria* ('salvation') label rescues from danger, and physical or mental healings, as well as spiritual redemption (for example Matt. 8.25; Mark 5.23; Luke 19.9–10; Acts 4.9; 14.9; 16.30–1; Heb. 11.7; cf. Mark 2.1–17). Jesus' name is itself the Greek form (*Iesous*) of the Hebrew name Joshua, meaning 'Yahweh is salvation' (Matt. 1.21).[1]

---

1 'Yahweh' is the proper name of Israel's God, revealed to Moses at Ex. 3.13–15. In Hebrew texts it is written without vowels as YHWH, and is usually rendered in English versions of the Bible as 'the Lord'.

When salvation is thought of in this general way, practically all religious traditions may be understood as 'salvific' – even Buddhism with its emphasis on enlightenment. Religions are distinguished with reference to the predicament they say that humans need to be saved *from*, the aim or goal *for* which people are saved, and *how* this is to be achieved – the 'from what', 'to what' and 'by what' of salvation (Clark, 1978, pp. 10–69).

In Christianity, the 'to what' is understood in the Bible and later Christian theology in various ways:

- *shalom* (a this-worldly 'peace' whose fundamental sense is wholeness, health and security);
- God's rule in this world;
- a 'heavenly' state beyond this present world;
- some ultimate participation in God's own life, or absorption into God's own being.

The things Christians believe keep them away from this desired state or end of life also vary, for different people think that they need to be saved from different things. Among the candidates are ignorance (often presented as spiritual 'blindness' or 'deafness') and suffering of various sorts. But, traditionally, the most important has been sin.

The Theology of Sin

It is often said that, fundamentally, sin is anything that separates us from God. Nevertheless, our disobedient transgression against God's moral and religious law has become the paradigm (supreme example) of sinfulness. Our *guilt* lies in having rebelled against God's will, or even in contravening it unintentionally (cf. Lev. 5.2).

According to the Bible, although at first 'God saw everything that he had made, and indeed, it was very good' (Gen. 1.31), things went badly wrong. Not only the human race but also the whole creation were turned away from God as a consequence of human sin. This catastrophe is most strongly represented in the narrative-metaphor ('myth') of Genesis 3; although chapters 4—11 also deal with human sin and God's response (Cain and Abel, Noah's flood, the Tower of Babel).

The Bible is realistic about human beings. 'Crowned . . . with glory and honour' they may be (Ps. 8.5), but they are still deeply flawed. The fall of Adam ('man') follows from a primordial temptation to doubt the goodness of the creator, leading to a first act of self-assertive disobedience. This results in expulsion from the Garden of Eden, and God's curse on the serpent and the ground. Henceforth, the lives of Adam and his partner Eve ('life') are subjected to (increased?) travail and to death – although many scholars argue that death was natural to creation from the start. This dramatic narrative is obscure in places, and is not referred to elsewhere in the Old Testament. However, disobedience, arrogant defiance, selfishness, untruthfulness and faithlessness are key elements throughout the rest of its literature.

Judaism itself produced no fully developed idea of original sin, although it regarded God as creating an 'evil inclination' in humans. Paul, however, clearly draws out the story's implications that 'sin came into the world through one man, and death came through sin, and so death spread to all because all have sinned' (Rom. 5.12). Thus 'one man's trespass led to condemnation for all', and 'by the one man's disobedience the many were made sinners' (Rom. 5.18–19). But this also falls short of a doctrine of original sin.

The early Greek Fathers acknowledged a transmission of human sin as a wound in human nature, but offer no hint that mankind shares Adam's *guilt*. It was the Latin West that accentuated the fall, ascribing to it spectacular effects, Augustine attributing original righteousness and perfection to Adam. Through his fall came the corruption of the entire human race, which through his 'ancient sin' became 'a universal mass of perdition'. (Augustine read Rom. 5.12 in a poor translation that suggested that Adam was the one *in whom* all sinned, not that all are guilty *because* they sin like Adam.) According to Augustine, we all share a 'seminal identity' with Adam because we were all already present 'in his loins' (genes?), when he disobeyed God.

God created man [humanity] aright, for God is the author of natures, though he is certainly not responsible for their defects. But man was willingly perverted and justly condemned, and so begot perverted and condemned offspring. For we were all in that one man, seeing that we all *were* that one man who fell into sin through the woman who was made from him before the first sin. (*City of God* xiii, ch. 14)

In traditional Western theology, Adam's fall had four results for all humans: (i) *original sin* (our inherited tendency to sin), (ii) *original guilt* (our inherited guilt for Adam's sin), (iii) *natural evil* (pain, suffering and death that is God's punishment for the fall, and for our individual sins thereafter),[2] and (iv) *the defacement of the image of God* in humans (though Gen. 9.6; 1 Cor. 11.7 and James 3.9 suggest that it is not wholly lost).

Conscious of the power of sexual passion in his own life, Augustine believed that original sin was transmitted by concupiscence: that is, lust that 'aims at enjoying one's self and one's neighbour, and other corporeal things, without reference to God' (*On Christian Doctrine* iii, chs 10 and 16). As a further by-product of our fall, from now on we can only freely do wrong – psychologically, we *can* only sin. And God's will *predestined* (or foreordained) from eternity the salvation of those he mercifully chooses (the 'elect') – creating their faith by preparing their wills to respond. Without God's grace, therefore, all are on the road to hell.

In contrast to such views, the British layman Pelagius (a fashionable teacher at Rome) argued that our free will remains unsoiled by original sin, and God doesn't condemn us for another's (Adam's) sin. Adam would have died even if he had not sinned; and it is now human culture – emulating the poor example of Adam – that propagates disobedience. God's grace does not predestine us to holiness, nor does it have any internal effect on the soul. It is offered to all in baptism and penance, and in reason and revelation. But for Pelagius, it is *resistible*; whereas Augustine eventually concluded that there is no true freedom of the human will in relation to grace.

Pelagianism, 'with its excessively rosy view of human nature and its insufficient acknowledgement of man's dependence on God' (Kelly, 1968, p. 361), was condemned at a variety of Church councils in the fifth century; although Augustine's complete account of sin and grace was never accepted as dogma. Theologians frequently complain that the Pelagian heresy remains widespread within the Church.

Augustine's theology had a profound influence on medieval theology and the Protestant Reformers. The latter placed even more stress on the 'total depravity' of humanity after the fall. Calvin explicitly taught a 'double predestination': 'Some are preordained to eternal life, others to eternal damnation; . . . each has

---

2 Augustine himself thought that Adam and Eve were *created* mortal, but that after their sin God withheld his gift of immortal spiritual bodies.

been created for one or other of these ends, ... predestinated to life or to death' (*Institutes of the Christian Religion* iii, ch. 21, 5). Classical Calvinist theology further exalted the freedom and sovereignty of God as the sole author of human salvation, and stressed the heinousness of Adam's fall and his subsequent loss of free will. But such views were opposed by the sixteenth-century Jacob Arminius (hence 'Arminianism'), John Wesley, Bishop William Laud and the Puritan John Milton. They argued that people are truly free to resist God's grace, so that God's 'election' to salvation must be conditional on our own response and co-operation. But even on this view, salvation cannot be *earned*. It is still regarded as due to the unmerited love, forgiveness, favour and assistance of God.

The image of God is that within us that reflects God. It has often been thought of as our reason or freedom, including the ability to transcend ourselves morally and spiritually. Its purpose is to obtain knowledge of God, to 'image' God's character better, and (most importantly) *to form a relationship with God*. Luther saw the image as our life's complete orientation towards God, and declared it lost at the fall as humanity turned away from God. For Calvin, it was not annihilated but 'so corrupted, that any thing which remains is fearful deformity' (*Institutes* i, ch. 14, 4).

Irenaeus, and others in Eastern Christianity, distinguished the 'image' and 'likeness' of God (synonyms in Gen. 1.27). The first includes our natural rational and moral capacities, which are retained at the fall; the second is our intended spiritual conformity to God's true likeness, which we may become by God's grace. Irenaeus viewed the fall as one of children; it evoked God's compassion for Adam, 'a little one ... his discretion still undeveloped' (*Proof of the Apostolic Preaching* ch. 12).

In Chapter 5, we touched on the social nature of sin. This perspective is expressed very strongly in the Bible, and is part of the explanation why children suffer on account of their parents' sin (Ex. 20.5). Eventually, however, the responsibility of the individual and the current generation is more clearly affirmed (Ezek. 18). But 'no self begins with a clean slate' (Paul Sponheim), if only because we are born into a corrupt and corrupting society.

> The meaning of original sin is not original guilt but that all people sin, from the first humans until now, and thus all are born into a broken and fallen world. Theirs is original ... also in that the effects of sin are passed down.... Children do not inherit the guilt of their parents ... They do, unfortunately,

bear the brunt of the consequences of the guilt of their parents. (Stiver, 2009, p. 231)

EXERCISE

- In light of this section, how do you understand the origin and significance of human sin?
- Is your interpretation of Adam and Eve affected by claims about human evolution?

Going Beyond Sin?

If salvation is about healing the wounds of the human condition, it concerns much more than the forgiveness of guilt. There are many other elements to our existential woundedness, and a range of related notions of what is involved in our salvation (cf. Borg, 1997, ch. 7; 2003):

- renouncing *unfaithfulness* and returning to our true love, which leads to . . .
- the experience of God's love, overcoming our sense of worthlessness and being *unloved*;
- liberation from the *spiritual bondage* of the law, and other dominating powers that oppress us as false gods (see below);
- 'coming home' to God and coming to rest 'in Christ', and so overcoming our sense of *separation*, *alienation* and *exile* from what gives our lives meaning and a sense of belonging;
- enlightenment from spiritual *blindness*, and the fear, loneliness and sense of *being lost* – the effect of not being able to find God in the world and other people;
- opening our *hard, closed hearts*, caused by the self-protective suit of armour that protects our ego, to be made vulnerable to gratitude, awe, compassion and love;
- resurrection or new birth from our old, self-centred lives and our spiritual *deadness*;

- having our *hunger* satisfied and thirst quenched, by satisfying our deepest longings for what gives us life;
- entering a personal relationship in which we truly know God by encountering him, rather than just by possessing truths about him in a *distanced knowing*;
- coming to live under the kingship of God, sharing its overturning of *the values of the world*;
- healing our *spiritual illness* by quelling our *rebellion* against the inevitable limits, transience and pains of life – a rebellion that turns our suffering into *bitterness*;
- overcoming our excessive *pride* and self-centred presumption, allowing us to adopt a realistic view of our own significance, and a proper humility before God and our neighbours.

A broad, multifaceted interpretation of Christian salvation is expressed by the sixteenth-century poet and Catholic martyr, Robert Southwell:

O dying souls, behold your living spring;
O dazzled eyes, behold your sun of grace;
Dull ears, attend what word this Word doth bring;
Up, heavy hearts, with joy your joy embrace.
From death, from dark, from deafness, from despairs,
This life, this light, this Word, this joy repairs.

EXERCISE

- It is said that people are less concerned nowadays about their need to be saved from sin. Is this your experience? How would you react to the claim?
- Which of the elements listed above rank as most significant in your own theology and spirituality? Are there other ills (and corresponding concepts of salvation) that you would wish to add to this list?

A New Creation

Because it originates in such concerns, the doctrine of salvation (studied in *soteriology*) relates closely to the depth of many people's Christian experience. Salvation was an experience well before it became a doctrine; just as prayer began as a primal cry of the soul that was only subsequently transformed into orchestrated masses performed in concert halls. For the first Christians, Jesus was somehow responsible for this experience. Those who flocked to him, sought out his touch and listened to him 'with delight' (Mark 12.37) undeniably experienced some form of being made whole, and a new closeness to God's Spirit.

Even after his death and resurrection, he retained this power to bring healing. For all who experienced it, Jesus was good news indeed ('gospel' translates the Greek *euangelion*, literally 'good news'). In and through his words, and at his hands, and even through his continuing presence in the prayer, worship and fellowship of the Church, people felt released and healed, accepted and free. It is no wonder, then, that Christians very quickly began to make big claims, even interpreting their 'redemption' or 'deliverance' as a reversal of the current state of creation.

> if anyone is in Christ, there is a new creation: everything old has passed away; see, everything has become new! All this is from God ... in Christ God was reconciling the world to himself [or 'God was in Christ reconciling the world to himself'], not counting their trespasses against them, and entrusting the message of reconciliation to us. (2 Cor. 5.17–19)

But Christian theology speaks as much of continuity as of a break between creation and redemption. As God never abandoned his world, this new creation is seen as a *re-creation*: a renewal of the original promise and orientation towards God that the creator had built into the universe at its inception. Theologians often put it like this: God always gives himself to us, in and through the creation; but because our separation from God has made us hostile to and alienated from him, he must come again to us. The God from whom we are alienated is the only power that can overcome this separation. 'We cannot be saved by a better theology, a better *idea* of God. God must *come* to save us' (Forde, 1984, p. 67). In redemption, God becomes present to us 'in a concrete and specific way, to overcome the evil', and to allow us to respond. In redemption, then, we encounter 'the God who is present for people in their own history as a reality which calls to them, says something to them and about them, and so makes a difference for the character of their lives' (Norris, 1979, pp. 73–4).

And this time – as they say – it's personal.

Grace Received

We are exploring doctrine 'backwards' in this book, beginning with the more concrete and experiential before moving on to abstract processes and concepts. It is appropriate, therefore, to work within this chapter from the 'subjective human appropriation' (this section) to the 'objective divine act' (the next section), of what theologians sometimes call the overall 'economy' or 'dispensation' – the ordering or management – of God's saving activity.

Humanity is in a wrong relationship with its creator that can only be put right, so that we can be 'in the right' and 'vindicated' by God, by our finding pardon and acceptance through God's free, forgiving love (grace). This is a major theme in Paul's letters to the Romans and Galatians, for in his own experience God had 'justified the ungodly' (see Rom. 3.19–28; 8.28–39; 10.1–4; Gal. 2.15–21; 3.10–14; 5.1–6). It was also crucial to the Reformers.

Classical Protestantism, and its contemporary heir 'evangelical theology', developed this Pauline theology by laying great stress on the *past dimension of human salvation* ('we *have been* saved'). This is understood as conversion united with a particular 'one time event' of reconciliation between God and the individual. In this tradition, this moment of *justification* is normally understood as involving God's gift of forgiveness, together with his declaration of a right relationship with himself ('passive righteousness'). We are not only forgiven for our own actual sins by this act, we are also released from the inherent *fault* – and, for some, the inherited *guilt* – of the original sin into which we are born, which alienates all people from God. Justification is frequently described as a 'forensic' concept: that is, one that relates to courts of law. In that context, being justified is a matter of being vindicated and acquitted as innocent, so that the judge declares the prisoner 'just' or 'righteous'. In evangelical thinking, this is often expressed in terms of God *imputing* (Christ's) righteousness to us. 'Imputing' ('reckoning', 'regarding') is actually a metaphor from accounting, and means entering something into an account. Tom Wright contends that 'imputed righteousness' should be understood in more Pauline terms.

> There is indeed a sense in which 'justification' really does *make* someone 'righteous' – it really does create the 'righteousness', the status-of-being-in-the right, of which it speaks – but 'righteousness' in that law court sense does not mean either 'morally good character' or 'performance of moral good deeds', but 'the status you have when the court has found in your favour'. (Wright, 2009, p. 71)

This past event is said to be accompanied by a special gift of the Holy Spirit that empowers a *regeneration* of the spiritual life; in the view of Pentecostals and charismatics this is always a separate event – a 'baptism of the Holy Spirit' that should show itself in phenomena such as speaking with tongues. For all Christians, this regeneration and new presence of the Spirit empowers a continuing process of *sanctification* – literally, a 'making holy'. This is conceived as the inward transformation of the believer into a righteous, Christ-like character and life. It represents *the present dimension of salvation* ('we *are being* saved'). Whereas Catholics often refer to this stage as a 'growth in grace', Lutherans and others tend to restrict the language of grace to God's favour in the initial act of justification. Wesley held that a full perfection of believers in this life (an 'entire sanctification') is a real possibility; it is a gift of the Spirit for which we should pray and strive. This is not a state of sinlessness, however, but a purity of intention – a 'perfection in love'.

The final, *future dimension of salvation* ('we *shall be* saved'), is the future glorification of the saved, when they are made free of all sin and perfected in their new resurrection life (see Chapter 10).

Protestants insist that both salvation and sanctification are down to God. Since there is no way that a human being can deserve God's forgiveness or regeneration, neither event is in any sense a *reward* for human piety or any other 'good work'. Salvation is thus entirely *by grace alone through* (that is, accepted and appropriated by) *faith alone*, where both grace and faith are God's gifts (see Rom. 3.21–8; Eph. 2.8–10). The offer and acceptance of grace is essentially an experience.

Grace strikes us when we are in great pain and restlessness. . . . Sometimes at that moment a wave of light breaks into our darkness, and it is as though a voice were saying: 'You are accepted. *You are accepted*, accepted by that which is greater than you, and the name of which you do not know. Do not ask for the name now; perhaps you will find it later. Do not try to do anything now; perhaps later you will do much. Do not seek for anything; do not perform anything; do not intend anything. *Simply accept that fact that you are accepted!*' If that happens to us, we experience grace. After such an experience we may not be better than before, and we may not believe more than before. But everything is transformed. In that moment, grace conquers sin, and reconciliation bridges the gulf of estrangement. And nothing is demanded of this experience, no religious or moral or intellectual presupposition, nothing but *acceptance*. (Tillich, 1962, pp. 163–4)

Faith is presented here as the simple matter of putting out one's hand to receive God's gift. By faith, we accept that we are accepted.

It is easy, however, to turn human faith into yet another 'work', whose exercise deserves or even guarantees our salvation. But faith is not a *condition* of justification. Rather, faith ultimately liberates us to produce good works, and will then show itself in them as a fruitful faith – as 'faith working through love', freely and graciously (Gal. 5.6, 22–6; see also James 2.14–17, 26).

Luther was mainly opposed to a view within late medieval Catholic theology that suggested that justifying grace must be earned. This was not representative of Catholic theology in general. Many, however, followed Augustine's reading of Paul, and interpreted justification not only as a forensic justification of believers, but also as a *making righteous* of those who were sinners – by God's love redirecting the sinner's desires. In recent years, scholarship has helped to heal the rift of the Reformation over this point, by arguing that Luther's own position actually lay quite close to this view. He understood justification both as an imputation (a declaring just) *and* as an 'impartation' (a making just) – both events being the consequence of God's action. Hans Küng has famously argued that 'today there is a fundamental agreement between Catholic and Protestant theology, precisely in the theology of justification' (Küng, 1964, p. 271).

Coming to Terms with Theology:
Salvation

Terms particularly used within Orthodox Theology

Deification/divinization (*theosis*) – the view that participation in God's blessings can lead to Christians being progressively conformed to the likeness of God, and ultimately to their heavenly transformation. Often described as resulting from the reconciliation of God and humanity in the incarnation of the Logos in Jesus Christ, which leads to a divine re-creation of our human nature in union with God.

Terms particularly used within Protestant Theology

Conversion – the individual's response to God's calling, involving repentance ('turning' or 'changing one's mind') and the embrace of faith.

Election – God's initiative in choosing and calling some (or all) to salvation.

Glorification – the final transformation of the believer.

Justification – being declared or 'reckoned' righteous by God's grace. It is normally said to be received by faith alone.

Predestination – God's foreknowledge about and/or foreordination of those individuals who will be saved.

Simul iustus et peccator – 'both righteous and a sinner at the same time': that is, always needing to pray for (and always receiving) God's mercy; always 'a sinner in fact, but righteous by virtue of the reckoning and certain promise of God' (Luther).

Sola fide – 'by faith alone'.

Roman Catholic Emphases

Catholics too have insisted on the **priority of grace**. A person, for example, cannot 'be justified before God by his own works [or] . . . the resources of human nature' (Council of Trent, *Decree on Justification*). However, Catholics insist on the believer's power either to respond to God's invitation and grace, or to resist it. For Catholic theology, God's 'prevenient grace' can awaken and mend the freedom of the human will, so that it can co-operate with God's grace, regardless of the person's merit.

Faith (see Chapter 2) is more a matter of belief than of active trust and commitment. Thus justification is said to be by 'faith furnished with love', which also helps explain the claim that God *makes* the sinner righteous (by means of 'sanctifying grace'), as well as accounting him righteous.

Justification is a broader concept here than it is in Protestantism, comprising not only the remission of sins 'but also the sanctification and renewal of the interior man'. It is also, therefore, more gradual.

The Words and Work of Salvation

The verse quoted on p. 114 is from Southwell's 'The Nativity of Christ', which indicates that salvation may be associated as much with Christ's birth as with his death – and not just because anyone who is to die has first to be born.

For much Eastern Orthodox thought, the *incarnation* itself is part of Christ's saving activity, for it embraces and 'recapitulates' our human experience – 'gathering up' human history and repairing the damage caused by Adam's disobedience. It thus *effects*, as well as demonstrates, the reconciliation of divinity and humanity.

According to Irenaeus and Athanasius, 'God became man in order that man might become God' (cf. 2 Peter 1.3–4). Salvation is perceived here as 'participation in the divine life' and 'the union of the created with the uncreated' (Zizioulas, 2008, pp. 70, 108). This is often expressed in terms of *theosis* ('deification', 'divinization'), the ultimate end for human beings. Although this can only be fulfilled in heaven, in this life there is a synergy ('co-operation') in our union with God that results in a gradual transformation and re-centring of our selfish human nature within the divine life, as we respond to the Holy Spirit – 'the forming of those who participate, into the likeness of what they participate in'

(Maximus the Confessor, *Questions to Thalassius*). 'What is deified in Christ is His human nature assumed in its fullness by the divine person. What must be deified in us is our entire nature, belonging to our person which must enter into union with God' (Lossky, 1957, p. 155).

For many others this may seem dangerous stuff, unless it is interpreted in terms of forming a Christ-like character. But in the East, Christianity often thinks in terms of 'natures' rather than ethical concepts.

For Western Christianity in general, and Protestant theology in particular, the experiences and ideas about salvation are much more intimately associated with the *death of Christ*. In its most convincing formulations, this is never separated from his resurrection; and explicitly linked with his historical teaching and ministry, which were already the expression and means of God's healing, accepting love.

In the New Testament, a wide range of imagery is used to express the experience of salvation, besides justification. Christians are described as receiving 'adoption as children' – and therefore as heirs – instead of remaining as slaves (Gal. 4.5–7). They are also 'bought with a price' (1 Cor. 6.20) and 'liberated' or 'redeemed' (literally 'bought back'), implying that they are no longer slaves of whatever had kept them from God but now belong to him. In Mark 10.45, Jesus speaks of giving his own life 'as a ransom for many'. The 'many' is to be contrasted with 'few'; it is not meant in the restrictive sense of 'not for *all*'. The 'for' is literally 'instead of' in Greek, though some understand it in the sense of 'for the good of' (cf. Mark 14.24; Rom. 8.32; 1 Tim. 2.6). This text is set within the context of Jesus' servant role, which possibly relates to Isaiah's 'suffering servant' (Isa. 52.13—53.12).

Freedom-bought-by-payment is best understood as a powerful metaphor, rather than a process worked out in terms of a particular transaction. The same may be said of the sacrificial language employed in the New Testament. This is abundant in the Letter to the Hebrews (see 9.11–28; 10.11–23), where the author argues that 'without the shedding of blood there is no forgiveness of sins' under the Jewish law (9.22). Paul explicitly describes Christ as having been put forward by God 'as a sacrifice of atonement [or 'a place of atonement'] by his blood, effective through faith' (Rom. 3.25; cf. 1 Cor. 5.7; 1 John 2.1–2; 4.10). This is an *expiation* for human sin – a 'covering', 'putting away' or 'wiping'. ('Propitiation' denotes appeasing an angry deity; whereas the object of 'expiation' is sin, not God.)

The idea of sacrifice implies that the victim is offered in some sense for and on behalf of the worshippers. The idea of an 'inclusive representative' (Burnaby), personifying true, faithful Israel, lies close to this theme; and the anointed king or future Messiah was a representative of his people in this sense, as was the suffering servant and the 'one like a son of man' in Daniel 7. For Paul, Jesus fills this role not just for Israel but for the Church, for which and to whom he gave up his life. As all Christians are 'in Christ' and make up the 'body of Christ', 'one has died for all; therefore all have died . . . so that those who live might live no longer for themselves, but for him' (2 Cor. 5.14–15). Jesus gives himself *to* God, then, *for* us.

Scripture provides equally striking accounts of Jesus' death and resurrection as a victory. This conquest is not just over his human enemies, but also over the supernatural forces of sin and death, the demonic force of legalism and the corrupt angelic powers behind nations, all of which enslave people (1 Cor. 2.6; 2 Cor. 4.4; Gal. 4.3; Eph. 2.2). The picture being painted here is of a great cosmic battle between God and created supernatural spirits who have rebelled against God (Col. 1.15–20; 2.13–15). Christians may enter into Christ's victory by putting themselves under the protection of the conquering hero, receiving the benefits of his conquest.

Down the centuries of Christian thinking and worship, this treasure house of imagery has been drawn on in a variety of ways, as Christians have attempted to explain what is sometimes called *the work of Christ* and the '*atonement*' (literally 'at-one-ment', William Tyndale's word for 'reconciliation'). Following the general pattern for the development of religious language (see pp. 44–6, 55–60), the profound biblical *narratives, themes, images and metaphors* of salvation were made more suitable for the purposes of theological explanation by being developed into more stable, systematic and long-lasting *models* – a half-way house on the road to abstract, technical *concepts*. These models found a place in various conceptual *theories* about how the death of Christ could effect our atonement with God. 'Theories arise because there are questions to be asked . . . Atonement theory is an attempt at an explanation which arises directly out of the fact that what God did about human sin is both extremely surprising, and gives rise to many questions and objections' (Sykes, 1997, pp. 12, 50).

This development entailed loss as well as – and sometimes more than – gain. It occasionally involved the translation of dramatic biblical stories, and allusive religious poetry and symbolism, into rather wooden and confusing theological prose, cut off from its linguistic roots. While 'the metaphor cannot be lost without losing some vital grasp on the reality' to which it refers, 'if the metaphor is taken literally the reference is equally lost' (Dunn, 2009, p. 89). Many of these stories and metaphors remain effective in promoting appropriate attitudes in spirituality and worship. Some of the subsequent models and theories, however, leave many people cold – or worse: 'the story of the passion retains its appeal; any doctrine of the passion is more likely to appal' (Wiles, 1974, p. 62).

The Church as a whole has never opted for any one model or theory of atonement, declaring it a 'dogma' (see Chapter 1). This allows us to speak of the atonement in a 'multi-model discourse', utilizing several metaphorical images, instead of struggling to perfect and defend any single overarching perspective. Theories of atonement 'give the answers they give because of the questions they ask' (Wright, 2007, p. 211). It is just as important, however, to affirm that the centre of a truly Christian understanding of salvation is 'not a metaphor but a personal history' (Hart, 1997, p. 193): the life, death and resurrection of the Christ. By comparison, 'all theories of reconciliation can be but pointers' to God's activity *there* (Barth, 1966, p. 116).

Christ as Ransom

Pressing the New Testament analogy of the ransom, early Greek theologians began asking to whom this ransom was due. Both Origen and Gregory of Nyssa took the answer to be the devil, with the latter twisting the story by adding that Christ's humanity was the 'bait' hiding the 'hook' of his divinity. This is only one of many 'trap' metaphors, in which Satan was thought of as exceeding his proper authority in attacking Jesus. (Augustine pictured Christ holding out his cross 'like a mouse trap' baited with his own blood.) Irenaeus joined the ransom model with his idea that Christ's incarnation in fallen humanity effects our redemption by recapitulation, leading to our divinization. On this view, the cross is seen as a part of Christ's wider, obedient self-offering.

Even allowing for the mythological transaction pictured in the model, we may ask why God has to do this; and should we think of God as a deceiver – even of the devil?

Christ as Sacrifice

The theme of Christ as the perfect sacrifice, offered 'once only' and 'accomplished in its entirety' (Athanasius), developed into a view of considerable importance. The act is often presented as *vicarious* ('done for another'). While Augustine identified Christ as 'the true Mediator' between God and humankind, he insisted that *God* was the real actor in the drama. 'In union with the Father, with whom he is one God', Christ was 'both the priest, himself making the offering, and the oblation [offering, sacrifice, victim]' that extinguishes our guilt (*City of God* x, ch. 20). As Christ was also human, his offering may be seen as taken from our sinful human nature.[3]

Sacrifice (Hebrew *zebhah*, 'slaughter') is largely alien to most people today. Yet it retains the potent symbolism of returning the gift of life (as blood) to the God who created it – not as a bribe, but an act of homage. Sacrifices in general were presumably once seen as restoring a relationship with God (by sharing a meal, or making a restitution for a wrong). And the sin and guilt offerings that developed after the exile were special expiatory sacrifices considered capable of removing sin.

Christ as Conqueror

The image of the devil's deception also relates to this wider theme of Christ's death as a victory, the consummation of a cosmic battle waged against the powers of evil throughout Jesus' ministry, and exhibited in his exorcisms (for example Mark 1.23–8; 5.1–13; 9.20–9). Christianity saw this decisive victory as given *by God* 'through our Lord Jesus Christ' (1 Cor. 15.57). In Colossians, the 'principalities and powers' are disarmed and defeated at the crucifixion (Col. 2.15). In Ephesians, the enmity and barrier between Gentiles and Jews was destroyed on the cross, by the abolition of the law (Eph. 2.14–16). The Lutheran theologian,

---

3 The 'threefold office' of Christ, first framed in the early Church and much developed at the Reformation, included the idea of Christ as *priest* representing humankind before God and God to humankind (Heb. 4.14), as well as being the complete and perfect sacrifice. This priestly role was placed alongside Christ as *prophet*, proclaiming (as well as being) God's word of salvation; and Christ as *king*, the messianic ruler now exalted in heaven.

Gustaf Aulén, described this most objective theory of atonement (from the New Testament and Luther) as the *dramatic or classic view*.

> Christ – Christus Victor – fights against and triumphs over the powers of the world, the 'tyrants' under which mankind is in bondage and suffering, and in him God reconciles the world to Himself.... [This view] represents the work of Atonement or reconciliation as from first to last a work of God Himself, a *continuous* Divine work; ... It does not set forth only or chiefly a change taking place in men; it describes a complete change in the situation, a change in the relation between God and the world, and a change also in God's own attitude. (Aulén, 1970, pp. 4–6)

One positive feature of the model is that it views the crucifixion through the lens of God's vindicating act of resurrection. But identifying the crucifixion as a mythological battle-ground presents other difficulties for the modern believer (cf. pp. 131–2).

Christ as Supreme Example

This radically subjective analysis draws on passages such as Mark 8.34; 10.39; Philippians 2.5–8 and Hebrews 12.1–2. It commends our imitation of the cross, interpreting it as the most appealing exhibition of God's love. It found a place in the thinking of the twelfth-century theologian, Peter Abelard, though it is secondary there to the cross's redemptive character. (Abelard insists that we are saved by God's grace, not our own unaided will.)

> We have been justified by the blood of Christ and reconciled to God in this way: through the unique act of grace manifested to us – in that his Son has taken upon himself our nature and persevered therein in teaching us by word and example even unto death – he has more fully bound us to himself by love; with the result that our hearts should be enkindled by such a gift of divine grace, and true charity should not now shrink from enduring anything for him. (Abelard, *Exposition of the Epistle to the Romans* ii, 3, 26)

For Auguste Sabatier, 'the cross is the expiation of sins only because it is the cause of the repentance to which remission is promised' (Sabatier, 1904, p. 127).

On this *moral influence* or *exemplarist theory*, we are converted by looking on Christ's passion. 'Christ's death is the supreme expression of the love of God . . . The Cross is the ultimate sign of man's hatred; and in that very focal point of hatred the love of God accepts him despite the worst that he can do, in his most extreme sinfulness and bitter enmity' (Lampe, 1966, p. 190).

The usual criticism of subjective theories of the atonement is that they do not allow that the passion 'actually does anything'. Although it is true that 'in the world of historical experience, the passion has done much and continues to do much' (Wiles, 1974, p. 80), critics are usually looking for some more objective victorious and/or reconciling event.

Christ as Satisfaction

Anselm of Canterbury's influential work, *Cur Deus Homo?* ('Why God became Man?'), completed in 1098, was perhaps the first systematic theory of atonement. It drew on the medieval concept of 'satisfaction' (to 'satisfy' means literally to 'make enough'). Disobedience to a feudal superior is a slight upon his honour that needs to be satisfied by some acceptable gift or penitential act. Without this satisfaction, punishment is due. For Anselm, sin was simply equated with the insult of not rendering to God the absolute obedience that all sinners owe.

But because God is the lord of the universe, and because we *already* owe God perfect obedience, it is impossible that we can ever repay this debt of honour. Nothing less than 'something greater than all the universe besides God' could satisfy God's impugned honour. *This* satisfaction, therefore, is one that 'none but God can make'; it is also, however, one that 'none but man ought to do' (Anselm, *Cur Deus Homo?* ii, 6). It therefore follows that only Christ, 'the God-man', can make it – and he *must* make it. Anselm imagines God the Father saying 'to the sinner doomed to eternal torments and having no way of escape: "Take my only begotten Son and make him an offering for yourself"' (ii, 20).

Although based on a way of thinking now largely meaningless to us, this theory strongly influenced the idea of atonement as an abstract *transaction*, involving God, Christ and ourselves (an idea already implicit in the ransom model). This takes seriously the notion of some objective barrier between God and his creatures that can only be overturned by an objective action, as changes in the believer's subjective feelings cannot accomplish that task on their own.

The transactional approach has proved especially attractive in the next version of atonement theory.

But however mighty he is, why can't God just show mercy – without demanding something first? Isn't the atonement an exercise of power here, rather than love? Jesus' death also seems disconnected from his life – all he has to do is die! And although Anselm found the idea of a retributive balance 'fitting', 'sweet and desirable', many nowadays recoil from the 'indescribable beauty' of his scheme.

Christ as Substitution

Both this theory and the last are sometimes labelled *juridical*. The substitutionary theory of Christ's death as punishment or penalty (hence *penal substitution*) arose within Protestant theology in the sixteenth century. It drew on the understanding of law and the idea of objective justice prevalent at that time, in order to understand passages such as 'for our sake he [God] made him [Christ] to be sin who knew no sin, so that in him we might become the righteousness of God' (2 Cor. 5.21).

As in the previous approach, punishment cannot be set aside. God cannot simply go ahead and forgive the sinner – a price must be paid. But again, the price is paid *by God*. In the law court of divine justice, God can and does provide a substitute who will bear the sins of the world for us. God sends his Son to suffer our punishment in our place – hence Jesus' cry of dereliction on the cross. 'Our sin must be Christ's own sin, or we shall perish eternally' (Luther, *Galatians Commentary*).

Calvin writes that man is 'estranged from God by sin . . . [and] excluded from all hope of salvation'. But Christ interceded for him, and 'took the punishment upon himself, and bore what by the just judgement of God was impending over sinners' (*Institutes* ii, ch. 16, 2). For Calvinists this is a *limited* atonement that extends only to the elect. For some other Protestants – and most other Christians – it is in principle *universal* in scope, if not in its 'application' (if only those who believe in Christ are actually saved).

Even many evangelical thinkers nowadays prefer a less forensic account, concerned that law seems to determine God's action here rather than grace, or that the theory portrays an odd understanding of justice. Some draw on insights in the psychology of forgiveness to improve the model; while others emphasize the representative or vicarious nature of Christ's death. (This may mean that Christ's offering is accepted by God for the benefit of others, rather than that Christ bears their penalty.) Wright endorses the model, not in the world of 'some arbitrary law court', but in the context of a biblical narrative of the story of Israel and of Israel's representative Messiah. He sees that story as climaxing in the death of Christ as a victory, which he takes to be the overarching atonement model within which substitution can make its proper point.

> Jesus was taking upon himself the direct consequences, in the political and in the theological realm alike, of the failure and sin of Israel . . . Jesus died in a representative capacity for Israel, and hence for the whole human race. . . . The cross is not just an example to be followed; it is an achievement to be worked out . . . But it is an example none the less . . . the template, the model, for what God now wants to do . . . It is the start of the process of redemption, in which suffering and martyrdom are the paradoxical means by which victory is won. (Wright, 2006, pp. 53, 56, 62)

Soteriological Doubts?

In some recent interviews with churchgoers, only those who declared themselves evangelicals subscribed to the substitutionary theory of the atonement. They had clearly been specifically taught the theory and used its set phrases. However, they were no more likely than other interviewees to reflect on it in any theological depth.

About a quarter of the sample articulated some form of exemplarist theory of the cross. A third 'just accepted' soteriological themes, without any attempt at explanatory atonement theology. But a further third found atonement theology a considerable stumbling block. Many 'never felt that being "a sinner" has prevented them from entering into a relationship with God . . . [They argued:] If God is loving and forgiving now, and always has been, then why was Jesus' death necessary?' (Christie and Astley, 2009, p. 191). Some interviewees even spoke of the crucifixion as 'totally unnecessary', 'preposterous' or too 'horrendous' to be interpreted positively. For one, God seemed 'a bad person and a cruel Father-figure to actually put [Jesus] through that'.

Academic theologians have expressed similar concerns. Feminists have sometimes recoiled from any power-and-violence transaction, as expressing 'not a God of love but a sadist and a despot' (Hopkins, 1995, p. 50). Some have even suggested that atonement theology can present God as a divine child-abuser. Other scholars have criticized the fact that the paying of penalties does not necessarily affect the relationships involved; or bemoaned the impersonality of much atonement theology. According to one liberal theologian:

> The basic fault ... of the traditional understandings of salvation within the Western development of Christianity is that they have no room for divine forgiveness! For a forgiveness that has to be bought by the bearing of a just punishment, or the giving of an adequate satisfaction, or the offering of a sufficient sacrifice, is not forgiveness at all but merely an acknowledgement that the debt has been paid in full. But in the recorded teaching of Jesus there is, in contrast, genuine divine forgiveness for those who are truly penitent and deeply aware of their own utter unworthiness. (Hick, 2008, p. 110)

Hick adds that the father in the parable (Luke 15.11–32) does not say of his returning, penitent son, 'I cannot forgive him until someone has been duly punished for his sins.'

Certainly, most people now argue that retributive punishment doesn't restore any true 'moral balance'. In personal relationships, what needs to happen is that the 'offence' or 'hurt' be ultimately *transformed*, 'by creating something new and better out of it ... through recreation and redemption' (White, 1991, p. 99).

Other Insights?

1   The French philosopher of social science, René Girard, argues that something like the scapegoat ritual in the Old Testament (Lev. 16.21–2) represents a universal phenomenon in ancient cultures. Human beings were expelled or even murdered, as *surrogate* victims, to avert violence and maintain social unity.[4] Girard contends that the story of Jesus' passion offers a unique critique of this practice, by clearly proclaiming the innocence of the victim. Jesus allows himself to be the scapegoat who is sacrificed for the community (John 11.50); but

---

4 He interprets the Gadarene madman of Mark 5.1–20 as a demonized member cast out from the community in this way, which explains why the townsfolk are not pleased with his healing.

through his resurrection the process is shown to be absurd, and the truth that only non-violence and forgiveness can bring peace is revealed (John 20.19).

2   Donald Baillie emphasizes the inevitable cost that the *one who has been offended* must pay for the sake of any reconciliation. Forgiveness cannot simply ignore the hurt caused by any great wrong that another has done. The one who forgives must suffer the sinner's shame, while not condoning the offence. God's free pardon is infinitely costly, then, and 'God alone bears the cost.'

> In whatever way the process of salvation through the Cross is conceived, God's merciful attitude towards sinners is never regarded as the *result* of the process, but as its cause and source. It all took place because God so loved the world. (Baillie, 1948, pp. 175, 188–9)

3   God in Christ takes the experience of the cross into his divine experience, and this allows him to engage in a redeeming relationship with his creatures. In Moltmann's notable definition of God as suffering love, God takes the world's suffering to himself in his Son, identifies with it and vindicates his righteousness in the world. On the cross:

> All human history, however much it may be determined by guilt and death, is taken up into this 'history of God', i.e. into the Trinity, and integrated into the future of the 'history of God'. There is no suffering which in this history of God is not God's suffering; no death which has not been God's death in the history on Golgotha. Therefore there is no life, no fortune and no joy which have not been integrated by his history into eternal life, the eternal joy of God. (Moltmann, 1974, p. 246)

4   One way of going beyond substitutions and external relationships is to find our salvation in some sort of participation in Christ, as a 'corporate person'. 'In Christ' and 'in the Lord' language is very common in Paul; and John writes of a mutual indwelling (for example 6.56; 14.17, 15.4–7). According to H. A. Hodges, 'our mystical union with Christ' can alone overcome the diseased will that prevents our full repentance. 'Since we cannot do it alone and He [Christ] cannot do it instead of us, it must be both together who do it, He in us and we in Him.' It is the new self that results from this union that finds acceptance before God. Hodges quotes the eucharistic hymn: 'Look, Father, look on His anointed face, /

And only look on us as found in Him' (Hodges, 1955, pp. 55–9). Citing Colossians 3.3, Charles Cranfield comments: 'God in his mercy has decided to see us in his Son' (Cranfield, 2004, p. 46).

5   Vincent Brümmer distinguishes between truly personal relationships and 'tacit agreements of rights and obligations'. Bearing a punishment or making satisfaction for sin can restore a balance of rights and obligations between people, but that is a matter of *earning* reinstatement; it is not *forgiveness*. 'Broken fellowship can only be restored by penitence and forgiveness', a sincere repentance coupled with an answering forgiveness (Brümmer, 2005, pp. 43). The justice of God is 'restorative not retributive'. As God's forgiveness is always 'on offer', *we* must recognize our need to bridge our estrangement from God. This can only come by God's enlightening, empowering and inspiring us to 'seek his will joyfully out of love and not merely out of duty' (Brümmer, 2005, pp. 50, 60).

6   The idea of an objective reparation for sin – a 'making amends for', or repairing, a wrong – may be understood as *our* bearing, in a Christ-like life, the consequences of our own *and of other's* sins, including Pilate's and those of the Chief Priests. 'The consequences of sin (whether one's own or other people's) borne in the spirit of Christ can be transformed so as to become eventually not a curse but a blessing' (Hanson and Hanson, 1981, pp. 127–8).

7   Many look to a 'demythologized' conquest model. Walter Wink writes of spiritual powers, not in terms of distinct angelic entities, but as 'the spirituality at the core of . . . institutions and structures'. This 'soul' of a system can be caring; but it is often 'demonically' perverted, betraying its divine vocation 'for a selfish, lesser goal' (Wink, 1998, pp. 4, 29, 197). Whether there are actual supernatural principalities or not, we are certainly in spiritual bondage to such false gods. The deepest spiritual mistake is that of valuing the concerns of our own self above all others. But even our concern for our family or our own health *can* come to tyrannize us, if we commit ourselves to these values too absolutely. Lacking in faith (trust) in God, we seek security in what is less than God. And we also come to fear – and rebel against – the adversity and death which are natural and necessary parts of God's material creation.

To refuse to idolize any being . . . is to deprive that being of any possibility of acquiring demonic power. . . . This Christ finally does in giving himself utterly in the passion and death . . . [bringing] God's constant self-giving for his creation right into the creation (Macquarrie, 1977, pp. 319–20).

For Macquarrie, this last element makes such an account 'objective'.

8   Meeting force with force, evil with evil, even (especially?) when right is on your side may cause the enemy to retreat or surrender. But it will not stop his evil intentions. The true 'overcoming' of evil occurs in the heart of the enemy. We have sometimes seen that happen when people have passively resisted evil, as with Gandhi's *ahimsa* movement in British India and Buddhist monks elsewhere. Evil received without retaliation was accepted and absorbed, and the hearts of the unjust aggressor *eventually* changed. Is this partly true of the cross (see Mark 15.39)? Jesus resisted, and angrily battled against, the pains and slights that were inflicted on others; but when they turned on him, he accepted them – and thus morally and spiritually neutralized them.

9   Our salvation may involve several other subjective elements.

(a) Recalling his passion, we may be strengthened by one who suffered before us at Gethsemane and Golgotha, 'released from anxiety as we endure it' (Moltmann, 1980, p. 54). 'Carrying in the body the death of Jesus . . . being given up to death for Jesus' sake', perhaps we too can *live* through evil. 'As having nothing, and yet possessing everything', we may enter into his victory. (2 Cor. 4.10–11; 6.10.)

(b) We may view the cross as the revelation of the truth about the world, including the 'injustice of justice' and the foolishness of our reliance on human gods. In Pilate, 'it is the State as such that is disgraced' (Barth, 1966, p. 111).

> Jesus absorbed all the violence directed at him by the authorities and the Powers but still loved them. . . . if God loves us unconditionally, there is no need to seek conditional love from the various Powers who promise us rewards in return for devotion. (Wink, 1998, p. 92)

(c) We may learn that God is God, and that God alone is to be trusted. 'This is the promise God gives us: I am there for you' (Barth, 1966, p. 19). Our separation from God (sin) is a result in part of our lack of trust in his love, which often leads to our hiding from and refusing grace. The crucifixion, as the completion, fulfilment and fullest application of Jesus' life and teaching, serves as a supreme revelation of God's love for us ('No one has greater love than this': John 15.13). But Jesus' resurrection is the supreme revelation of the trustworthiness of God, and the confirmation of the victorious power of the love of God over the values of the world. 'God is not more powerful than he is in this helplessness' (Moltmann, 1974, p. 205).

(d) Our vision may thus be restored. The instinct lies deep in us that love – as the power to give, empower and create – is the only power *we can or wish to trust*. But can it conquer all, destroying even our estrangement and self-protective separation? Well, 'we can feel certain that no *other* power can overcome the evil in the world' (Burnaby, 1959, p. 31). And from the Easter dawn, we see that – again, despite appearances – sin was not victorious over the Christ. So even the cross may now be seen in depth, as God's victory over the world's sin, which can no longer come in the way of our redemption. The shooting continues, but we now perceive that this war is already won.

10   Subjective themes often have an objective dimension.

(a) Viewing the life–death–resurrection of Christ as a supreme revelation of God's love may lead to our discovering that our false gods do not any longer have any power over us. As our spiritual anxiety truly begins to fade, we might then truly claim that we are 'objectively' released and liberated.

(b) Christ's accomplishment on the cross, even when analysed in subjective terms, at least has this sort of objectivity: that it genuinely expresses the real love of the true God. This is true whether anybody 'believes it or responds to it', in the way that 'the objectivity of [a] writer's achievement is beyond dispute, in spite of the fact that it does not become actual communication until someone is interested enough to read it' (McKeating, 1970, p. 113).

But the writer writes in order to be read; and God's love is only completed in a response of love. God has made the first and biggest step; but if he will never force his love on us, there must always be two poles, two agents and two directions. Which eventually must come together into one.

EXERCISE

- Which elements from these theories and ideas about the 'work of Christ' do you respond to most positively?
- How would you describe the effects of the death of Christ, and how people can 'enter into' them?

Suggestions for Further Reading

Introductory

Doctrine Commission of the Church of England, 2005, *Contemporary Doctrine Classics*, London: Church House Publishing, pp. 275–447.

McGrath, A. E., 2007, *Christian Theology: An Introduction*, Oxford: Blackwell, chs 13, 14.

Wright, N. T., 2006, *Evil and the Justice of God*, London: SPCK.

Advanced

Brümmer, V., 2005, *Atonement, Christology and the Trinity: Making Sense of Christian Doctrine*, Aldershot: Ashgate.

Fiddes, P. S., 1989, *Past Event and Present Salvation: The Christian Idea of Atonement*, London: Darton, Longman & Todd.

Gunton, C. E., 1988, *The Actuality of the Atonement: A Study of Metaphor, Rationality and the Christian Tradition*, Edinburgh: T. & T. Clark.

7

Reading Christ: Unpacking Faith in Jesus

Origins

The study of the doctrine of the 'person of Christ' is called *Christology*. Within Christianity, the experience of the *effects* of Jesus – the 'work of Christ' – has normally preceded reflection on the *nature* of the figure whose birth, teaching, life, death, resurrection and proclamation gave rise to these effects. 'Christology is a function of soteriology' (Tillich, 1968, vol. 2, p. 174). We are following the same order in this text.

While the New Testament contains the essential primary documents for any Christological study, the teaching of the Church about Jesus is no mere summary of this material. It is a reflective development that also draws on philosophical categories, as well as the Church's continuing experience of its living Lord. The results of this combination of influences can sometimes seem rather remote from the (admittedly) mixed messages that originate in the plethora of events, titles, parables, teaching and confessions contained within Scripture.

Before trekking down the centuries of our Christological journey, we should briefly look at some of these data (while ignoring most of the vast scholarly literature they have provoked). In particular, we should note the great *variety* of views contained within the New Testament on this topic, as on many others. New Testament scholar James Dunn argues that contemporary Christology 'should recognize that from the first the significance of Christ could only be apprehended by a diversity of formulations which though not always strictly

compatible with each other were not regarded as rendering each other invalid'
(Dunn, 1989, p. 267).

Christians very quickly came to pray to and worship Jesus the Christ (Messiah);
and to call him – as they did Yahweh God – *Kurios*, 'Lord' (Acts 5.19; Rom. 10.9),
as well as 'Son of God' (John 1.18; Heb. 1.2; 1 John 5.20) and even 'God' (John
20.28; Rom. 9.5). Yet although Jesus is Lord in bearing the supreme authority of
God, he is never simply identified with Yahweh.

John Knox has provided helpful summaries in diagram form of four *early
Christological positions*, for which there is some evidence in the New Testament
(Knox, 1967, chs 1–3). Even though that evidence is contentious, these accounts
are helpful in illustrating certain *logical options* that found champions in the
later history of theology. (In interpreting the diagrams below, note that movement up the page represents a closer relationship to God, while movement down
signals a closer relationship to human beings.)

Adoptionism

There are hints of this 'exaltation Christology' in the early speeches in Acts (for
example 2.36; 3.13–15) and perhaps elsewhere (Rom. 1.3–4). For this view, the
man Jesus is exalted to divine status from the time of his resurrection, although
later adoptionists identified his baptism (cf. Mark 1.11) or some other key
moment. Knox calls this 'the original two-act drama' (1967, p. 14).

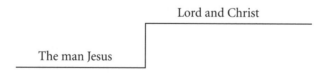

Lord and Christ

The man Jesus

Kenoticism

The drama of this 'humiliation–exaltation' Christology begins further back in
time, by the addition of a 'prologue'. This provides the background information
to explain the meaning of the rest of the play, by speaking of Jesus' divine *pre-*

existence. This was rapidly assumed to be the case, at least in some sense. In this second ancient Christology, the pre-existing heavenly Christ gives up his divine status to become, or 'take up', a fully human existence (at the level assumed in the earlier version). As before, he is later exalted, but this is now a restoration to the state he had prior to his earthly life. This simple, 'primitive kenoticism' (the Greek word *kenosis* means 'self-emptying') is only evident in traces: as in Philippians 2.5–11 and possibly Hebrews 1.1–4; 2.9 (texts that likely incorporate pre-Pauline, Christian hymns).[1]

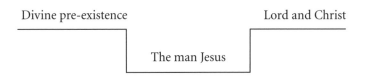

Docetism

However, the introduction of the prologue soon begins to affect the whole play. Inevitably, it becomes a new first act in its own right, so that the (second) act of Jesus' earthly life has to be rewritten. The most extreme rewriting is represented by Docetism. This view was rejected by the New Testament authors and by later Christian orthodoxy, but it seems to lie behind the thinking of some of Paul's opponents at Corinth and elsewhere, as well as the warnings in 1 John 4.1–3. In Docetism, the three-act drama portrays a Christ who does not truly 'come down from heaven' in the sense of becoming a true man, but only 'seems' to be human (Greek *dokein*, 'to appear'). This divine figure is not subject to the risks of a human life, and the humanity he possesses is no more than a disguise for his divinity.

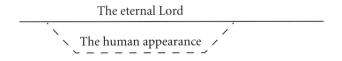

---

1 Some scholars think of Christ's pre-existence at this stage as 'ideal', rather than 'personal' – intending only to affirm that 'Christ's earthly life was an embodiment of grace from beginning to end'; 'It is the act and power of God which . . . pre-exists' (Dunn, 1989, pp. 121, 209).

Incarnationism

The final revision produces the Christological model of the incarnation ('making flesh' or 'enfleshing') of Christ. This idea, or better narrative pattern, is found in several forms in the New Testament. By far its most complete version is in John's Gospel, where the Logos ('word') of God's utterance and self-expression becomes a particular individual reality (John 1.1–18; 16.28; 17.5). Perhaps something of this shape appears, in a much less developed way, in the other Gospels, wherever the line of the second act is 'lifted' by revealing the earthly Jesus as the heavenly Son of God through his life, miracles, teaching and passion, and events such as the transfiguration.

Divine pre-existence   Lord and Christ

The man Jesus

In John's full incarnationism, the 'sharp corners' of the earlier diagrams are lost, morphing into a smooth curve. This illustrates the less abrupt changes here compared with those suggested in kenoticism, for the human Jesus *remains* the divine Logos-Son even while on earth, although he takes up a real human existence. (See, for example, the 'I am' sayings, such as 8.58; 11.25; 14.6; the raising of Lazarus in 11.1–44; and the Son's uninterrupted relationship with the Father, portrayed throughout this Gospel.) In John, 'the divine Logos leaves heaven on an arc which will inevitably return him there' (Knox, 1967, p. 38).

In the more qualified 'incarnationism' of Paul's epistles, however, the resurrection–exaltation is still a more abrupt and significant motif, and the human career of Jesus is presented as in stark contrast to it. Dunn thinks it more probable that Paul's meaning 'did not stretch so far' as to endorse the incarnation of 'a heavenly being who had pre-existed with God from the beginning' (Dunn, 1989, pp. 46, 255).

Christological Problems and Approaches

However Christians understand the different New Testament accounts of Jesus (in the different forms that scholarship recovers them), their own Christology will inevitably reveal their own way of seeing and valuing. 'The claim that Jesus is my Lord says something about me as well as a great deal about him' (Astley, 2007, p. 116). Christians are all involved, therefore, 'in an unending conversation about Jesus'. But how Christians think and talk about Jesus has greatly changed 'over time and from one cultural setting to another' (Borg, 2006, pp. 310–11).

EXERCISE

- How would you now answer Jesus' two questions to his disciples in Mark 8.27–30?
- How has your Christology changed over the years, and why?
- Which three New Testament passages best capture your vision of Jesus?

Over the next four centuries, Christological *narratives and metaphors* became *doctrines*. As reflection on the person of Jesus Christ moved out of the Jewish thought world, in which titles such as 'son of God' had originally applied to wholly human beings such as the Israelite kings, Hellenistic (Greek) influences rapidly became dominant. Assumptions about pre-existent divine beings then transformed the question, 'Who do you say that I am?', into one about how God's divine Son – '*the* Son' – could take on human nature. Many soon came to accept the invitation of one first century writer, 'We ought so to think of Jesus Christ as of God' (*2 Clement* 1.1). But this was not without its difficulties. The central problems for Christology are these:

- If Jesus was human, how could he have been and how can he be divine?
- If Jesus is or was divine, how could he ever be human?

People's theology often depends on their 'viewpoint' or 'perspective', the position from which they survey the topic at issue.

There are, somehow, two sides to everything that Jesus did and was. From one point of view, Jesus is God-with-us. From another and equally legitimate point of view, he is us-with-God. And he is both of these things at the same time: humanity revealed in God, and God revealed through humanity. (Norris, 1979, p. 165)

Throughout much of the history of Christianity, Christology has been approached *from the side of God*. Speaking metaphorically, it has moved or looked 'from above' downwards. From that vantage point, Jesus was first assumed to be in some sense God, and it was his humanity that needed explanation. 'If he is God, how can he also be human?' The approach has often resulted in a 'high Christology' wedded to an inadequate account of Christ's humanity, as compared to his divinity. But there is no doubt that it represents the traditional approach, and is widely held by both ordinary theologians and scholars.

However, many ordinary Christians, and a sizeable number of academic theologians, prefer an approach *from the side of human beings* – a Christology 'from below'. Assuming that Jesus was fully human, this asks, 'In what sense was he also of God?' Of course, the danger now is the exact opposite of the previous one, in that a Christology from below can easily lead to an extreme 'low Christology' with an inadequate emphasis on, or notion of, the divinity of Christ. Nowadays, however, many find it difficult to talk about Christology *without* taking his kinship with us – his humanity – as the decisive factor.

EXERCISE

Before proceeding further, reflect on which of these two approaches you yourself favour, and why.

The doctrine of the person of Christ soon became a hot topic of debate within the Church. It was not a theoretical matter, or at least never solely that. The Christology hammered out at the Council of Nicaea in 325, like its later interpretations and defences, represents 'a cosmological confession and a soteriological confession simultaneously'. Its underlying conviction was that 'only he who created the universe could save man, and that to do either or both of these he himself had to be divine and not a creature' (Pelikan, 1971, p. 203). So the debate is still focused on salvation; but also on the scribes' question, 'Who can forgive sins but God alone?' (Mark 2.7).

Although this book offers a topical rather than a historical account of doctrine, it is helpful to give some detail of the different beliefs about Christ that developed in the early history of the Church, and their locations across the Christological spectrum. *(Please note, however, that most of this detail is provided solely for reference purposes. It is the general shape, and final 'resolution', of the debate about Christ that matters.)*

To the Classical Solution

In the chart below, the location of the different theologies across the width of the page represents the relative position occupied by these diVerent schools of thought, in their attempts to solve the basic Christological problem of combining humanity and divinity in Christ. Thus:

a location to the left	a central location	a location to the right
represents a greater emphasis on *humanity* at the expense of divinity	represents a *balance* between divinity and humanity	represents a greater emphasis on *divinity* at the expense of humanity

←————————————————————————————→

'Christologies from the side of human beings'   *'Christologies from the side of God'*

Second Century

Ebionitism	Docetism
A Jewish Christian sect which viewed the divinity of Christ as representing nothing more than a special dignity conferred on Jesus because of his goodness, etc.	Christ was a divine being who only appeared to be involved in the evil world of flesh, and could not have truly suffered
	Influenced by Hellenistic ideas about an impassible (unchanging) God
	Docetism later led to the full-blown heresy of **Gnosticism**, which viewed matter as a corrupt reality from which true believers can escape with the help of a secret *gnosis* (knowledge) brought by Christ the Redeemer

---

'Spirit Christology'

The pre-existent Spirit of God united himself with human nature

'Christ the Lord . . . being first of all spirit, became flesh'
(*2 Clement*)

'Logos Christology'

It is the Logos (pre-existing Word) of God that becomes flesh

Influenced by Greek notions of a reason immanent in the world, as well as Old Testament ideas of the role of God's word in communication

Sometimes Christ is designated 'another God' (Justin Martyr)

The Logos doctrine was retained, and taken up into the notion of a pre-existent divine *Son*

(These two Christologies overlapped with each other; the Logos Christology overlapped with and eventually displaced both forms of Monarchianism)

Third Century

Dynamic Monarchianism/ Adoptionism	Tertullian (c.160–225)	Modalistic Monarchianism
Jesus was a good man who received the power of God	Christ possesses two natures, with distinctive functions, but is only one person	Father, Son and Spirit are three 'modes' of the one God, appearing in sequence – temporary theophanies (mere manifestations of God)
'Mary did not bear the word . . . what she bore was a man equal to us, but superior in all things as a result of the holy spirit' (Paul of Samosata)	The Logos 'assumes human flesh', with a human soul (*ignored by Eastern Church*)	For example Sabellius, Callistus

Fourth Century   'SON CHRISTOLOGY'

Arius (250–336)

Christ is subordinate to God – a supreme creature, but not properly a man: a unique demi-god

'There was when he was not'

As the Logos/Son changes (is 'passible') he could not be God, only *like* God

He is therefore not of the same substance (*homoousios*), only of a similar substance (*homoiousios*)

Council of Nicaea (325)

resolved that *Christ is fully divine*

Enshrined at Council of Constantinople (381) in the **Nicene Creed** (the Son is *homoousios* with the Father: 'true God from true God', 'begotten not made')

Athanasius (c.296–373)

Defended the view that the Son is fully divine

A champion of the Nicene party's *homoousios* against its later Arian opponents (through five banishments!)

---

triumph of
full divinity of Christ

The non-biblical word *homoousios* ('of the same substance') was suggested at Nicaea by the Emperor Constantine to end the controversy over the Arian question. An ambiguous word, it was used to mean that what the Father was, so essentially was the Son.

Apollinaris (c.315–392)

In Christ there is no human will, mind, spirit or soul

The Logos replaced them, adopting a human *body* not a human person ('in a man the life which is given by God cannot be found')

Theodore of Mopsuestia (350–428)

Christ has a human body, spirit, soul and will

The Logos adopts a perfect man, not just a body

Gregory of Nazianzus (329–390)

'If anyone has put his trust in him as a man without a human mind, he is really bereft of mind . . . For that which he has not assumed, he has not healed; but that which has been united to his Godhead, is also saved . . . Let them not then begrudge us our complete salvation, nor clothe the Saviour only with bones and nerves and the portraiture of man'

---

leads to
triumph of
full humanity of Christ

Fifth Century

(These movements first began up to two centuries earlier)

Antiochene Christology	Alexandrian Christology
A 'word–man' tradition	A 'word–flesh' tradition
Stresses two full natures in Christ	Stresses the unity of Christ
Christ's humanity is seen as being as important as his divinity	The work of Christ = an act of God
The Logos is not the subject of the human activities and experiences of Christ	The Logos is the subject of all Christ's. activities and experiences
Tends to give an inadequate account of the union of the two natures, reducing incarnation to mere inspiration	Tends to reduce the humanity of Christ to a theophany (a mere manifestation of God)

Nestorius (c.381–452)	Cyril of Alexandria (c.378–444)
Stresses the humanity of Christ	Stresses union between the two natures: 'But we are accustomed to worship Emmanuel with one single worship, not separating from the Word the body which was personally united to him'
Word–man Christology	
Mary is the mother only of Christ's human nature, and therefore is not *Theotokos* ('God-bearer', 'Mother of God')	Mary is *Theotokos*
	Word–flesh Christology – 'tacitly reduced . . . to a subject-attribute Christology' (Norris)
	Human nature never had a separate existence, but belonged entirely to the Logos from conception

Nestorius condemned at
Council of Ephesus (431)

Eutyches (c.378–454)
Human nature of Christ is absorbed in divine nature
There is only one nature after the union

Nestorianism	Pope Leo (d. 461)	Eutycheanism/ Monophysitism
Christ is two persons, with two subjects	Christ is 'one person in two natures' But as the peculiar and proper attributes of each of the natures are attributed to the same person, the divine Word can be said to be (e.g.) 'hungry' (*communicatio idiomatum*, the exchange of properties)	Christ is one nature only (the divine) – but they probably meant one 'person'!

unity of Christ
defined (but not resolved) at

Council of Chalcedon (451)

- condemns Nestorianism, Eutycheanism, Apollinarianism

- steers between Alexandrian and Antiochene Christologies

- **'Chalcedonian definition'**:

Christ is *homoousios* with the Father in his Godhead, and therefore *truly God*

and *homoousios* with us in his humanity, and therefore *truly human*

These *two natures* exist, 'without confusion, without change, without division, without separation', 'in one person (*prosopon*) and *hypostasis*'

This defines the
hypostatic union of the two natures of Christ.

Sixth and Seventh Centuries

The debate continued over the nature of this union of the two natures. The view of Leontius of Byzantium that the human nature of Christ had no personal centre of its own, but achieved personalization only in the Logos, was endorsed by the Second Council of Constantinople (553). The Third Council of Constantinople (680–1) resolved the controversy over the wills of the incarnate Christ, by ruling that he had two wills but that his human will was always 'subject to his divine and omnipotent will'. As John of Damascus put it, the human will 'wills of its own free will those things which the divine will wills it to will'.

The *Chalcedonian definition* of 451 defines the *hypostatic union of the two natures* of Christ. He is one individual with two natures, human and divine.

As the Council of Nicaea had pronounced over a century earlier, Christ is fully divine. He is of the *same* substance (*homoousios*) with the Father, not just of a *like* substance (*homoiousios*). 'In this iota ["i"] the whole of the Gospel was at stake' (Barth, 1966, p. 85). Hence the 'Arian view', which understood the Son to be a creature, was rejected. God had come *in person*.

But Christ was also fully human – with a human will, mind, spirit, soul. His humanity is *homoousios* with our nature. 'He not only resembles us . . . He is the same as us' (Barth, 1966, p. 97). The humanity is therefore no mere appendage to, or manifestation of, divinity; and the divinity is not simply an 'inspiration' of the humanity. This is a true union of two very different natures, with neither just 'taking over' the other. Even so, orthodox Christology veers slightly away from the centre, towards the right. For it is the Logos, God the Son, who is 'in charge'; and orthodoxy suggests a sort of *mixture* of two substances in which each retains its identity, but with the divine predominating in a 'personal unity'.

Nevertheless, after Nicaea and Chalcedon, the Church accepts that there is 'one subject, one agent or actor, one person', and therefore no 'separation or division between the eternal Son of God and the man of Nazareth' (Burnaby, 1959, p. 79).

Coming to Terms with Theology: *Christology*

Communicatio idiomatum – the sharing of the attributes of the two natures of Christ, so that what is said of the divine nature may also be said of Christ's humanity, and vice versa. The one person may be described as *both* 'eternal' *and* 'born' or 'created'.

Homoiousios – being 'of like substance', that is a similar kind of thing.

Homoousios – being 'of the same substance': originally meaning, perhaps, 'the same kind of thing', but later the same thing (numerical identity).

Perichoresis, co-inherence – 'mutual indwelling or interpenetration' of the two natures of Christ, without blending or fusion.

Subordinationism – the view that the Son is less than the Father. (Origen called the Son 'the second God'; Arius thought of him as a creation of God.)

Modelling Christ

Chalcedon didn't *explain* the incarnation, it only *defined* it – as 'two natures in one person'. But did it give Christological debate 'a direction' (Bernhard Lohse), or simply serve as a compromise? It plainly left unresolved the actual character of the union between such disparate realities as humanity and divinity.

Some commentators feel that the two-nature Christology is a philosophical step too far, remote from the language of the Bible and Christian devotion. It relies on a distinction within Aristotelian philosophy between two notions of 'substance': (i) a particular, individual reality or thing (*hypostasis*, 'person'), and (ii) a generic, universal reality that exists (and can only exist) 'in' such particulars (*physis*, 'nature'). Such terminology foregrounds Christ's substance, essence or being – his 'ontology'. The obvious danger is that this will distract us from his saving activity, as expressed in his teaching, ministry and passion. Therefore current theological thought – while paying some sort of homage to the Chalcedonian definition – sometimes seeks to articulate Christology in rather different ways.

Psychological Models

Among 'Chalcedon-based models', John McIntyre distinguishes the two-nature model from more recent 'psychological' and 'revelation' models.

Psychological models are concerned with the mind of Jesus. Faced by claims about the divinity of Christ, many ask, 'How much did Jesus know?' Did he, for example, know everything that contemporary biblical scholars know about the authorship of the Old Testament; or what scientists now know about mental illness, or the origins of the universe? Were there *human* limits to the knowledge of Jesus? (He admits some ignorance in Mark 13.32.) On most accounts of kenoticism (see below), the Logos 'gave up' his omniscience (all-knowing power) at the incarnation. Or perhaps Jesus had two 'streams of consciousness', one human and the other divine; but if so how did they relate to each other – in Gethsemane, say, or on the cross? On some psychological models, 'it is difficult to avoid the conclusion that [the divine person] both knows and does not know the same fact at the same time' (McIntyre, 1998, p. 139).

And how did Jesus think about *himself*? What did he believe about his relationship to God, what was going to happen to himself and so on? Those who think that Jesus could not, as a real human being, have thought of himself as either divine or pre-existent (see below) also raise psychological challenges for Christology.

But focusing on the mental life of Jesus – itself, surely, largely irrecoverable – also gives rise to metaphysical issues about the nature of mind. If God is wholly Spirit (see Chapter 9), while humans are embodied spirits, selves or minds, any union between them is not well modelled in ways that suggest two pieces of matter or 'stuff' coming together (cf. p. 146). Minds are 'thinking things', for which agreement in thoughts ('having a common mind') may be more significant than any other sort of union. But this would hardly give us a *unique* relationship between God the Father and Christ. A more orthodox model has been proposed in terms of one person constituted by 'a connected sequence' of the 'eternal experience of the Logos . . . intentionally "joined on" to the earthly experience of Jesus' (White, 1991, p. 83).

Revelation-Salvation Model

Many have argued that the really important feature of Jesus Christ is something about his function or activity, rather than his being or nature. It is frequently claimed that in the New Testament the question, 'Who is Christ?', meant 'first of all, "What is his function?"' (Cullman, 1963, p. 4).

Well, Jesus *reveals* the true nature of God to us. Some insist that God reveals all of himself *through himself* (in the person of the God-man Jesus), so that Christ is thought of as both the medium and the subject of revelation – 'through God alone can God be known'.

Theologians sometimes describe Jesus as the one who both reveals the character, and truly *expresses* the love of God. I have tweaked McIntyre's title, 'revelation model', both to include the idea that this revelation is itself salvific, and to allow us to say that the salvation that Jesus brings also covers other aspects of his work (see Chapter 6).

Functional Models Criticized

Where ontological accounts of God's relationship with Jesus seem to protect the claim of Christ's *uniqueness*, distinguishing Christianity from other religious faiths, many functional accounts are open to a *degree Christology*. Here Jesus differs only in degree from prophets and other religious figures, and not in kind. Is this true of such activities as forgiving sins, or healing human woundedness?

But 'the finality or decisiveness of revelation in Christ is ... threatened the more that knowledge of God is accessible before or independently of Christ's coming' (Tanner, 1997, p. 265). Even on a functional account, it is possible to speak of Christ's work as *somehow* final or distinctive. We may view Jesus as a man 'in whom the glory of God was manifested *fully*'; or say that he is 'the *paradigmatic* revelation of God's love for us and of God's willingness to pay the price for reconciliation with us' (Ward, 1977, p. 255; Brümmer, 2005, p. 92 – my italics). Would that guarantee that 'Jesus does not just bring a word from God; he brings the whole word and the total God' (Schwarz, 1984, p. 263)?

Functional models *can* permit absolute outcomes. In tuning an analogue radio receiver, incremental changes in wavelength (differences 'in degree') will at some point result in a difference 'in kind' – hearing the broadcast programme, compared with not hearing it or not hearing it 'clearly enough' to understand its real message.

Christology often declares that, even if we begin with *function* we must end up with *ontology*. Jesus Christ 'does what he is and is what he does' (Barth, 1956b, p. 405). What must the inner identity of Christ be, if he can act as the agent – or even only the medium – of God's revelation and salvation? Can he function as the revelation of God *only if* he is God incarnate? But the same functions can be compatible with very different ontologies, as science illustrates. The function-to-ontology route can only be assured of leading to an orthodox destination if the function is interpreted in certain specific ways.

Linguistic Models

Does the Chalcedonian definition *require* the ontological speculation of the two-nature model? Perhaps we should move Christology from the mysterious realm of metaphysics into the world of language analysis. Chalcedon 'sets a "bound-ary" on what can, and cannot, be said' (Coakley). It lays down 'the rules ... for talking about the relations between God the Father and Jesus Christ' (Ramsey, 1965, p. 43; see above p. 47). It tells us that we need to speak both of the human and of the divine in Christ; that we should not emphasize either at the expense of the other; and that we must maintain the unity and distinctiveness of this *one* figure.

Can the two natures of Christ best be understood in terms of two languages: 'not two storeys but two stories' (Wiles, 1972, p. 9; Robinson, 1973, p. 117)? The 'complementarity' of wave-language and particle-language in discussions about electrons could serve as a parallel. Physicists have found it illuminat-ing to use both languages, as both reliably represent different aspects of the electron's behaviour, while leaving the electron's 'true nature' unresolved. Is the God–Christ relationship likely to be any simpler?

One linguistic model treats the doctrine of the incarnation as *a myth* (see Chapter 3). Of the 'two stories', one is then historical (the human story) but the other mythological. Christological story-metaphors about God's 'coming down at Christmas', being 'born of a virgin' and 'made flesh', express the significance of Jesus – as 'God for us', or 'the human face of God'. Perhaps this language should not be pushed further, by attempting to draw inferences from these powerful, poetic narratives about the divine technology and hardware involved?

In the controversial collection, *The Myth of God Incarnate*, Hick characterized the Church's conception of Jesus as God incarnate as no more than 'a mytholo-gical or poetic way of expressing his significance for us'.[2] The 'truth' of this myth depends on the appropriateness of the attitude it invites in its hearers (Hick, 1977, pp. ix, 178). For a myth to be 'true', Wiles claims that there must be *some* 'ontological truth corresponding to the central characteristic of the structure of the myth'. Although this takes the linguistic model in an ontological direction, Wiles does not travel far along that road. He supposes that the notion of a 'union of divine and human at the heart of the human personality', as in the experience of grace, may be all that Christology requires (Wiles in Hick, 1977, p. 161).

---

2 Others have responded that, although certain biblical narratives may be called myths, it is wrong to assign a doctrine to this literary category. Rather, the incarnation is a doctrine that is *expressed* in myths. Hick also speak of incarnation as a 'metaphor' (Hick, 2005).

Kenoticism

A number of British theologians of the nineteenth and twentieth centuries drew on this theme to develop moderate versions of kenotic Christology. Some understood the incarnation as involving the Son of God laying aside the infinite powers of God, omniscience, omnipresence and omnipotence (see Chapter 10), while retaining – or enhancing – God's character as self-giving love. Kenoticism has been criticized for proposing some odd mythological transformations, particularly when we imagine Christ once again taking up these powers. Others argue for a progressive growth or filling of Christ's humanity by the Logos during Jesus' life. In both cases, 'the Logos was filled with as much Godhead as the humanity could bear' (Torrance, 2001, p. 212, citing Irenaeus). The Son might have 'set aside the style of a God, and took the style of a servant', by the 'retraction' of certain attributes 'from actual to potential', rather than by their renunciation or concealment (Forsyth, 1909, pp. 306–8).

But if God divests himself of these distinctively divine attributes, doesn't this imply that he *ceases* to be divine? One might deny this on the grounds that what makes God 'God' is a love that leads to a humble *giving up* of power. In response to the question, 'Who looks after the world during Jesus' life?', one might also appeal to a Trinitarian concept of God that allows for more distinctions between Father and Son (see Chapter 9).

Pre-existence, Humanity and the 'Virgin Birth'

Whereas earlier Christians were often content to emphasize the divinity of Christ at the expense of his humanity, it seems more natural today to begin with his humanity. 'To say that Jesus was not God but like God at least says something, and something important. To say that he was not man but like man is to condemn his entire life as a charade' (Robinson, 1973, p. 39). Many consider beliefs about Jesus' pre-existence and 'virgin birth' *incompatible* with the belief that he is truly human.

The New Testament's language of *pre-existence* (for example John 17.5; Col. 1.15–17) may have originated in a natural desire to make claims about Jesus that paralleled those voiced by Jewish sources about God's *torah* (Law), *sophia* (Wisdom) or *ruach* (Spirit) (cf. Gen. 1.2; Ps. 33.6; 139.7; Prov. 8.1, 22; Ecclus. [Sirach] 24.23–7). Was Paul, too, only saying that 'Jesus is the exhaustive embodiment of divine wisdom' (Dunn, 1989, p. 195)? Others treat these early beliefs in the pre-existence of Christ as 'the equivalent in Greek terms of his "foreordination"' (Robinson, 1962, p. 143), expressing the affirmation that Jesus was 'in God's mind from the beginning' as part of the eternal plan of salvation. 'He was not an afterthought in the divine plan for the world' (Braaten, 1984, p. 546) but 'already latent, already predestined, in the primaeval swirling cloud of particles' that burst out from the Big Bang (Macquarrie, 1990, p. 392).

However it arose, pre-existence is now seen by many as a challenge to Jesus' full humanity. 'We can have the humanity without the pre-existence and we can have the pre-existence without the humanity. There is absolutely no way of having both' (Knox, 1967, p. 106). But is this true? Those who accept Indian religious teaching about reincarnation (around 15% of the world population?) presumably think that their own pre-existence – admittedly usually unremembered – is quite compatible with their real humanity.

The *virginal conception of Jesus* is the accurate way of referring to the event related at the beginning of Matthew and Luke (and nowhere else in the New Testament). Though often taken to be a foundation – even a 'proof' – of Christ's divinity, it has played only a minor role in traditional teaching about the person of Christ. While the Virgin Mary appears in both the Apostles' and Nicene Creeds, 'the virgin birth does not belong at the centre of the gospel' (Küng, 1993, p. 44). There are parallels in ancient pagan religion (although these are of physical intercourse with a god) and, paradoxically, the doctrine was used in early Christian debate against the Gnostics to prove Jesus' true *humanity*. But today, a physical 'virgin birth' seems to throw doubt on this. Many scholars espouse agnosticism on the topic; others deny the doctrine, arguing that Jesus shares the pre-existence *we* have, within the genetic ancestry of humankind.

More conservative voices contend that 'the non-biological conception of Christ . . . is essential to the Christian faith' (Zizioulas, 2008, p. 103). Karl Barth accepts the doctrine, but rejects any inference that Christ's human nature is not 'identical with our nature as we see it in the light of the Fall' (Barth, 1956a, p. 153). Others agree. 'The Son of God took on the fallen nature of man' (Zizioulas, 2008, p. 109) for 'what Christ did not take, he did not redeem' (Gregory of Nazianzus). The view that Christ must have taken *unfallen* human nature at the incarnation lies behind the nineteenth-century Roman Catholic dogma of the *immaculate conception* of Mary. This states that, though conceived in the normal way, Mary was by God's grace 'kept free from all stain of original sin'. However, if Christ 'in every respect has been tested as we are, yet without sin' (Heb. 4.15), his nature must have been the sort that we have – one that is capable of sin.

The Centrality of Christology

Christological debate often starts at the wrong end. We seem to have been asked to do the impossible, rather like drawing a two-dimensional figure that is both a square (man) and a circle (God). But how do we know the 'shape' of God?

> In confessing the divinity of Jesus Christ, we do not attribute to him a notion of deity which we have derived beforehand from our own philosophical specu-lations. We do not look at Jesus and call him God because he conforms so remarkably to our preconceived idea of what a God must be. Jesus is not the fulfillment of our prior notion of God. He *is* God for us. We apprehend the final meaning of God in Jesus, and nowhere else. (Braaten, 1984, p. 537)

Is this the real challenge of Christology – to rewrite the doctrine of God?

EXERCISE

Look back to your notes from the earlier exercises in this chapter. How does your own vision of Jesus, and general approach to Christology, relate to:

(a) the different Christological models;
(b) your views on the pre-existence and 'virgin birth' of Christ?

Remember, 'To succeed in Christology is only not to fail too badly' (Turner, 1976, p. 130).

Suggestions for Further Reading

Introductory

Astley, J., Brown, D. and Loades, A. (eds), 2009, *Christology: Key Readings in Christian Thought*, London: SPCK.

Borg, M. J. and Wright, N. T., 2007, *The Meaning of Jesus: Two Visions*, San Francisco: HarperSanFrancisco.

Macquarrie, J., 1998, *Christology Revisited*, London: SCM Press.

Advanced

Gunton, C. E., 1997, *Yesterday and Today: A Study of Continuities in Christology*, London: SPCK.

O'Collins, G., 1995, *Christology: A Biblical, Historical and Systematic Study of Jesus*, Oxford: Oxford University Press.

Pelikan, J., 1999, *Jesus through the Centuries: His Place in the History of Culture*, New Haven, CT: Yale University Press.

8

Believing in the World: Finding God in the Mud

Introduction

Salvation and incarnation take place on this muddy, material earth. Most religious traditions claim that 'the world' (that is, the whole universe, the 'cosmos') is God's creation. It is, therefore, intended and planned, crafted, sustained and developed, by God. In the creeds, God is 'the maker of heaven *and earth*', of '*all* things'. The Christian doctrine of God's relationship to the world revolves around this notion of *creation*.

Although physicists sometimes use the term in their theories, the *doctrine* of creation does not work like a scientific, causal explanation of the 'how' of the world. This is not a scientific theory like the 'Big Bang'. It is 'not a story devised for the sake of satisfying mundane curiosity about how everything began' (Haught, 2007, p. 109); nor is it a theory or 'an intellectual, speculative notion' (Brueggemann, 1997, p. 533). It operates at a different level altogether – or, rather, at two levels.

- *Theologically* and *religiously*, it serves as a personal, purposive explanation of the 'why' of the world; and a perspective on our place within it, as creatures who depend on God's gift of existence.
- *Metaphysically*, it works as an all-embracing interpretation of that which undergirds and explains all things: the ever-present, all-pervading, cosmic reality that goes beyond the empirical world.[1]

---

1 'Empirical' covers what is perceived by or can be inferred from, and may be tested by, sense experience.

Although the Bible begins with creation in Genesis 1 and 2 (two different narratives written at different times and expressing rather different theologies), this does not mean that this theological theme ranks first in significance. We should think of creation, rather, as a preface and presupposition to the history of salvation that follows, as in Isa. 40.28–31; 42.5–7. The nature of creation is 'simply its equipment for grace' (Barth, 1958a, p. 231). 'The Hebrew people . . . found God as he acted in history and it was because they were convinced that God is the Lord of all nations that they were led to see that he is the Creator' (Hordern, 1969, p. 78). Much theology argues, therefore, that it is a mistake to split apart the doctrines of creation and redemption; for creation is also a 'redemptive act', and 'creation and salvation are one continuous process' (Lampe, 1977, p. 180). Some even use the hybrid term 'creative redemption' to stress the unity of God's action in creating the world and redeeming his children.

This is reflected in the New Testament claim that Christ is the agent of creation (John 1.1–5, 14–18; 1 Cor. 8.6; Col. 1.15–20; Heb. 1.2–3). For the Christian, 'what Jesus did and said points to the underlying meaning and purpose of the creation' (Hefner, 1984a, p. 290). The 'new creation' in Christ is a renewing or restoration of creation (2 Cor. 5.17). For Aquinas, therefore, 'grace does not scrap nature but brings it to perfection' (*Summa of Theology* 1a. 1, 8).

Picturing God's World

The dominant view within Christianity, usually called *theism* (or 'transcendent theism'), is that God and the universe are connected by a one-way relationship of dependence. The world 'depends' on God for its existence (literally 'hangs down' from God); but God's existence does not depend on the world. This asymmetrical relationship has been expressed in two simple subtraction sums (Temple, 1934, p. 435):

$$\text{The World} - \text{God} = 0 \qquad \text{God} - \text{the World} = \text{God}.$$

However, this way of thinking is often criticized for portraying a distant deity who relates to his creation only through his action – 'at arm's length', one might say.

Paul seemed willing to speak of a God in whom 'we live and move and have our being' (Acts 17.28), suggesting a closer and more intimate relationship. *Panentheism* has developed this image, depicting a more interdependent association – with the universe existing in a God who 'includes the world but is more than the world' (Hartshorne, 1976, p. 90). ('Panentheism' literally means 'everything-is-*in*-God-ism'. It must be distinguished from the 'everything-is-God-ism' of *pantheism*, which treats the universe as another name for God.)

There are many varieties of panentheism. Augustine described creation as like a huge sponge existing within, penetrated by, and 'filled through and through with the waters of [the] boundless sea' of the infinite God (*Confessions* vii, 5). A metaphor often employed today is that the universe serves as God's cosmic body, with the events in the world revealing and expressing God's will, as our bodies reveal and express our embodied 'selves' or 'minds'. *Process theology* (see Chapter 9) has a particular interpretation of panentheism, and of the related metaphor that 'the world lives by its incarnation of God in itself' (Whitehead, 1926, p. 156). On this view, God is to be thought of as changing to some extent, affected by and caused by the changing world. But there is another pole to God's reality that lies outside time and is unchanged by the events of the world. 'We are truly "outside" the divine essence, though inside God' (Hartshorne and Reese, 1953, p. 22).

Some process thinkers follow Whitehead in regarding the world as having always existed, like God. In this case, although God is the ground of all its novelty and its supreme influence ('lure'), God does not actually bring it into being. Others hold the traditional view, conceiving God as 'being the reason that entities occur at all' (Cobb, 1966, p. 211).

Charles Hartshorne argues that the world affects how God is because the world is *a part of God* ('What is in the parts is in the whole': Hartshorne, 1953, p. 511). But Augustine rejected an identification of the two that would imply that 'anything which anyone treads underfoot would be a part of God' (*City of God* iv, ch. 12). Arthur Peacocke also denies that the universe is 'of the same stuff or "substance" as God himself', for 'the world is "in" God, but not "of" God' (Peacocke, 1993, p. 371; 1996, p. 13). Even so, he has produced a striking analogy of the world being created *within* Godself.

> The concept of God as Creator has, in the past, been too much dominated by a stress on the externality of God's creative acts – he is regarded as creating something external to himself, just as the male fertilizes the womb from

outside. But mammalian females, at least, create within themselves and the growing embryo resides within the female body and this is a proper corrective to the masculine ... God creates a world that is in principle and in origin, other than him/herself but creates it, the world, within him/herself. (Peacocke, 2004, p. 142)

During her pregnancy, however, a mother does think of the baby as 'a part' of herself; and ontologically it *is* made of the same human stuff (even though it is genetically different). But then all metaphors have their limits!

Deism takes a position at the other extreme of the spectrum of interrelatedness, asserting that God brings the universe into existence but then has no further dealings with it. This understanding of God 'as an absentee landlord' or 'retired potentate' (McGrath, 2001, p. 184) was influenced by the closed, determinist view of nature that flourished in the seventeenth and eighteenth centuries. The dominant picture then was of a clockmaker-God whose handiwork can continue to exist and run effectively, despite its maker's absence. Only a poor craftsman would need to hang around to repair his works; a truly powerful, skilful God could safely leave his creation in the hands of the laws of physics that he had also created. In its extreme form, deism denies not only this sort of 'intervention' in nature, but also the idea that the universe requires *any* continuing contact with God to keep it in existence. By contrast, theism deems the world to be more like an electric clock that must remain plugged into the mains if it is to continue to operate.

Coming to Terms with Theology: *God's World*

Deism – the belief that God brought the universe into existence once in the past, but has no continuing contact with it.

Immanent – closely involved with, indwelling.

Naturalism – the belief that reality is understandable without reference to supernatural events or beings.

Panentheism – a form of theism, for which the universe exists 'within' God.

Pantheism – the belief that God is identical to the universe.

> **Theism** – the belief that God creates a separate universe, and continues to keep it in existence.
>
> **Transcendent** – that which excels or surpasses; what is above and beyond the universe, and human experience, language and thought.
>
> **Voluntarism** – (here) the belief that God's will *directly* causes every event in the world, rather than working through natural causes.

Adopting another analogy, we might think of God effecting changes in nature like a computer program produces changes on a screen. But then every event in nature would be a new and direct creation of God, wholly uncaused by previous events of nature. Such *voluntarism* has usually been regarded as unorthodox. Alternatively, God could be pictured as analogous to a snooker table, lying beneath and supporting the ricocheting balls of all natural events. Their first movements were initiated by God at the beginning of the 'game', but now they continue in movement under the influence of physical laws. This 'undergirding' God captures the idea of one who has 'the whole world in his hands', and humanity's reliance on God's 'everlasting arms' (as Deut. 33.27 is translated in some versions; cf. Ps. 95.4–5).

EXERCISE

Like all other theological models, those outlined above give *some* insight into God's relationship with the world, but they have limitations and cannot be pressed too far.

- Reflect on the *positive* and the *negative* analogies (see Chapter 3) in each of the above models (pp. 156–8).
- List other metaphors and analogies that might describe the God–world relationship, and note *their* positive and the negative aspects.

The following is by no means an exhaustive list.

Sub-personal models include creation out of the divine substance itself (*ex divino*); and as a series of *emanations* of an increasingly degraded nature, somewhat analogous to rays emanating from the sun (as in Gnosticism). Such models suggest that the world is made of the same substance as God, or is only an 'appearance' of God; and that it does not depend on God's *will*.

Personal Models

(i) a gardener – who designs, nurtures, tends (and selectively destroys?) an independent creation with its own nature;

(ii) a lord or king – who rules over a 'dependent' world by the exercise of sovereign power;

(iii) an architect or designer – who creates the plan, but not the finished artefact;

(iv) a builder, sculptor, potter or artist – who both plans and manufactures ('creates') a work of art or craft, out of pre-existing materials;

(v) a speaker, actor, musician or dancer – as in (i) to (iv), their creations are expressions of their creators; but these creations only exist *as they are created*. Here creation is not so much the work of God, 'as the "play" of God, as a kind of free artistic expression … [of] God's good pleasure' (Migliore, 2004, p. 112);

(vi) a novelist, dramatist, poet, composer or choreographer – whose creations are semi-independent, and so cannot be 'made' to behave in ways contrary to their characters;

(vii) 'suicide-in-reverse' (William H. Poteat) – where a person's suicide is the destruction of their whole world;

(viii) the 'soul' of a world that is here analogous to God's body. God may be thought of as like a discarnate spirit who could exist without a world (Richard Swinburne), or as an essentially embodied 'person' who could not exist without *some* world (as argued by Grace Jantzen). On this second view, God may need the world for God's self-expression and 'full' life;

(ix) *parental analogies:*

(a) in procreation – the loving of a child into existence;

(b) in nurturing a child's independent personhood to maturity and relative independence, through a relationship of continuing self-giving love and care.

You will have noted that some negative analogies are inevitable in all such models, including the limitation of an inherent dualism – as humans can 'create' only by manipulating things that already exist. Significantly, perhaps, the Hebrew verb for God's act of creating (*bara*) is not applied to human activity in the Bible.

God in Action: Creation

EXERCISE

Attempt to summarize in a single sentence your present understanding of the doctrine of creation. What does it imply about the world and God?

Most definitions refer to God *bringing* the universe into existence at the beginning of time; but in many ways the more fundamental element is God's activity in *sustaining* the universe after it was first made. God is therefore still 'at work' (Ps. 104.29–30; John 5.17; Col. 1.17; Heb. 1.3). This second element is sometimes referred to as *continuing* or *continuous creation*, 'the incessant act by which [God] preserves the world in existence' (Mascall, 1956, p. 132). According to Aquinas, even if the world had always existed, it should still be described as 'created' if its *present* existence depends on God.

Dependence, Independence and Nothing

However, accentuating the world's dependence on God for its very being (its 'ontological dependence') does not necessarily deny it *any* measure of independent existence or causality, as voluntarism does. While some extend God's sovereignty to a total control over all events in his creation, others insist that through creation God 'limits Himself by the fact that the world over against Himself is a real existence' (Brunner, 1952, p. 20). On this second view, the world is at least *semi-autonomous*; and when God creates active agents with some measure of free will, God limits himself even more. The 'risk' intrinsic in such creation expresses the 'openness of God' (Thomas Torrance). These two positions are described by evangelicals as 'meticulous' and 'non-meticulous' providence.

God's *primary causation* is God's sustaining of all things in existence. This activity of God is necessary for anything and everything to happen. But this is not sufficient on its own to produce the effects that nature produces, if there is genuinely independent causal activity within the world (*secondary causation*). Continuous creation is essential, then, but it is no more than God's 'uniform enabling of the secondary causes' power to act' (Wiles, 1986, p. 34). Even though 'God makes things make themselves' (Charles Kingsley), God must take a great deal of responsibility for the world's activity. For without God's preservation *nothing* would ever exist or happen. And that is even true of our free actions.

You may have used the word 'nothing' in your definition of creation. Most Christians take it as fundamental that God did not create the universe out of any 'pre-existing' something, any reality that already existed independently of God. That view was held by Plato. It was also widespread in the 'conflict' creation myths of other ancient peoples – themes from which are picked up in the Old Testament (for example Ps. 74.12–17; Isa. 51.9–10). The motif is also suggested by references in Genesis to 'a formless void', 'the deep' and 'the waters'; and reflected in the more ancient narrative of human creation (Gen. 1.2; 2.7, 22–3).

From Irenaeus and Theophilos of Antioch (both late second century) onwards, Christianity has insisted that God created 'out of nothing' (Latin *ex nihilo*). This idea can be traced even earlier, in the Apocrypha (2 Macc. 7.28) and possibly in the New Testament (Rom. 4.17; Heb. 11.3). It implies that the universe *now* 'depends on a divine thread of preservation above the abyss of nothingness'; and that 'at any moment God can let it fall into nothingness' (Brunner, 1952, p. 34). This is a powerful image: 'if [God] withdrew his action from them, all things would be reduced to nothing' (Aquinas, *On the Power of God*, 5, 1).

Creation *ex nihilo* is nevertheless denied, not only by most process thinkers, but also by others who trace natural evil back to some raw matter out of which the universe arose, and which continues to resist God's will – seeking 'to descend once more into chaos' (Vardy, 1992, p. 122).

But does traditional theology actually mean that *nothing* exists prior to God's initial act of creation? There was certainly no matter, energy or laws of nature; but what of 'laws of logic' or 'laws of morality'? Many think of these as human creations, others as norms that must be true in any universe there could be. Augustine argued that God created time: 'at the time of creation there could have been no past, because there was nothing created to provide the change and movement which is the condition of time. The world was in fact made *with* time, rather than *in* time' (*City of God* xi, ch. 6). However, the idea of God being 'outside time' creates other problems (see Chapter 9).

Implications of Creation

1 The doctrine denies not only any *ultimate* dualism (belief in two primary forces), but also 'monistic' views such as naturalism and pantheism. Ultimately, there is only God with no competitors, and no intermediate category between created and uncreated reality.

2 Creation is incompatible with the claim that matter is evil (see Gen. 1.31) – in distinction from philosophies such as Platonism, Gnosticism and Manichaeism.

3 In transcendent theism, God is ontologically distinct from the world and the existence of the world is dependent on God's *will*: 'the world exists just so long as God wills it to' (*Summa of Theology* 1a. 46, 1). Creation is neither divine nor an inevitable emanation from God, but a purposeful production. But is that purpose 'for us' or 'for nature'? Or is creation just intended for *God's* delight? Moltmann argues that 'the whole work of creation was performed for the sake of the sabbath' – God's rest, which is the 'feast of creation's redemption', and creation's meaning and destination (Moltmann, 1985, p. 277).

4 'If God made the world, then God's "signature" . . . may be found within the created order' (McGrath, 2008, p. 52). Human beings are created in God's image (see Chapter 6). Many argue that they represent the goal of creation.

5 Creation implies a sacramental view of nature (see Chapter 4).

6 Creation may be said to have value implications, if it implies that God is

generous, and creation a 'benefit' or 'gift' to which we should respond with reverence and gratitude. Yet the earth still *belongs* to God and we only hold it in trust, which suggests ecological implications for our responsible stewardship.

7 As the processes of creation are 'reliable and trustworthy', the universe may be thought of as a home, 'rather than an uncaring or even hostile environment' (Hefner, 1984a, p. 271).

8 Perhaps creation is itself a divine *kenosis* – a self-emptying and self-limitation undertaken by God for the sake of humans, and possibly other creatures.

9 Creation implies that God as creator is *transcendent* over the world, but also necessarily *immanent* within it (see Chapter 9).

God in Action: Providence and Miracle

Michael Langford (1981, pp. 5–24) distinguishes six different ways in which God may be said to be active in the world. These are the (initial) *creative activity of God* and God's *continuing sustaining activity*; *God's action as final cause* (in the sense of providing the general 'direction' and purpose of creation); and three more direct expressions of God's plan – *general providence, special (or particular) providence* and *miracle*.

The word 'providence' derives from the Latin *providere*, 'to see before' (for God's foresight, see Chapter 9), or 'to see for, on behalf of'. This doctrine takes God's care beyond the relatively impersonal and universal ideas of making and preserving creation, to develop an understanding of God as one who has a concern for nature (including evolution) and, in particular, for the history of individuals and peoples.

Although continuous creation may be said to represent God's 'caring hand', most Christians have wanted to affirm a closer and more personal activity. *General providence* is the name given to God's general 'ordering', 'regulating', 'leading', 'directing' or 'steering' of the course of nature, evolution and history. This 'government' takes place according to the universal laws that God has laid down: so that (say) humans evolve more sophisticated brains, and nations move towards more peaceful relationships. This level of care – which may still seem rather distant and impersonal – is something we think essential in a parent's love for her children, exercised by paying the mortgage or doing the washing.

Special (or particular) providence is this divine care expressed in more specific, ad hoc events that aid particular individuals or communities. These events appear to be designed 'for this particular purpose' – as in apparent 'answers to prayers' for healing or rain, or the 'coincidence' of a doctor being in the theatre when an actor suffers a heart attack. While the events of general providence are routinely predictable; special providence can be unexpected. But neither set of events is scientifically inexplicable. This steering of nature may take place, for example, within chaotic weather systems or at the level of the indeterminacy built into nature at the subatomic level (where a gentle nudge from God would give one result rather than another). Yet this is still analogous to a boatman changing the path of his boat as he sails down a wide river, while remaining within the defined limits of its banks. Although particular providence is often slated for portraying God as acting arbitrarily and spasmodically, and tending towards favouritism, it cannot be criticized for picturing God as a creator who breaks his own natural laws.

Theologians disagree as to the measure of freedom God allows his physical and human creation. Is there true 'randomness' at the subatomic level, and real 'libertarian freedom' of the human will? Many, especially those influenced by Calvin, think not – for God controls everything. But proponents of 'non-meticulous providence' (see above) allow a real openness in a world that God guides, but does not wholly determine.

Defining and Defending the Miraculous

There seem to be two essential aspects to the idea of a miracle – it is both a striking 'wonder' and a religious 'sign'.

1 Miracles are *scientifically inexplicable*: a miracle is an unusual event for which no natural explanation can (yet) be offered – an exception to the known laws of nature. Now the boatman pushes the boat out of the river altogether, transcending the boundaries of the laws of nature by pulling it across dry land.
2 They are *religiously significant* and of *moral worth*: a miracle is an event that gives rise to religious awe, gratitude and wonder; so that people say, 'the gracious, loving God has acted here.'

EXERCISE

- Which of these aspects is more significant for you?
- Do any problems arise if we accept only one part of this definition?
- Do you agree that 'miracles can be perceived and identified only by personal faith within the tradition, story and community of faith . . . [this] means that God does not force himself on people' (Jenkins, 1987, p. 30)?

For a long time, people have played down or reinterpreted miraculous elements in the Bible. Schleiermacher held that 'miracle is simply the religious name for event . . . all events alike are miracle' (1958, pp. 88, 114). Many argue that, even if God does work miracles, God is no more present in a miracle than in the regular working of the laws of nature; although (as with our own actions) some events express God's character better than others. Perhaps miracles are God's *extreme anomalies*. A pianist playing a piano normally plays the notes as set down in the score; occasionally, however, he improvises – playing new notes that surprise the listener. But each and every note (whether 'natural' or 'miraculous') is equally his work.

David Hume (1711–76) insisted that our human testimony in favour of a miracle must always be balanced against the evidence (actually the human testimony) that established the law of nature which it 'violates'. It is not surprising, therefore, that he thought that the decision should always go against any supposed miracle. Especially as you just can't trust religious folk: 'violations of truth are more common in the testimony concerning religious miracles' (*Enquiry Concerning the Human Understanding*, sect. x, ii).

Hume correctly saw that there must be a proper historical and scientific prejudice against miracles, since these disciplines are founded on assumptions about regular and reliable ('probable') patterns of cause and effect. Even theories of indeterminacy in the behaviour of free human beings and subatomic particles do not overturn these assumptions. Science and history, therefore, can't include 'supernatural events' in their subject-matter. However, neither can they outlaw the *possibility* of miracles. And now that physical nature has been shown to be open and indeterminate at the subatomic level, it is possible that God may work within the gaps of a flexible natural world. Are miracles *interventions*?

That word implies interfering or manipulating a closed system. But God's 'inter-action' at this level doesn't seem much different from the sort of steering activity we discussed above, with God guiding the universe 'by purposive choices among its alternative pathways' (Ward, 1990, p. 69). Under such circumstances, God's action would also be *necessarily hidden* 'within the cloudiness of the intrinsic-ally unpredictable' (Doctrine Commission of the Church of England, 2005, p. 239).

But *must* we have miracles? The theological advantage of moving away from miraculous theology is that we avoid this criticism: if God can and does perform miracles, why does he not do so more often? Why can a God 'who can reserve parking spaces for his chosen ones' not also 'divert a few Nazi death trains' (Hab-good, 1986, p. 111)?

Does God 'answer prayer'? It is not just conservative Christians who argue for the possibility of God doing so in a miraculous or particular providential way. Peter Baelz argued that 'our asking in faith may make it possible for God to do something which he could not have done without our asking' (Baelz, 1968, p. 118). Others, however, prefer to interpret prayer 'for things' as seeking only psy-chological (spiritual) 'answers' – by strengthening our concern for the person for whom we pray; our own willingness to accept whatever happens as God's will; and something that sustains us 'which does not depend on the way things go, namely, the love of God' (Phillips, 1965, p. 120).

EXERCISE

- Where would you place yourself along the theological spectrum of God's *cumulative* activity (below)? What is preventing you moving to the right – or left? (Those in the extreme left-hand column are deists; those in the extreme right-hand column accept miracles, *as well as* the four other levels of God's activity.)
- How do you respond to the following claims?
  - (a) In a fundamental sense 'there is only one act of God, namely the continuing creation of the universe' (Wiles, 1994, p 156).
  - (b) We should only identify as 'acts of God' those events that God does not only cause, but also intends.

A Spectrum of Views of God's Activity

CREATION		PROVIDENCE		MIRACLE
				'intervention' + special/particular providence +
			special/ particular providence +	
		general providence +	general providence +	general providence +
	preservation +	preservation +	preservation +	preservation +
initial creation (making-creation)	initial creation (making-creation)	initial creation (making-creation)	initial creation (making-creation)	initial creation (making-creation)

The Problem of Evil

We may distinguish between:

- a 'theological' or 'intellectual' *problem of explaining* evil in God's creation; and
- a 'practical', 'spiritual', or 'pastoral' *problem of facing and coping with evil* in human life, perhaps with the aid of religious, social and moral practices.

Theodicy is usually taken to be that part of theology that deals with the intellectual problem of evil, by presenting an abstract 'defence of the justice of God'. Some criticize this as 'a merely theoretical undertaking', contrasting it with a theodicy that allows 'the screams of our society to be heard' (Surin, 1986, p. 52). 'No statement, theological or otherwise, should be made that would not be credible in the presence of the burning children' (Irving Greenberg, cited by Surin, 1986, p. 147).

A *theodicy of protest* accepts that life is 'outrageous' and 'tragic'; and that we are justified in reacting with anger and refusing to 'explain away' or justify it. As close kin to this approach, *protest atheism* does not deny the existence of God, but protests against the human condition of suffering and injustice – and the activity (or lack of it) and character of God. D. Z. Phillips argued that we need 'reactions or responses' to replace our questions about evil, not 'answers' to them (Phillips, 1993, p. 166).

At their best, Christians have always acknowledged the tragedy of evil, and related it to the affliction of Christ's cross. This 'allows us to conceive of all suffering as the presence of God to us through the world (both natural and social), and enables us to find God's love in and through the events of this life' (Allen, 1990, p. 207). Such a religious response to evil is as much about 'coping with it' as 'explaining it'.

> It is sheer nonsense to speak of the Christian religion as offering a solution of the problem evil. . . . Rather Christianity takes the history of Jesus and urges the believer to find, in the endurance of the ultimate contradictions of human existence that belongs to its very substance, the assurance that in the worst that can befall his creatures, the creative Word keeps company with those whom he has called his own. (MacKinnon, 1968, pp. 92–3)

Rowan Williams claims that in the authentic spiritual tradition of Christianity, there is 'no route to God which does not pass under the cross'.

> To discover in our 'emptying' and crucifying the 'emptying' of Jesus on his cross is to find God there, and so to know that God is not destroyed or divided by the intolerable contradictions of human suffering. He is one in the Spirit, and in that same Spirit *includes* us and our experience, setting us within his own life in the place where Jesus his firstborn stands, as sharers by grace in that eternal loving relation, men and women made whole in him. In the middle of the fire we are healed and restored – though never taken out of it. As Augustine wrote, it is at night that his voice is heard. To want to escape the 'night' and the costly struggles with doubt and vacuity is to seek another God from the one who speaks in and as Jesus crucified. (Williams, 1979, p. 80)

Varieties of Theodicy

Evil is what human beings disapprove of and avoid, and what they ought to react to in these ways. When we call a situation or act 'evil', it means that 'intrinsically' (in and of itself, if it existed alone) it is a bad thing, even if 'instrumentally' it leads to other good things. (It does not necessarily imply that an agent is respons-ible for it.) We may distinguish the natural, moral and metaphysical origins of evil – evil from nature, free agents and createdness.

Coming to Terms with Theology:
Evil

Natural evil ('physical evil') – events of nature (such as disease, famine, earthquakes) that give rise to physical pain and mental suffering.
Moral evil – human wrongdoing (sin), and the pain and suffering it causes.
Metaphysical evil – the unavoidable imperfection, limitation and death of a material, finite, contingent (non-necessary) universe.

Either God cannot abolish evil or he will not. If God cannot then he is not all-powerful; if he will not then he is not all-good. Evil only requires an expla-nation in the context of certain beliefs about God and the world: that evil really exists; that there is only one God who is the supreme creator of everything; and that this God (a) can know everything that can be known (is 'omniscient') and can do anything that can be done (is 'omnipotent'), and (b) is all-loving and perfectly good.

A theology in which God is *not* the supreme creator *ex nihilo*, but merely ordered and formed the cosmos out of a pre-existent chaos, can easily explain natural evil. It arises from the recalcitrant ('obstinately disobedient') nature of the co-eternal, pre-existing material from which the world was fashioned. Justin Martyr and others held this view in the second century, as do many process theologians today. But God could be limited (finite) in other ways, perhaps in possessing only finite knowledge, skill or power. 'Creative skill, wonderful as it is, was not sufficiently perfect to accomplish his purposes more thoroughly' (Mill, *Theism*, part II); '[God] did not will or even know particular events such as *this* death and *this* birth' (Cowburn, 1979, p. 38). But critics ask whether such a God would not be 'open to a charge of gross negligence or recklessness' for creating any world (Mackie, 1982, p. 176).

Yet what if God *is* all powerful and all knowing?

Must an omnipotent, omniscient God be able to prevent or eliminate all evil?
If 'God is limited by the universe he has chosen to create' (Vardy, 1992, p. 124),
then natural evil is 'an inevitable consequence of [this] sort of world' (Ward,
1990, p. 55). Perhaps God could not create a *physical* world, subject to law-like
interactions, *without* natural evil; and natural selection surely requires a world
in which the maladapted do less well. Materiality involves imperfections – a
tendency to disorder, decay, fragility and mortality. According to Austin Farrer,
natural evil results from the fact that material objects occupy space, in that the
unavoidable interaction and collision of material objects causes pain in creatures that feel pain (for example the cancer in the lung and the fungus in the
foot). 'The mutual interference of systems ... [is] the grand cause of physical
evil'; and 'the physical universe could be delivered from the mutual interference
of its constituent systems, only by being deprived of its physicality' (Farrer, 1966,
pp. 50–1). In order to avoid such suffering, God could have restricted himself
to creating only minds or spirits that do not occupy space (such as angels). But
then he would not have created *us*.

Another suggestion begins with the claim that notions like 'pleasurable',
'happy' and 'good' only have an application in a universe where there are situations for which such terms are not used.

EXERCISE

Plot your experiences (say of drinks) on this 'hedonic scale' (Greek
hedone, 'pleasure'):

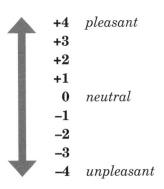

+4	*pleasant*
+3	
+2	
+1	
0	*neutral*
−1	
−2	
−3	
−4	*unpleasant*

Can God remove those experiences you evaluate as lying on the lower
half of the scale, while leaving the scale itself intact?

The expected reply is that, if all the unpleasant experiences were taken away, we should inevitably reassess the remaining ones so that some of them would now be ranked as negative ('to be avoided'). However, the suffering caused by pain is not in fact 'on the same scale' as pleasant and unpleasant experiences: the pain of drinking acid is not just different in degree from the experience of drinking something you don't particularly like, such as cranberry juice.

Karl Barth argues that the divine act of rejection of chaotic evil (*das Nichtige*) – that is, God's decision *not* to create evil – gives it its virulent existence. As God's 'No' is as powerful as his 'Yes', God's rejection of evil bestows a sort of negative existence. Evil's reality is that of an 'excluded and repudiated thing, the reality behind God's back' (Barth, 1966, p. 57).

Must an all-loving God wish to prevent or eliminate all evil?
Does God have a 'morally sufficient reason' (a good enough reason) for allowing evil? God would have such a reason, if a universe in which evil is permitted is in some way *better* than a universe with no evil at all.

1 *The free will defence ('FWD')*. This traditional solution to the problem of moral evil allows that it is better that God should have created free responsible beings who might do wrong, rather than programmed automata who could be guaranteed never to do so. This is because free will is either good in itself or a condition of other such goods (e.g. forgiveness, compassion). Defenders of this view require a 'strong view' of freedom, one that applies only to 'agents whose choices do not have fully deterministic precedent causes' (Swinburne, 1977, p. 86). Moral evil is the risk God takes in creating beings with real free will. This FWD has been applied in several contexts.
(a) *Individual wrongdoing*. Many claim that there is a contradiction in saying that God is the cause of our acting as we do *and* that we are free beings. Certainly, God could not truly value our responses if we were simply puppets or hypnotized patients acting out his will.
(b) *The fall of man*. As we saw in Chapter 6, Augustine traces natural evil as well as moral evil back to Adam's fall. He admits no undeserved suffering. But this 'Augustinian' account raises many difficulties.

- One is the idea of a single historical figure as the progenitor of the human race, living in 'original righteousness' in a perfect past without suffering or death (which is a driver for evolution). On the contrary, 'We appear to be rising beasts rather than fallen angels' (Peacocke, 1998, p. 373); and sin seems to be rooted in the selfish instincts that have inevitably evolved through natural selection.
- It is difficult to defend the view that a child should suffer for the sins of its father: 'I cannot be guilty in respect of the sins of another' (Swinburne, 1998, p. 41).
- Augustine and Calvin appear to deny the reality of real human freedom after Adam's fall.
- There is a strong tradition in Scripture of a 'moral providence' within this world, which unfailingly punishes the sinner – for example 2 Kings 13; 16 and Psalm 37.25. However, Job's criticism of this theology is more convincing (see Job 21.17, 29–30; also Eccles. 9.11; Luke 13.4–5; John 9.2–3).

(c) *The fall of angels.* Though the Bible offers no consistent doctrine of 'the satan' (Hebrew *hasatan*, 'the adversary'), some have argued for a 'pre-mundane' (before the material creation) fall of angelic beings. After turning against God, they embark on their career as strong spiritual sources of natural evil and temptation. 'It seems perfectly reasonable for the Christian to maintain that the free will of heavenly beings also limits God's power' (Vardy, 1992, p. 180). While their actions are their own responsibility, God is responsible for creating them as free beings and allowing their continued evil existence. Some therefore contend that 'the picture of a God who permits his creatures to fall into the grip of a supernatural irredeemable malicious spiritual agent is not ... religiously or theologically plausible' (Hebblethwaite, 2000, p. 74).

(d) *The world in process.* In process theology, *all* natural events are centres of spontaneity and self-creation, with some degree of freedom and unpredictability. So the FWD can apply to the whole universe!

2 *The vale of soul-making.* John Keats preferred this phrase to the idea of 'a vale of tears'. This theodicy is an essential element, coupled with a FWD of individual wrongdoing, in the liberal alternative to the traditional Augustinian theodicy – characterized by John Hick as the 'Irenaean tradition' (see pp. 175–7).

It may be said to imply that natural evil is necessary if the world is to provide an environment for free human beings, created as immature creatures, to develop morally and spiritually into the 'likeness of God'.

- In order to be properly describable as 'good', humans must be liable to temptation, not immunized from evil.
- The world is not intended to be a cage for a pet (a hedonistic paradise), but an environment for moral and spiritual growth. Courage and compassion are 'higher-order-goods' that could not exist, except 'in the face of bad states' such as pain and danger (Swinburne, 1998, p. 162).
- If God forever *intervened* to prevent natural evil, there would be 'no prediction, no prudence, no accumulation of ordered experience, no pursuit of premeditated ends' (Tennant, 1930, p. 199). (But see pp. 166–7.)
- If God always fended off the effects of moral evil, we should develop no sense of the wrongness of our evil intentions – for our 'wrong' acts would never have 'bad' consequences.
- Swinburne argues that natural evils must also exist in order for humans to have knowledge of how to create or prevent moral evils (e.g. we need to know about the effects of wounds, and of eating poisonous toadstools).

Therefore any vale of soul-making must contain evil. By contrast, in a painless world:

> There would be nothing to avoid and nothing to seek; no occasion for co-operation or mutual help; . . . The race would consist of feckless Adams and Eves, harmless and innocent, but devoid of positive character and without the dignity of real responsibilities, tasks, and achievements. (Hick, 1985, pp. 306–7)

This argument implies the value-judgment that 'one who has attained to goodness by meeting and eventually mastering temptations . . . is good in a richer and more valuable sense than would be one created *ab initio* in a state either of innocence or of virtue' (Hick, 1985, p. 255). It also appeals to *mystery*, in that suffering has to be distributed randomly or it would not serve this soul-making function. The reason for this is that if a sufferer's specific pain were clearly seen to be for her ultimate good (or as part of a deserved punishment), it would not evoke our sympathy or caring help. And if we were faced by instant suffering for our own wrongdoing, we would not battle against evil – nor do good simply because it was right to do so. But encouraging these virtues and behaviour is God's main reason for creating a world containing evil. 'The fact that natural evil is not morally directed, but is a hazard that comes by chance, is thus an intrinsic feature of a person-making world' (Hick, in Davis, 2001, p. 50).

Others, however, demur – rejecting the 'instrumentalist nightmare' of 'a conception of God ... as a creator who experiments with his creatures' (Phillips, 2004, p. 225).

3   *The value of pain.* Much pain has survival value, as the mutilated bodies of lepers who have lost feeling in their limbs shows. But pain such as that caused by terminal cancer is not 'useful' in this way.

4   *The aesthetic analogy.* The Augustinian tradition often treats evil as analogous to the dark parts of a painting, arguing that they should be seen in the context of the whole work of art – as a necessary contrast to the brighter areas. 'The whole universe is beautiful, if one could see it as a whole, even with its sinners' (*City of God* xi, ch. 23). But such impersonal analysis ignores the human beings who suffer under these 'darker pigments'.

5   *An eschatological justification.* Is God justified in allowing evil if it is only a *temporary* condition? Here the theodicist may encourage us to see the 'bigger picture' as extended through time, so as to embrace the last things (*eschata*) of heaven and hell (see Chapter 10).

Contrasting Theodicies

The chart below summarizes John Hick's main points of contrast and agreement between two theodicy 'families'.

'AUGUSTINIAN' THEODICIES	'IRENAEAN' THEODICIES
(Augustine, Aquinas, Calvin, Leibniz, and many traditional Catholic and Protestant accounts)	(Irenaeus, Schleiermacher, Tennant and many modern liberal accounts)
Responsibility for evil rests on created beings (angels and/or human beings) who have misused their freedom. Moral evil is *their* fault, and natural evil is the inevitable consequence (punishment) for that moral evil.	It is explicitly recognized that *God is ultimately responsible for the evil in the universe.* Moral evil is the fault of free human beings that God has created and permits to sin. God has deliberately put natural evil in the world to create the best environment for soul-making.
This tradition appeals to the following metaphysical views.	*This tradition holds no such metaphysical views.*
• Evil is 'non-being' (God only creates good; evil is a going wrong of good, or is to be found where things are at the limits of existence).	
• While some parts may be ugly, the whole picture is more beautiful as a result of the contrast they provide.	
• *The principle of plenitude*: it is better for God to create at all possible levels of existence, so that the universe is as full as it can be of beings – including those that suffer evil, or cause it.	
God's relationship with the universe is impersonal. Humans are created to complete the list of types of being.	*God's relationship with the universe is essentially personal.* Humans are created for fellowship with God.

Looks to the past (the fall) for an explanation of the origin of evil.

The fall is central to this theodicy: Adam was created perfect in a perfect world, but deliberately sinned (see Chapter 6).

The present world is not what God intends it to be. It should be a paradise without suffering and death. Human beings need to be saved from it.

Our behaviour in this world will determine *our ultimate destination in heaven or hell*.

Looks to the future (heaven) for a justifying end, when God brings good out of evil.

The fall is less important, or is denied altogether. Some argue that the fall of Adam was like the sin of a child; others that mankind was created or evolved as 'fallen'. (Down here in the mud of the world, we are free to grow towards God without being overwhelmed by the divine presence.)

The world is more or less what God intends. It is a world with real temptations and risks. This is the only sort of world in which we can freely develop faith and virtue, and learn obedience through suffering, in co-operation with God's grace.

This tradition is *more likely to reject the notion of hell*. In the end all will be saved, perhaps through a continuing process of soul-making after death (see Chapter 10).

EXERCISE

- Which elements and arguments from these various theodicies do you
  (a) welcome most warmly?
  (b) reject most strongly?
  How would you justify these responses?
- If someone were to ask you why God allows their child to suffer, how would you respond?

Suggestions for Further Reading

Introductory

Astley, J., Brown, D. and Loades, A. (eds), 2003, *Creation: A Reader*, London: T. & T. Clark.

Astley, J., Brown, D. and Loades, A. (eds), 2003, *Evil: A Reader*, London: T. & T. Clark.

Astley, J., Brown, D. and Loades, A. (eds), 2004, *God in Action: A Reader*, London: T. & T. Clark.

Advanced

Davis, S. T. (ed.) (2001), *Encountering Evil: Live Options in Theodicy*, Louisville, KY: Westminster John Knox Press.

Langford, M. J., 1981, *Providence*, London: SCM Press.

Ward, K., 1990, *Divine Action*, London: Collins.

9

Embracing Mystery: The Deep Nature of God?

EXERCISE

Write down as complete a list as you can of the things that Christians say about God, by completing the sentences:

God is . . . .   God is not . . . .

Now mark those attributes and activities that:

[✓]   form a very significant part of your concept of God;

[–]   are not really important in your concept of God;

[X]   form no part of your concept of God;

[?]   you are puzzled about.

Sources of the Doctrine of God

We arrive now at a more limited and specific understanding of the word 'theology' – as the doctrine of the nature of God (Greek *theos*). It is routine to identify two bodies of discourse as the sources of the Christian doctrine of God:

- **a religious source** in biblical revelation and the Church's traditions of worship, spirituality and piety – this in the main gives rise to the *religious and moral attributes* of a personal, active God (for example, God's love and justice);

- **a philosophical source** in the Greek philosophy that greatly influenced most theologians of the patristic and medieval periods – which framed the accounts of the *metaphysical attributes* (for example, God's changelessness and omniscience).

There has always been some tension between these two categories. This partly relates to the polarization between revelation and reason, and 'Jerusalem' and 'Athens', that we noted in Chapter 2. Adopting the distinction made famous by Blaise Pascal in the seventeenth century, Christians have often asked whether the 'God of Abraham, God of Isaac, God of Jacob' is or is not 'the God of philosophers and scholars' (Pascal strongly rejected the identification). Yet it *is* possible for two such disparate sets of properties to belong to the same God; just as it is quite possible for anatomists, physiologists, biochemists or accountants to describe a human being in one way; while her parents, children, lovers and colleagues describe the same person in very different – and much more personal – terms.

Another major conflict within theology has been the Greek view of divine perfection, which quickly found its way into Christian thinking. This was largely couched in impersonal terms, and treated God as unchanging. It does not map easily on to the biblical figure of God as a personal, loving agent – as we shall see.

EXERCISE

Mark the descriptions of God from the earlier exercise, depending on whether you think they are best described as:
[A] *personal / religious / moral* or
[B] *impersonal / technical / philosophical*.

God's Religious and Moral Attributes

This set of properties portrays the response to the question, '*Who* is God?' God is an 'intentional agent', and as such may be modelled as *personal*. In Scripture, *God's character* is expressed, identified, represented or 'rendered' in his acts of creation, care and deliverance; and other aspects of a personal relationship with his children.

Love, goodness and grace

Central to Christian belief is the claim that 'God is Christlike and in him is no un-Christlikeness at all' (Ramsey, 1969, p. 98). For most Christians, this means that God is absolutely good, morally perfect, and infinitely loving and compassionate. In the Gospels, the *moral perfection* of God 'lies in the unrestricted, unlimited character of his loving' (Richardson, 1999, p. 22). According to 1 John 4.8 and 16, 'God is love'. Here, and in many other places in the New Testament, the Greek word used for the love of God is *agape*. It is often said that this labels an unconditional, universal, self-giving love far removed from the type of love (*eros*) that is only evoked by the attractiveness or 'loveableness' of its object. Unlike human love, God's love is unlimited and unchanging. Hence 'only God, my dear, / Can love you for yourself alone / And not your yellow hair' (Yeats, 1952, p. 277). Yet *agape* is no mere emotional attachment, but an activity directed towards another's good. God loves us because we are; and we are because God loved us into being, holds us in being, guides and protects us.

A radical distinction between the 'direct opposites' of unselfish *agape* (which 'freely spends itself', bestowing itself 'on those who are not worthy of it') and egocentric *eros* (representing 'a will to have and to possess, resting on a sense of need') was made by Anders Nygren (Nygren, 1932, pp. 165, 171). It has been challenged by claims such as the following (Brümmer, 1993, pp. 240–2):

- 'giving without receiving is not love but mere beneficence';
- 'it is only through need-love . . . that I can bestow value and identity on your person and your love'; and
- 'only by needing us can God bestow value on us and upon our love for him'.

Does God need to need us?

Fatherhood

In the creeds and much patristic theology, God is exclusively Father to 'his only Son', Jesus Christ. This is the 'metaphysical sonship' (Lohse) of the doctrine of the Trinity, which we shall explore later. But the metaphor has a wider usage. It is likely that Jesus taught his disciples to call God – in Aramaic, their common language – *Abba* (cf. Mark 14.36). This is usually translated 'dear Father' or even 'Daddy'. The first Christians used this form of address in their prayers (Rom. 8.15; Gal. 4.6); and many scholars think that this word also lies behind the Greek word *pater* in the Lord's Prayer. Although 'Father' was applied to God within Judaism – as, indeed, was *Abba* – it is used much more frequently in the New Testament (over a hundred times in John's Gospel alone, although mainly in a Christological usage as Father of 'the Son').

In its wider senses, the metaphor is appropriate because God, like a good human parent, both initiates our existence and preserves it (the doctrine of creation); as well as seeking our welfare and assisting our growth to maturity (providence). According to Irenaeus, the universal creator was called Father because of his love. Like all figurative language, however, the image has its limitations: not least for those whose experiences of parental 'care' has been essentially negative, or non-existent. There is also the more general problem that 'father'-language is 'sexed' or 'gendered'.

Feminist theologians have sought recognition for a wider range of gendered language about God, to complement the 'patriarchal' language of king, father, husband and master; or to go beyond it with gender-free metaphors such as friend (cf. Jer. 3.4). The Old Testament does sometimes use explicitly female imagery for God (for example, Deut. 32.18; Isa. 66.13); and in the 'Priestly' creation narrative both 'male and female' are said to be created in God's image (Gen. 1.27). Jesus employs female imagery for God's activity in Luke 13.20–1; 15.8–10.

The use of 'Father' does not imply that God is biologically male, and the Bible never speaks of God's fatherhood in terms of *physical* fatherhood. If God exists without a material body, God is necessarily beyond sexual distinctions – and therefore can be neither male nor female (the Anglican Articles of Religion describe God as 'without body, parts or passions'). God is only *like* a human father, literally neither a 'he' nor a 'she'.

But what of God's 'gender', using that word to label a person's cultural or social role, or even personality stereotype? While *female* is a term that denotes biological sex, the adjective *feminine* is applied to qualities that society generally takes to be 'womanly'. Stereotypically feminine characteristics include compassion, which is a rich biblical image for God's activity (Deut. 30.3; 2 Kings 13.23; Jer. 12.15). (The Hebrew word for compassion, *rachmin*, derives from the word for 'womb', *rechmen*.) The imagery of the *parental* loving kindness of God in Hosea 11.1–4 is stereotypically feminine, but without any explicit female language. A number of theologians, including Moltmann (1981, p. 164), use the language of a 'fatherly Mother' and 'motherly Father' of God.

EXERCISE

- Survey your lists of metaphors of God (p. 55) and sentences describing God (p. 179), highlighting any female or feminine images. With the help of a concordance, can you list similar imagery that is applied to God in Scripture, prayers or hymnody – whether in explicit words or phrases, or by implication?
- What arguments might be employed *both* in favour of *and* against:
  (a) avoiding referring to God as 'he'?
  (b) applying explicitly female or feminine images to God?
- Some translations of the Bible have called God both 'she' and 'he'; some modern prayers begin, 'God our Parent' or 'Dear Mother God'; and some theologians use the language of a 'motherly father'. How do you react to such language – and why?

The most important implication of parent language is to underscore the claim that God can be thought of as *personal*. Naturally, God is not literally 'a person', for human persons are created, finite beings. But God may be said to be personal in the sense that God is a free, responsible centre of experience, activity and response – a 'Who' as well as a 'What'. Drawing on the language of the Jewish philosopher, Martin Buber, we can have a real 'I–Thou' (or 'I–You') mutual relationship with God, 'the eternal Thou', as we do – or should do – with all human beings. But we can only have an 'I–It' relationship with objects that we view wholly impersonally, in analytical detachment or abstraction, as separate from us. 'When *Thou* is spoken, there is no thing' (Buber, 1958, p. 4).

God is an – or rather *the* – unlimited and uncreated, personal Soul, Spirit or Mind. Although some theologians think of the world as God's body, and all insist that in some sense Jesus is 'God incarnate', most accept that God is 'essentially bodiless . . . although he may sometimes have a body, he is not dependent on his body in any way' (Swinburne, 1994, p. 127).

Justice

In many religious traditions, God is described *both* as gracious and merciful, *and* as righteous and just. Theology often resolves this paradox by stressing that these contrasting themes can both be understood as aspects of God's goodness – since God could not be good without being fundamentally opposed to what is evil. And love does not always mean getting what we want, though it might imply getting what we need. Theology often adds that, while God offers an unlimited infinite mercy to all, God must respect the freedom of those who reject this offer (see Chapter 10).

The divine response to human sinfulness is sometimes presented in the Bible in terms of the anger or *wrath of God* (see Deut. 9.7; Ps. 90.7–9; Isa. 13.6–13; Luke 3.7–14; Rom. 1.18–23, 28–32; 5.9; 1 Thess. 1.10). According to some scholars, Paul understood this as an impersonal, inevitable response to wrongdoing, built into the moral order of the universe. The wrath of God is not the personal anger of God, nor a system of rewards and punishments. Doctrine sees it as a condition of humanity. It is something we have done to ourselves in placing ourselves under sin, turning away and thereby putting ourselves 'so to speak behind the back of God's grace' (Barth, 1966, p. 117) – with disastrous consequences for ourselves and for others. There is certainly a sense in Scripture that there is something inevitable about God's wrath. The idea is set, however, within the deeper intention of God's *compassion* for his creation. So the repeated prophetic denunciations are always accompanied by promises of restoration (for example Isa. 10.33—11.12; 12.1; Hos. 11.1–11; Amos 9.8–15).

Worthy of Worship

This may be regarded as the quality that best defines God from our human perspective. To worship is to ascribe supreme worthiness. Unless we acknowledge that God is 'worship-worthy', we do not treat *the* God as *our* God.

This chapter outlines a 'definite' or 'identifying' description of the Christian God: that is, it unpacks its meaning (or 'connotation') in such a way that it has only *one* designation, 'denotation' or reference. Theology defines or describes God as the supremely valuable reality or the ground of all perfections, and thus as 'worthy of worship'. Why? Is this a response to God's *personal* characteristics as good, loving, gracious and merciful; or are these titles bestowed because of God's *metaphysical* nature as 'that than which no greater can be conceived' (as Anselm put it) – an infinite reality, with a power that is unlimited by anything beyond itself?

This question matters because monotheism involves more than just agreeing that there is only one God; it includes *worshipping* that (the) God. We must not worship the wrong God (cf. Rom. 1.25). Even Paul acknowledged that 'there are many gods and many lords' – complaining that, for some, 'their god is the belly' (1 Cor. 8.5; Phil. 3.18-19). This doesn't mean that they worshipped a Great Stomach in the Sky, but that they ascribed supreme worth to their own selfish appetites. Luther goes to the hub of the matter: 'Confidence and faith of the heart alone make both God and idol. … Whatever your heart clings to and confides in, that is really your God' (*Large Catechism*, first part, first amendment). Hence, 'to have a god is nothing else than to trust and believe him with our whole heart' (*Book of Concord*).

In practical Christianity, the metaphysical idea of God counts less than does the character of God, for it is the character of God that makes the God our God. It is the values expressed in the character of God that make God worthy of worship – as the *morally and spiritually* greatest reality. The real 'falseness' of our false gods may be said to lie 'not in their failure to exist, but in their unworthiness' (Astley, 2004b, p. 29). The most serious form of atheism is value-atheism: worshipping a God who is not truly worthy of worship.

Holiness and Mystery

These attributes, like the last one, occupy a bridging position between the religious and metaphysical attributes of God. According to Rudolf Otto, God is known in a 'numinous experience' of profound *awe* (dread, terror, godly fear) tempered with *fascination*. The one who is encountered in such an experience is 'the Holy One', the daunting-but-entrancing 'Wholly Other'. There are different levels to this experience, and secular analogies as well – including the 'uncanny' and 'spooky', and the horror and 'shudder' of ghost stories. But at its best, it may become 'the hushed, trembling, and speechless humility of the creature in the presence of – whom or what? In the presence of that which is a *Mystery* inexpressible and above all creatures' (Otto, 1925, p. 13). This is the *mysterium tremendum*; and Otto argues that this *experience of the holy* forms the basis of all worship and all religion.

EXERCISE

• The following passages have been proposed as examples of numinous experience (some by Otto). What features justify their selection?

Ex. 3.1–6	Ex. 4.24	Deut. 5.26	Job 38.1—42.6
Isa. 6.1–8	Mark 9.2–8	Mark 10.32	Mark 16.1–8
Luke 24.36–7	Heb. 10.31		

• In your experience, what other passages of Scripture can give rise to or express something like a numinous experience? What about poems or prose; hymns or choruses; music, drama, dance, film, sculpture, architecture; or other experiences involving people or nature? Reflect on *why* these things awaken this response in you.

Mystery is a deeply felt aspect of much religious experience and devotion. According to Otto, numinous experience is essentially unique and unanalysable, and provides an authentic mark of the divine presence. He argues that when religious people attempt to speak of their experiences of the holy, they 'schematize' the elements of allure and entrancement in terms of *moral goodness*, and those of dread and awe in terms of *transcendence*.

God's Metaphysical Attributes

Certain aspects of God's nature are couched in language that is both relatively impersonal, and often both technical and abstract – with some terms especially coined to apply only to God (see p. 52). Taken together, these constitute the 'What God': the concept advanced to answer the question, '*What* is God?'

If the religious and moral attributes describe God in personal relation to God's creation, those we consider in this section describe God as God is 'in himself' (better, 'Godself'), independently existing as an 'absolute' or 'ultimate' reality. God is clothed here in metaphysical language: that is, language about an all-encompassing, supreme entity that surpasses our sense experience, and whose description greatly exceeds the range of our earth-bound analogies and metaphors.

Transcendence

As we have seen, the experience of God's holiness and mystery is partly a recognition of God's transcendence. God is transcendent in going beyond our experience, our language and our created universe. In this sense, God is 'other', and is often metaphorically portrayed as 'outside' or 'beyond' the world – as 'far off' or 'high' (see Ps. 97.9; 113.4–6). This does not mean that God is literally in outer space; but that God is *utterly different* from the created universe. As the uncaused, independent *creator*, God is definitely in 'a class of his own'. Everything else that exists differs from God because everything else is a part of God's caused, dependent *creation* – including the human race (see Isa. 40.12–28) and even such beings as angels. In panentheism and process theology, God's 'primordial nature' or essence still transcends the universe in this way.

Within Judaism and (especially) Islam, this belief in the supreme otherness of God led to resisting pictorial representations of the divine. Christianity itself has had something of a rocky relationship with images. These are never thought of as idols, in the sense of objects of *worship*, even where – as with Orthodox icons – they are 'venerated'. Even Orthodox iconography suffered two periods of 'iconoclasm' ('the smashing of images'); and many statues, murals and much stained glass of Western Christianity have suffered greatly at the hands of radical Protestants such as Puritans.

Immanence

God is not only transcendent but also 'immanent'. In biblical teaching, God was never isolated from humans, but worked for their good and revealed himself, often by messengers (angels) and his *Powers* of Wisdom, Word and Spirit. God's immanence is a function of God's self-revelation: God so makes himself known that he is 'nearer to us than we are to ourselves' (Barth, 1966, p. 38).[1] God is also intimately associated with the whole of creation, in sustaining and caring for it (Ps. 139.1–18; Acts 17.22–8). 'God exists in everything . . . as an agent is present to that in which its action is taking place' (Aquinas, *Summa of Theology* 1a. 8, 1).

So the God who is 'far off' and 'beyond' (that is, different from the world) is *also* 'near', 'with' (even 'within') and 'present' – acting 'towards' or 'in' every one of the events of the world. The metaphors may point us in opposite directions, but the theological truths they describe arise together as two implications (or parts) of one single idea. Both follow from the very idea of creation, which envisages an infinite, independent creator holding in existence all finite, dependent creatures (Chapter 8).

Omnipresence

Traditional dualist philosophy treats minds, unlike bodies, as being neither located within nor spread across space. If God is 'non-corporeal' (bodiless) and 'immaterial' (non-physical), God is not limited as we are – at least in this life – to any particular place. It would perhaps be more accurate to say that there is nowhere (no 'where', no place) that God is, or that God is not. Nevertheless:

- omnipresence is a corollary of God's creative immanence – God *acts* wherever there is anything else ('everywhere'); he is 'present to' all things and events, as their continuing, sustaining cause;
- God may also *act* 'anywhere' by providentially steering parts of the universe, and perhaps also through miracles;
- God can be *known* 'anywhere', in a revelation mediated through any part of God's natural and human creation; and
- those who understand the universe as God's body may include in their concept of omnipotence the identification of the whole universe as a part of God.

---

1 Quoting Augustine? The Qur'an (50.16) puts it thus: 'God is close to man, nearer to him than his jugular vein.'

Omniscience and Omnipotence

As we saw in Chapter 8, claiming that God possesses unlimited knowledge and power is something of a hostage to fortune. Yes, God has no rivals; but it is a mistake to say that God can know and do *anything*. An omniscient God can know all that can be known. An omnipotent God can do all that can be done. But God cannot create a 'contradiction in terms'; nor can God know anything that it is in principle impossible to know – a category that might include the future free acts of human beings. Further, 'if God can be what he does not will to be, he is not omnipotent' (Augustine). God's omnipotence is therefore limited by his character, if God is to remain 'God' (cf. 2 Tim. 2.13). 'God's omnipotence . . . is thus the power of the God who is in Himself *love*' (Barth, 1966, p. 49).

However, some thinkers reject even this understanding of an *infinite* God as spiritually unworthy. Others cannot reconcile it with the quantity of evil in the world. They might picture God as very much wiser and more powerful than we are, but as having *insufficient* wisdom or power to complete his purposes – at least not yet. This theology of a *finite God* is one way of acknowledging limitations within God.

Taking a more orthodox line, commentators often point out that the credal term 'almighty' is essentially poetic. *Pantocrator* ('ruler of all') in the Greek original of the Nicene Creed, and *omnipotens* in the Latin of the Apostles' Creed, were originally 'adjectives of "glorification", which in the mouth of the suppliant or worshipper express little more than the contrast between human weakness and divine strength', or sovereignty (Burnaby, 1959, p. 27). See Job 38; Isaiah 40.18–31.

Self-existence

God is *independent* of all other realities, which depend on God for their origin and continued existence. Unlike them, God's existence is said to be 'necessary' and not 'contingent'. This does not mean that 'God exists' is a logically necessary truth (one that is true by definition), as in the 'ontological argument' that the most-perfect-possible-being cannot be thought not to exist. (No propositions asserting existence can be true by definition.) Instead, the claim means that *if God exists, God exists with necessity*: that is, *if* there is a creator-God-with-independent-being, *then* God's existence is 'ontologically necessary'. Whatever we mean by God must have this sort of existence. So if you were ever to learn that God is to celebrate his birthday today, or that his friends fear for his health, you would know at once that this was not serious theology. Whatever these assertions refer to, it could not be the uncreated God. God has never had a beginning and will never have an end, and nothing can threaten God's existence. God is therefore also 'indestructible', 'incorruptible', 'everlasting' and 'immortal' (see Ps. 102.25–7).

It is sometimes said that God is his own cause, but it is better to say that God is uncaused and exists *a se*: that is, 'from or of himself'. Theologians therefore speak of God's *aseity* or self-existence (*a se esse* means 'being from oneself').

Eternity

The word 'eternal' may be understood as equivalent to 'everlasting': that is, as marking *unending duration* – an existence that is without beginning or end, but is still 'in time'. If God is in time, however, God's dimension of time must be very different from ours, *well* beyond our imagining.

Many assume, however, that God is *timeless*: that is, that God exists 'outside time' altogether. But timelessness seems to be incompatible with so many things that 'the theist wishes to say about God – that he brings about this or that, forgives, punishes, or warns' (Swinburne, 1993, p. 228). These are things we say of people who act in time, in response to something that has happened at a given time.

However, the idea of God's timelessness would allow theology to resolve its difficulty over God knowing our future free actions. For if God is timeless, then the whole of God's eternity is *simultaneous* with every part of time. According to Aquinas, God can 'observe' the past, present and future all at once, as an observer on a hilltop can see at one and the same time all the walkers on a road that winds around the hill – even when those striding out in front aren't visible to the laggards. On this scenario, God does not *fore*know our future actions – and certainly not by predicting them. Nor does God predetermine or 'predestine' them. God just 'timelessly knows' them.

Immutability (Changelessness)

God is the one 'who changest not'. In the hymn *Abide with Me*, God is contrasted with the 'change and decay' and 'earth's vain shadows' that we see all around us. When the Bible speaks of God as the solid rock amid the shifting sand (Ps. 62), this illustrates God's *moral* constancy or faithfulness (Mal. 3.6; James 1.17).[2] As early as Ignatius in the first century, however, this theme of changelessness was placed alongside philosophical notions (derived mainly from Aristotle) about impersonal, *metaphysical* or *ontological* immutability, expressing 'perfection' in terms of God's unchanging being. According to many critics, this sort of immutability conflicts with the personal model of God, for no 'person' could be unable to change.

Christian doctrine even took over Greek ideas about God's distance from human affairs and God's *impassibility* – the view that God does not experience the change of pain, suffering or sorrow. 'This concept was to be the clearest and most troubling mark of Hellenic interpretation within Christian theology' (Jenson, 1984a, p. 118). Although axiomatic in the early history of doctrine, divine impassibility is now widely rejected. 'The absolute God of Greek metaphysics was heartless, graceless, and faceless . . . and without compassion' (Braaten, 1984, p. 531). 'The personal God has a heart. He can feel, and be affected' (Barth, 1957, p. 370). As the twentieth-century Lutheran theologian and martyr, Dietrich Bonhoeffer, put it, 'only the suffering God can help' (1971, p. 361).

While our account of the nature of God would seem to make him immune from physical pain, corruption and death, and emotions such as fear, loneliness or guilt, the Christian doctrines of incarnation and Trinity impel us to think of God as suffering – and even dying – *in Christ*. In the ancient formulation, 'one of the Trinity suffered'. While Moltmann wrote of *the crucified God*, Jesus' death is not the death of God but 'death *in* God'. 'God himself loves and suffers the death of Christ in his love. He is no "cold heavenly power" . . . but is known as the human God in the crucified Son of Man' (Moltmann, 1974, pp. 207, 227). Moltmann even describes the doctrine of the Trinity as 'a shorter version of the passion narrative of Christ' (1974, p. 246). 'The death of the Son of God on the cross reaches deep into the nature of God' (Moltmann, 2000, p. 305).

Hence, 'the events summarized "cross" simply *are* God insofar as God becomes

---

2 This seems to be consistent with God mercifully changing his actual plans in response to human action (Gen. 18.22–31; Jonah 3.10).

our object, what we can see ... The mystery is not the mystic shimmer of distance; it is that God presents himself in sufferings' (Jenson, 1984a, pp. 182–3).

Classical Theism and Process Theology

Nevertheless, a so-called 'classical theism' developed under the tutelage of Aristotle's concept of God as the 'unmoved mover'. Its key idea was that God is an *immutable substance*: necessary, absolute, eternal and infinite – and utterly distinct from and independent of the world of space, time and change. The most abstract version of this theology is to be found in Aquinas, who understood God's nature as *pure act*, without any unrealized potentialities. Only as pure act can God be absolutely perfect, the sum of all perfections. God's relationship to creation was regarded as wholly one way, so that God had no real relation to creatures: 'being related to God is a reality in creatures, but being related to creatures is not a reality in God' (*Summa of Theology* 1a. 13, 7).

Extreme versions of classical theism have been severely criticized by process thinkers, who owe their greatest metaphysical debt to Alfred North Whitehead (1861–1947). In *Process and Reality* (1929) and other works, Whitehead offered a view of reality that he believed to be more scientific than the standard account of independent, discrete things. The key idea of process thought is that everything changes, including God. The world is dynamic, 'in process', made up of events not things – with every event interrelated. God is not the supreme anomaly, but the 'chief exemplification' (Whitehead), of this idea. The 'Process God' is therefore supremely *responsive* to the world. God's experiences change, because God receives from the world as well as contributing to it. All entities are co-creators of God's 'consequent nature'. Such a God is *relative, not absolute* – changing through sympathetic participation in the world. As God is genuinely related to the world in process theology, the world makes a real difference to God.

> Although on the process view God will always exist and is perfect in love, this God is not totally sovereign over nature, as it has its own freedom. Process thinkers are often scolded for this doctrine of a finite God: 'it is of little benefit to overthrow a tyrant if he is replaced by an ineffectual weakling' (Gunton, 1978, p. 223).

EXERCISE

Return to your marked-up list of descriptions of God from pp. 179–80. Reflect whether you want to revise any of your assessments of the role they play in your concept of God, and why.

Unity and Trinity

The Oneness of God

*Mono*theism affirms the existence of *one*, unique God. The Nicene Creed begins, 'We believe in one God'. Although people believed in family or tribal deities in the earliest history of Israel (the period of the 'patriarchs' Abraham, Isaac and Jacob), this was not a full-blown polytheism such as existed in Greek and Roman religion. From the time of the exodus, while other gods were acknowledged, Israel saw itself as covenanted with its own 'jealous' redeemer-God Yahweh (a situation sometimes called *henotheism*). This is the sense in which 'The LORD [Yahweh] is our God, the LORD alone' [or, 'the LORD is one'] (Deut. 6.4), and 'The LORD is God, there is no other' (1 Kings 8.60).

The conviction that other gods were to be 'as nothing' to Israel when compared with Yahweh, in concert with an increased tendency to ascribe the existence of everything to Israel's God, inexorably reduced these other deities to mere members of Yahweh's heavenly council. Eventually (in post-exilic times) their very existence was denied. The role that they held as 'rulers' of other nations and ideologies was then eventually filled by created beings – the angelic 'principalities and powers' of Chapter 6 – who in falling away from obedience to God come to exert a baleful influence on humanity. (See Ps. 82; Isa. 40.18–26; 41.21–9; 46.1–11; 48.1–13; Rom. 8.38; 1 Cor. 8.4–6; Gal. 4.8–10; Eph. 1.20–3; 6.10–12; Col. 2.15.)

> Philosophical theologians have sometimes developed the notion of divine unity in terms of God's perfect *simplicity*. This is not meant as a disparaging reference to God's IQ, but as an affirmation that God's 'own single and simple being' (Aquinas) cannot be corrupted by disintegrating into his composite parts. The idea of God's simplicity needs to be developed in ways that do not conflict with the doctrine of the Trinity.

The Threefold Nature of God

The Bible offers us no more than a 'soteriological trinitarianism' (Gordon Fee), 'primary trinitarianism' (Robert Jenson) or a 'trinitarian ground-plan' (J. N. D. Kelly). This is expressed in references to God, Christ and the Spirit as agents of salvation; and also in its rich and varied language about:

- the intimate relationship between Jesus as Son and God his Father (Matt. 11.27; John 1.1–18; 10.30; 14.6–7; 20.28; see Col. 1.11–20) – although the subordinate position of the Son seems to be assumed elsewhere (1 Cor. 8.6; 11.3; 15.24–8; Phil. 2.5–11);
- the relationship between God the Father, the exalted Christ and the Spirit (see Matt. 28.19; John 14.16–17, 26; 20.19–23; Rom. 8.9–17; 2 Cor. 1.21–2; 3.3, 18; 13.13; Gal. 4.4–6; Eph. 4.4–6).

Although speculative theology about the being of God plays little part in the perspective of the New Testament, it certainly did in later Christian thinking. A thought-through doctrine of the Trinity began to emerge in the second century and was partly defined by the Church at the Council of Nicaea of 325, which we met earlier in our explorations of Christology. We should now observe that the idea of the Trinity was developed in the context of these debates about who Christ really was – in particular, what was his relationship to God?

It was Nicaea that gave official sanction to the technical language that rejected the Arian alternative (pp. 143, 146), by affirming that the 'one Lord Jesus Christ, the Son of God' is not a creature, but part of the very being of God – 'begotten of the Father . . . God of God, Light of Light, true God of true God, begotten not made, of one substance [Greek *homoousion*] with the Father.' Although it is not wholly clear what the key term *homoousios* meant at the time, later debate came to defend it strenuously against the expression *homoiousios*, 'of like substance'. The latter word meant a *similar* kind of thing, not the *same* kind of thing.

> This distinction was to become even more pronounced in later centuries in the West, as the Church moved to the idea that there was a *numerical identity* between God the Father and God the Son. In other words, they were one and the same thing. That sort of identity might appear to be a step too far, *if* it collapses all distinctions between the two. The contrast between numerical and *qualitative identity* is captured in the bad joke about the philosophical shopkeeper who responds to a customer who requests 'a pen the same as this one', by saying, 'You are already holding it. We do, however, stock *similar* pens, identical to that one in all its qualities except their location in space – and the fact that they have more ink in them.' Numerical identity seems to be what we are looking for, but it must allow for some differences if we are to speak of threeness in God at all.

The language of threeness and oneness was developed in the Latin West (initially by Tertullian) speaking of three persons (*personae*) of one substance (*substantia*). Here substance unites, and person distinguishes – but doesn't separate or divide. Eventually, in the East in the fourth century, the 'Cappadocian Fathers' articulated this pattern by means of a new distinction between two Greek words that had previously been synonymous: one *ousia* (which was now defined as one *universal* essence or substance), and three *hypostaseis* (three *particular*, individual instances of this essence). *Homoousios* can now refer to the unity of God; the Trinity as such is God.

At the Council of Constantinople in 381, our present 'Nicene Creed' was formulated. This added that the Holy Spirit was one 'who proceeds from the Father', and is 'together worshipped and together glorified' with the Father and the Son.[3] So the Spirit too was God. This was a rather late confirmation of a position previously held by Athanasius (296–373), the Cappadocians and (in

---

3 In the early Middle Ages, the Western Church added Augustine's *filioque* clause – 'and the Son' – to the 'procession' of the Spirit. Eastern Orthodoxy rejects this doctrine of a 'double procession' within the eternal life of God.

other terms) by Augustine – all in sharp contrast to Arius' view that the Spirit (like Christ) was a creature.

Using the English word *person* for the individual identities, or concrete 'singular existences', of Father, Son and Spirit raises problems. In Trinitarian theology it operates as a technical term. Originally, the term only meant a distinct individual entity, or even 'a mask'. Nowadays, however, the word immediately brings to mind 'persons' of a particular, human kind. To us, persons are individual centres of (inevitably finite) agency and self-consciousness, possessing personality. As we shall see, however, in much modern theology 'the three divine hypostases are grasped as "persons" also in the modern sense' (Jenson, 1993, p. 245). Perhaps the use of the word 'father' of one of these persons encouraged this movement?

Coming to Terms with Theology
The Trinity

Appropriation – pre-eminently assigning to one of the persons an attribute that properly belongs to the whole Godhead. (Augustine appropriates 'unity' to the Father, 'equality' to the Son, and 'connection' to the Spirit.)

Binitarianism – the view that only the Father and Son are persons of the Godhead; the Spirit is no more than the bond or relation between them.

Economic Trinity – the view that God *becomes* three only in his dealings with creation. The divine persons are part of the history of salvation, revealing God through Christ and the Spirit. No threefold essence of God is affirmed; the threeness is only for the purposes of revelation (although the persons continue in being after their first 'extrapolation').

(**Economy** here is God's 'exterior' activity in the world and towards us, in salvation and revelation.)

Essential Trinity – the view that God is eternally and intrinsically three. The three persons are *homoousios*, and therefore co-eternal and equal in their very being. See *immanent Trinity*.

Homoiousios – being 'of like substance', i.e. a similar kind of thing.

Homoousios – being 'of the same substance': originally meaning, perhaps, 'the same kind of thing', but later the same thing (numerical identity).

Immanent Trinity – as for *essential Trinity*, but adding the idea of internal relations (of 'generation', 'procession') between the persons within the Godhead, and their *perichoresis*.

Modalism – the view that the Father, Son and Spirit are (only) three modes, manifestations or roles of the one God.

Perichoresis, co-inherence – the 'mutual indwelling or interpenetration' of the persons of the Trinity, so that each is 'in' the others. Safeguards the *appropriation* of attributes against denying God's oneness.

Person – both the Greek *hypostasis* and the Latin *persona* gradually came to mean an individual entity, and eventually an individual self-conscious agent.

Tritheism – belief in three distinct Gods.

Unitarianism – an anti-Trinitarian form of Christianity associated with Socinus (1539–1604), especially influential in England and the United States in the nineteenth century. Present-day unitarianism has no set creed.

Types of Trinity

There are two major approaches to the threeness of God.

- The *economic Trinity* (often called 'Sabellianism') is the older formulation, but is still widely held among ordinary theologians. It is an account of the Trinity that understands the divine persons as temporal rather than eternal, with the one God being manifested successively in three ways. The 'Modalistic Monarchians' (see p. 142) argued that God is not Father, Son and Spirit; but God *appears like* Father, Son and Spirit at different times, for different purposes.

- The ontological, *essential* or *immanent Trinity* tracks this threeness of God back behind God's economy of revelation and salvation. It affirms that these three persons have and always will exist in the inner essence and life of God. So God genuinely *is* threefold; and God in Christ is not different from God as God truly is. Both Christ and the Spirit reveal God in God's eternal being. The significant relationship is not now first *with us*, as in Monarchianism. It is the eternal relations *in the inner life of God* – as God generates, communicates, gives and loves within himself. It is this inner relationship, this trinity-in-unity, that relates to humankind.

The insistence on an immanent Trinity is an expression of a principle we have met before. 'What God is in his saving activity is what God is in the divine being itself' (Del Colle, 1997, p. 137): 'the one-ness of his being implies the one-ness of his operation' (Burnaby, 1959, p. 200). Karl Rahner famously argued that 'the "immanent" Trinity is the "economic" Trinity', and vice versa (Rahner, 1970, p. 22). In other words, the pattern of God's relationship to the world (as Father, Son and Spirit) must be interpreted as a revelation of God *as God is in Godself*. 'The work of God is the essence of God . . . God's work is . . . the work of the whole essence of God' (Barth, 1975, p. 371).

For Robert Jenson, the Trinitarian formula is the *proper name* of God ('Father, Son and Holy Spirit'), equivalent to 'Yahweh' in the Old Testament; and the doctrine of the Trinity elaborates this into identifying descriptions. The whole of theology, he claims, is the unpacking of the claim that 'God' is 'whoever raised Jesus from the dead' – thus identifying God by historical events, as Yahweh had been identified by the exodus (Jenson, 1984a, p. 91).

Trinitarian theology still reflects the ancient differences in emphasis between Christianity in the East and in the West. The heirs of Latin theology are more focused on the *unity* of the Godhead, while those more influenced by Greek theology lay greater stress on the *threeness* of the Trinity.

The *pluralistic view of the Trinity* draws on a *social analogy* developed by the Cappadocian Fathers. This likened the Trinity to three people enjoying mutual fellowship, who are one by virtue of their shared humanity. This approach bears fruit in accounts of an eternal plural Godhead in which love is both given and returned, so that God never exists in lonely isolation. Because 'God is the communion of this Holy Trinity ... God is love in his very being' (Zizioulas, 2008, p. 53); 'the divine identity is essentially constituted as a constant ("faithful") interrelationship' (White, 2002, p. 30).

> The *perichoresis* or 'co-inherence' of persons is understood here in terms of three (real) persons in intimate relation. However, the Cappadocians were emphatic about the absolute oneness of God, and the humanity of the three men was not for them an abstract concept, but represented 'one [really real] man'. And so too with God. (They offered other analogies – including three suns emitting the same energy of heat and light.)

Here the persons are distinct, discrete entities; but share the same divine nature. This social model of the Trinity has proved attractive to many contemporary theologians, including the German Protestants Moltmann and Pannenberg, and the Britons, Hodgson, Swinburne and Brown. Yet it faces strong criticism. According to some, a social Trinitarian 'union of love ... cannot avoid the charge of tritheism' (Brümmer, 2005, p. 105).[4] And it is 'not clear that it can be orthodox' on other grounds (Leftow, 1999, p. 249). This interpretation of the Trinity also speaks of 'personality *in* God' rather than of 'the personality *of* God', for which we need a second analogy.

On the *monistic view of the Trinity* the persons are distinct, but not discrete entities. The approach appeals to Augustine's *psychological analogy*. He suggested that the Trinity is well represented by the threefold working of a self-conscious human subject. For example, a person's memory, understanding and will (or love), are all those of a single subject.[5] Augustine was keen to safeguard the oneness of God's single divine essence, and therefore treated the distinctions between Father, Son and Spirit as *relational* distinctions.

---

4 A move surely encouraged by the famous fifteenth-century icon painted by the Russian monk, Andrei Rublev, which depicts Abraham's three visitors in Genesis 18 as three winged, angelic figures seated around a table, in an intimate pattern of inter-relationship.

5 Augustine even offers a psychological analogy that slides into the 'social Trinity' analysis – although this is far from his intentions – by speaking in terms of a Trinity of a loving subject, a beloved object and the bond of love between them ('a mutual love, wherewith the Father and the Son reciprocally love each other': *On the Trinity* xv, § 27).

> For Augustine there is an explicit, indivisible equality within the God-head: no one of the persons is greater than any other. Interestingly, Augustine treats his own analogies as no more than faint indications of the divine reality. He is even uneasy with the technical language of *personae*, declaring that the term may be used not for what it positively states, but 'so as not to be reduced to silence' on the subject of the mystery of the internal divine structure (*On the Trinity* v, § 10).

Augustine's Trinitarian monism is reflected in Aquinas and Calvin, and in recent times by Rahner and Barth. Barth prefers to think of three 'modes (or ways) of being' in God, rather than three persons. 'This one God is God three times in different ways' (Barth, 1975, p. 360). These three 'very distinctive modes of being' (God as Revealer, Revelation and Revealing) are not temporary appearances, however, but essential to the eternal divine nature. Barth's position is therefore not a form of classical 'modalism' or an 'economic Trinity' (see above). For Rahner, also, 'way of existing' is the preferred language: 'the one God subsists in three distinct manners of subsisting . . . the "personality" which makes God's concrete reality . . . meets us in different ways' (Rahner, 1970, pp. 109–10). Arguments ranged against this view include the criticism that in Gethsemane one consciousness seems to be praying to another, and the two wills are not yet 'at one'.

Getting the Point of the Trinity?

Why does any of this matter? Over the last 50 years or so there has been a remarkable recovery of interest in the doctrine of the Trinity, which permeates the work of most contemporary academic theologians. Many insist on it as an utterly central belief that rests at the heart of Christianity. This raises a number of general concerns.

1   This interest in Trinitarian theology has not spread far among ordinary theologians. In one survey, the majority of the sample of Anglican church-goers seem 'to manage perfectly well' without any thought-through Trinitarian doctrine, preferring a functional Christology that denies that 'Jesus is God' (Christie, 2007, pp. 183–4).

2   Critics of Trinitarian doctrine frequently regard it as speculative theology that transposes the melody of Jesus' relationship with his Father and the Spirit into an alien, ontological key.

3   Treating the doctrine as 'the armoury with which to attack theological puzzles' (Jenson, 1993, p. 245), modern Trinitarian theology often employs the idea of 'God in community' to illustrate or justify other Christian perspectives. Some evoke the image of an eternal divine dance, offering a life in which we may participate. Others relate its strong emphasis on mutual love to the Christian view of the equality of human persons – or at least their unity. This may be tied up with the idea that persons, unlike individuals, are social beings; by contrast with the individualism that the psychological analogy is said to promote. Colin Gunton therefore writes of our being able to understand the Church better by analogy with the Trinity, as 'the community which is called to echo at its own level the kind of being in relation – communion – that God is eternally' (Gunton, 1996, p. 194). How do you respond to such claims?

4   If religious life is primary and theology secondary, perhaps the doctrine of the Trinity too should be tested by its fruits. Theologians often assume that different theological models and theories have discernibly different expressions. But the evidence is against them. Different theologies often share almost identical practical and spiritual implications in terms of prayer, worship and Christian living. Ian Ramsey spoke of 'proving' our Trinitarian theology in 'Trinitarian living'; and adapted Wittgenstein's slogan into 'Don't look for meanings, learn the response' – in worship and Trinitarian behaviour (Ramsey, 1963, p. 39). But do doctrines of the Trinity really make that much difference in religious life?

5   However we develop our talk of God, we must allow that God must remain an ultimate mystery. The doctrine of the Trinity developed in the context of a threefold experience of God's activity (creation, redemption, sanctification), and a threefold revelation of a God for whom different language seemed appropriate ('father'; 'word' and 'saviour'; 'wind' and 'breath'). These activities occurred through three fairly *distinct* media (world, Jesus, Church). But the other triads are not that clearly separable. Clearly, the three encounters are 'ultimately one and the same encounter, God's own action' (Küng, 1993, p. 153); and the three revelations are at best three directions from which the one God may be seen.

Isn't that all we know? Perhaps we should be satisfied with an economic Trinity, and not seek to speculate beyond it into the inner workings of God, thus safe-guarding 'a genuinely religious form of knowledge against the pride of human self-assertion' (Wiles, 1974, p. 26).

6   In Christianity, the one thing we *must* hold on to is the insight that God, whom no one could possibly see, rightly bears the name of love (1 John 4.7–16). No doctrine must ever be allowed to obscure this. 'God is the mystery who is for us' (Norris, 1979, p. 49). Is this the real point of talk of the Trinity – and of all Christian doctrine?

EXERCISE

- How do *you* understand the doctrine of the Trinity?
- How does this doctrine fit with your beliefs about the person and work of Christ?
- What difference does it make to your Christian worship and life?

Suggestions for Further Reading

Introductory

Doctrine Commission of the Church of England, 2005, *Contemporary Doctrine Classics*, London: Church House Publishing, pp. 3–272.

McGrath, A. E., 2007, *Christian Theology: An Introduction*, Oxford: Blackwell, chs 9, 10.

Ward, K., 2002, *God: A Guide for the Perplexed*, Oxford: Oneworld.

Advanced

Brown, D., 1985, *The Divine Trinity*, London: Duckworth.

Davies, B., 1985, *Thinking about God*, London: Geoffrey Chapman.

Mackey, J. P., 1983, *The Christian Experience of God as Trinity*, London: SCM Press.

10

Christian Hopes: The Last Word for Christian Believers?

The Language of Hope

We began our survey of doctrines by looking at beliefs about what is closest to our Christian experience, the most familiar and palpable features of the Christian life. We have moved through increasingly abstract beliefs, and more rarefied and elusive themes, progressing from what is within our grasp to more elusive and mysterious topics. Nothing could be more mysterious than God, of course, and perhaps we should have ended our study journey with that doctrine. But God's future, and any life after this life, must run a pretty close second; so it still seems appropriate to close a book on doctrine with a discussion about our *end*.

There is a nice ambiguity in words such as 'end', 'last', 'final' or 'ultimate'. Speaking of 'ends' may specify something's limit in time or space, and therefore its final stage, its *conclusion*. Or it may serve to articulate its goal or *purpose*, the object for which it exists. Similarly, what is 'ultimate' may be the occasion that lies furthest off, but the word could also mean the fundamental happening. The 'last' thing comes after all the others, but it might also be something 'of the last [utmost] importance'. And 'final' events can be marked either by their lateness in time, or by the decisive, conclusive effect that fulfils the purpose to which they are aimed.

To talk of God or heaven as the end of life, or even to accept that 'death is the end', is therefore to make some claim about the purpose, value and meaning of our lives – in addition to saying what we believe will 'come next'. Expressed in terms of ultimacy and fulfilment of purpose, 'the end is that after which nothing further can happen . . . because there is nothing more to happen' (Robinson, 1968, p. 55). This is why eschatology has been called the doctrine of 'what is to be expected unconditionally' (Paul Althaus). As such, hope is a natural expression of faith. And yet it is inevitably associated with – and must be compatible with – a considerable amount of agnosticism. Luther helpfully pointed out that we know no more about our future life than babies in the womb know about theirs. 'The Christian has hope in God. It is a kind of confident expectation. But it is a confidence that never knows for certain how it is going to be answered. It doesn't need to' (McKeating, 1974, p. 47).

Eschatology in Scripture

'Eschatology' means the study of, or word about (Greek *logos*), 'the last things' (*ta eschata*). In traditional Christian theology, eschatology referred to the four 'last things' of death (and life after death), judgement, heaven and hell. More profoundly, it claimed that 'history was going somewhere under the guidance of God; . . . towards God's new world of justice, healing and hope' (Wright, 2007, p. 134).

Before we explore the range of doctrinal interpretations of these motifs, therefore, we need to say something more about eschatology as a general theme in the Bible. One of the major shifts in biblical scholarship during the last century was the recovery of the eschatological in the New Testament. But eschatology is not restricted to this part of Scripture; the Hebrew Bible is suffused with the theme of God acting in the history of Israel. Because Israel's history had been so chequered, a powerful hope gradually developed, as a fundamental theological virtue, for a future more firmly grounded in God. The promise to the patriarchs and their descendants, delivered out of slavery in Egypt, was the promise of a land. Yet Israel's settlement in her East Mediterranean location, as a small nation located at the crossroad of great empires, was repeatedly challenged. Throughout this troubled history, the prophets threatened Yahweh's judgement not only on Israel's enemies, but more significantly on Israel herself. They consistently accused her of courting disaster by her faithless response to God's faithfulness. Yet they usually also sounded a note of hope for those who repented; and after the calamity of Israel's exile in Babylon, this expectation was voiced with great beauty and spiritual sensitivity (see Isa. 40.1–11; 49.1–13; 52.7–10).

Later, after her conquest by the new Greek empire, Israel's expression of hope in God transmuted from this prophetic genre into a species of literature called *apocalyptic* – from the Greek for 'uncover' or 'reveal' – in which the truth about earthly history was conveyed by means of visions from a heavenly realm. The Book of Daniel was written at this time (although set at an earlier stage of history), and its text is full of markedly 'out of this world' accounts of judgement on Israel's enemies and God's vindication of his loyal people (see Dan. 7). This *transcendent* eschatological hope, which gave rise to a large number of literary works, formed part of the background of Jesus' ministry and many of the New Testament writings. These were all set within the context of Israel's final period of imperial oppression, under the heel of Rome (see, for example, Mark 13; 1 Thess. 5.1–11; 2 Peter 3.1–10; Rev. 21.1–8; 21.22—22.7).

The earlier, more *historical* hopes for a redemption of God's children had been expressed in terms of a restoration of Israel's earthly kingdom. This hope was sometimes associated with the figure of another anointed (earthly) king, God's future 'Messiah' (as in Isa. 11.1–9); or with the 'suffering servant' who seems to represent faithful Israel (Isa. 52.13—53.12). But in the later apocalyptic writings, this yearning for redemption became more radical and other-worldly, in the sense of an *overturning of history*, and was associated with heavenly dramas and figures including the suffering-and-vindicated 'Son of Man' of Daniel 7.13–14.

Eschatology dominated the earliest thinking of the Church. Both Jesus and Paul seem to have believed in an imminent and decisive end to the current state of things on earth (Matt. 16.27–8; Mark 9.1; Luke 12.35–40; 1 Cor. 7.25–31; 15.51; Phil. 3.20–1; 1 Thess. 4.15—5.11; 2 Thess. 2.1–10). They shared a radical hope in a radically different future, one that would be much closer than is this present life to God's heart's desire. Liberal scholars in the nineteenth and early twentieth centuries tended to underplay these eschatological elements, representing them as a mere husk – even distortion – of the true moral and spiritual message of Jesus. Scholars such as Johannes Weiss and Albert Schweitzer, however, reclaimed Jesus as an apocalyptic preacher, for whom a decisive eschatological climax was central to his teaching and mission – a figure far less congenial to modern tastes.

Jesus speaks many times of the 'kingdom of God' (or, in Matthew, 'kingdom of the heavens', which is simply a pious circumlocution to avoid speaking of

God) – the way things will be under the rule or reign of God. New Testament scholarship has vociferously debated how far Jesus thought that this kingdom was (a) an entirely future state, (b) one that had already arrived ('been realized') in Jesus' own ministry, or (c) (perhaps the most likely option in the Synoptic Gospels) something that had begun with Jesus but had yet fully to come 'in power' (a kingdom that was 'inaugurated but not completed'). Paul's eschatology also exemplified this tension between the 'already' and the 'not yet'; whereas John's Gospel eschews apocalyptic and has few references to the kingdom, preferring the language of a presently experienced 'eternal life' (John 5.24).

God's bringing in of the kingdom with power, and the 'second coming' (often called the *parousia*) of Christ, came to be thought of as a re-creation of life on earth under a millennial (thousand-year) reign of Christ (Rev. 20). As time went by, these elements were increasingly thought of as indefinitely deferred (compare 1 Thess. 4.13—5.4 and 2 Peter 3.1–10). This deferring of the eschaton opened up doctrinal space for the development of ideas about an 'intermediate state' for those who had died, prior to their general resurrection and the final judgement that was still assumed to accompany the return of Christ. However, from time to time (including our own times) Christians have appealed to biblical passages – plucked from their original context – that speak of such events, and interpreted them as predictions of an imminent final intervention of God.

EXERCISE

A study of over 400 English churchgoers in one town found that 78% accept a life after death, but this varied between 84% for the Methodists and 66% for members of the United Reformed Church (Francis, 2000, p. 181). Another survey among regular churchgoing Anglicans found that 87% of the sample of 5,762 lay people believed that there is a life after death (Francis, Robbins and Astley, 2005, p. 153). What about those who don't accept this belief?

- How do you imagine that the Christian beliefs and practices of the *minority* group would differ from those who do believe that there is a life after death?
- What do you think a future life after death might consist in, for a Christian?

Eschatology in Theology

The early Karl Barth complained that contemporary theology had muzzled eschatology, lulling us to sleep by completing its Christian dogmatics with 'a short and perfectly harmless chapter' on the subject (Barth, 1933, p. 500). He saw this as consistent with a general tendency to iron out the 'infinite distinction' between the heavenly God and his earthly creatures.

Things have changed. Wolfhart Pannenberg wrote of the 'eschatological self-revelation' of God, insisting that 'revelation is not comprehended completely in the beginning, but at the end of the revealing history' (Pannenberg, 1969, pp. 131, 135). Jürgen Moltmann's influential *Theology of Hope* argued that eschatology has practical and political implications; and that salvation included 'the realization of the eschatological *hope of justice*' (Moltmann, 1967, p. 329). For Moltmann, 'Christianity is completely and entirely and utterly hope' (Moltmann, 1980, p. 11).

By contrast with a Christian piety that understands the themes of eschatology as concerned entirely with God's actions beyond this life, indeed often beyond this world, much modern theology focuses on a more 'earthly eschatology' that recaptures the this-worldly emphasis of many of the Hebrew prophets – and which many argue is also dominant in Jesus' teaching. *Liberation theology* has underscored a Christian yearning for a future political and economic liberation of the poor and oppressed. The Roman Catholic phrase, 'a preferential option for the poor', is used widely of the hope for humankind implicit in the gospel:

> 'Christ the Saviour . . . willingly took [human misery] upon himself and iden-
> tified himself with the least of his brethren. Hence, those who are oppressed
> by poverty are the object of *a preferential love* on the part of the Church' . . .
> [He] invites us to recognize his own presence in the poor who are his breth-
> ren. (*Catechism of the Catholic Church*, pp. 523–4, quoting the Congregation
> for the Doctrine of the Faith)

Life after Death

Christians tend to forget that belief in a life after death for most of the Old Testament period was not an object of *hope*. Any afterlife was represented quite rarely, and even then described as no more than a gloomy, perhaps unconscious, half-existence in *Sheol* ('The Pit') – a subterranean location from which God was absent, and where darkness reigned (for example Job 10.20–2; Ps. 6.5; 88.1–12; Isa. 38.18). Israelite religion expected one to seek a relationship with God 'here'; and 'now' was when one would be blessed by God (cf. Gen. 25.8; Ps. 30).

It was during the time of the exile in Babylon, in the sixth century BCE,[1] that Israel's theology developed a fuller hope, perhaps influenced by beliefs about a life after death within the Zoroastrian religion. The affirmation in Psalm 139.8 that the psalmist will not be cut off from God's presence *even in the world of the dead* marks this theological breakthrough.

Hints of a new theology of trust in a God who will raise the dead to judgement (and thus to 'everlasting life' or 'everlasting contempt') only occur in very late Old Testament texts (Dan. 12.1–4; Isa. 26.16–19; possibly Job 19.23–7). Several convictions may have led to this development. But pre-eminent among them seems to have been the belief that a God of justice must restore some pattern of moral balance in another life. This view was particularly strongly felt at times when the righteous were being martyred for their faith. Ideas of salvation and judgement now began to shift, from being rooted in this life and in Israel's current history, as a this-worldly healing-wholeness, shalom-peace and flourishing, to embrace an intervention that would overturn this world. Hoping and praying in the teeth of their experience of blatant injustice and the oppression of non-believers, the faithful came to believe that God would vindicate the righteous dead who had not received their 'just deserts'.

By New Testament times, belief in resurrection and judgement was widely held, particularly by the Pharisees (Paul was a Pharisee, see Acts 23.6; Phil. 3.5) and the Essene sect (the community that produced the Dead Sea Scrolls). The more traditional, patrician Sadducees, however, who accepted only the written law and few other traditions, rejected the doctrine (Mark 12.18–27). For Christians, the resurrection of Jesus dominated their eschatological thinking. It was interpreted as a bringing forward of an event (the resurrection of *all*) that was expected in the future. It was natural, therefore, to claim that Christ had been raised as the 'first fruits', or guarantee, that his followers would also be raised (1 Cor. 15.20, 23).

---

1 'Before the Common Era' – equivalent to BC, 'Before Christ'.

In reading the New Testament, we should be cautious of misunderstanding the many passages that speak of a split – or even a state of warfare – within human beings, between the 'spirit' and the 'flesh' (for example Rom. 8.1–17; Gal. 5.16–25). These appear to suggest a *dualism* ('two-ism') of human nature, similar to the one we find in some Greek philosophy – in which our real selves are radically different from, and therefore able to escape, the prison of the material body and world. Plato's dualistic account of human nature stressed the superiority of the *soul* (which he regarded as the real person), and of its intellectual and contemplative life, over such mortal, changing and insubstantial things as the body, matter and the world of nature. It is an account that was very influential in later Christian thinking, and may also have influenced those Jewish Scriptures written in Greek around 200 BCE to 70 CE (the 'inter-testamental period').

Earlier biblical writers, however, viewed the human being as a unity. In Genesis 3, Adam is created from the earth and animated by God's Spirit or breath. There is little hint in such texts of any dualism of a physical body destined for death, wedded to a non-material mind or soul that is capable of independent existence. Rather, human beings are thought of as what would now be called 'embodied souls' or minds, or 'ensouled bodies'. These authors did not look to philosophy for answers to their key questions about the nature of humanity. Their questions demanded moral and religious answers about whether you – the whole of you – was, or was not:

- *open* in obedience *to God* as Spirit (whether you were 'spiritual'); or
- self-centred, corrupt and *oriented away from God*, following only 'natural' passions or desires (whether you were 'fleshly', 'carnal' or 'worldly' – see 2 Cor. 10.2; Gal. 5.19–21).

Although Greek thought was also concerned with moral and religious questions, it involved itself in more philosophical speculation about the inner nature or ontology of human beings.

Resurrection or Immortality?

The idea of life after death, as it arose within the Jewish world-view, envisaged something that closely resembled life before death, and was expected to take place *on earth*. The New Testament, too, overwhelmingly speaks of life after death in terms of this sort of *resurrection*, preceded by an interim period of waiting.

In the Latin 'received text' of the Apostles' Creed, Christians confessed a belief in the 'resurrection of the flesh'.[2] Within the early Church, a sturdy realism about resurrection sometimes contended that Christians rose in the flesh they possessed during their lifetime. A confession of belief 'in the life eternal/everlasting' was therefore added to the original Old Roman Creed, to gloss this affirmation of the resurrection. This shift from a rather unsophisticated physical understanding of resurrection also led to a shift in emphasis, 'from the idea of protracted existence to the blessed quality of the life of the world to come' (Kelly, 1972, p. 388). Eventually, attention became focused on a 'heavenly homecoming' *away* from any transformation of earthly, physical life: from heaven-on-transformed-earth to heaven-as-sharing-God's-space.

While *Jesus' own resurrection* fits the paradigm of an earthly resurrection, the New Testament accounts indicate that Jesus' resurrection-body was intermediate between a material body on earth and a wholly 'spiritual body'. (It appeared in locked rooms and was not always identifiable.) Liberal theologians routinely describe Jesus' resurrection appearances as consequent on his re-creation (or even the survival of his soul, mind or true self) in heaven; with Jesus manifesting his presence to the disciples through some form of telepathic communication to the disciples' minds that gave rise to an 'appearance' of his body. On this view, the resurrection appearances were 'waking visions of the living Lord' (Hick, 1976, p. 174). No physical body of Jesus was actually present on earth; but Jesus himself, alive in heaven, caused these images in the minds of the disciples. By contrast, more conservative scholars defend the historicity of the empty tomb and the 'bodily resurrection' of Jesus, pointing out that the Gospel accounts are very unlike stories of visions of spirits or ghosts – which would not have had the same profound effect on the disciples anyway. In the case of Paul, however, Jesus *did* appear in a vision from heaven, rather than as a resurrected person on earth.

---

2 However, 'body' is the intended meaning here. The Nicene Creed spoke less provocatively of the 'resurrection of the dead'.

Paul envisages the resurrection of Christians as involving a 'spiritual' body animated by God's Spirit, rather than by our present life-force. This new body will also be in a broad sense physical, but *non-corruptible* and therefore immune from death. Life after death thus involves transformation of our mundane bodies, which must 'put on immortality' – since corruptible 'flesh and blood cannot inherit the kingdom of God' (1 Cor. 15.35–57; 2 Cor. 5.1–10; Phil. 1.19–26; 3.21; cf. Rev. 20.11—21.4).

Many theologians welcome an emphasis on the doctrine of resurrection, believing that it safeguards *bodily identity*. They argue that to be the same person involves having a body that is 'identical to' or 'continuous with' our earlier earthly body; and also that a body of some sort is essential for persons to be able to act, communicate, enjoy experiences and recognize one another. Hick argues that we can imagine a person dying and his body and brain (and therefore mental powers) disintegrating, but then being *re-created* by God identical in every important respect to the person who has died. This 'replica' would consist of body and mind together, but would exist in 'another space': that is, another physical universe, with space-time co-ordinates different from this universe. If our future existence is in some sense 'bodily' or *corporeal*, it will require some sort of resurrection-world in which to dwell. This must be 'an actual world which will resemble our world of space, time and matter in all sorts of ways, even as it will be far more glorious' (Wright, 2006, p. 74). This view seems compatible with theories of 'multiple universes' in modern physics, and with the essentially embodied nature of life and mind as revealed by modern medicine.

Resurrection is the concept of life after death that is most easily imaginable and makes most sense to us; just because it is so like this life. We know how we would act, experience and communicate in this different 'resurrection world inhabited by resurrected "replicas"' (Hick, 1976, p. 285). Nonetheless, the resurrected body and the resurrected world would still need to be *very different* from this earthly body and world, in order for the concept of resurrection to be truly coherent. But this fits the Pauline notion that our resurrection does involve a fundamental change: it is a radical 're-creation', rather than a seamless 'continuation' of this life.

However, the influence of Platonic philosophy on Christian thinking eventually led to the biblical concept of resurrection being coupled with – and sometimes eclipsed by – the alternative doctrine of the *immortality of the soul*. The doctrine of immortality envisages the existence only of a *disembodied* mind or self. It is official Catholic doctrine and widespread in Eastern Christianity; Calvin and (to some extent) Luther also taught it, and it remains widespread among Protestants. On the whole, however, Christianity refuses to see the soul as 'naturally' immortal – its life depends on a gracious act of God. Yet immortality still does not speak of such a profound *reversal* of death as does resurrection. 'Resurrection means not the continuation of this life, but life's completion . . . a "Yes" is spoken which the shadow of death cannot touch' (Barth, 1966, p. 154). Traditionally, the two options have been rather uneasily connected, by treating the immortal soul as the afterlife state that we enjoy *until* the bodily resurrection of all (or only the just) at the last judgement.

The concept of a disembodied mind gives rise to its own philosophical problems. Does it make sense to say that a person can exist without a body? If we have no body at all in the afterlife, how does our mind perceive, act or communicate? The philosopher Henry Price developed an account of a disembodied afterlife that makes it very similar to our present dream experience, with 'post-mortem' (after-death) experiences like the perceptions we now enjoy in dreams. They would be mind-dependent and have their 'own space', with things having 'spatial relations to one another. But . . . no spatial relation to objects in the physical' (non-dream) world (Price, 1965, p. 12). We would 'act' in the afterlife as we do now in our dreams, by means of a 'dreamed body'. Price added that communication between disembodied minds could take place by telepathy, which might then give rise to an 'appropriate' (that is, recognizable) image of that person in the mind of the recipient.

Death

Not surprisingly, Christians share the ambiguous attitude towards death that is expressed in the clichés that most people give voice to in the face of another's death. We accept that death is inevitable. Often – especially after a distressing or painful illness – it is 'a blessing' and 'a relief'. 'She was ready to go', we say, or 'It was well past his time.' And sometimes, 'She's where she belongs.' On the other hand, those of us who are left behind must bear their loss. And even the 'passing' of the most grumpy old men and women will evoke more mourning than the onlooker, or even the mourner, might have expected. They, too, are 'sadly missed', 'gone but not forgotten', 'fondly remembered', 'forever in our thoughts' – as the *in memoriam* messages declare.

But death is also often viewed with resentment, even dread: whether our own death, or the impending death of those who are close to us, particularly when it comes too early or is too painful. The paradox of love is that the closer we are to other people the more we shall feel their loss. In a noble assertion of the value of human life, and what many see as a valid expression of the battle against natural evil in which the dying are often engaged (see Chapter 8), Dylan Thomas wrote of his father's death: 'Do not go gentle into that good night. / Rage, rage against the dying of the light.' But must we view death as 'never good ... always an outrage' (Zizioulas, 2008, p. 100)? This seems a long way away from St Francis's welcoming of 'Brother Death', and the assertion that 'our perishing, the terminating of our existence ... is the good order of God' (Barth, 1958b, p. 469).

Death is a natural part of the human condition, and biology sees it as an essential engine for evolution. Other positive purposes include:

- providing a boundary to make life manageable, as sleep does in breaking up our worldly life;
- providing a finite goal for human achievements, and our growth in spiritual and moral character – 'because time is limited it is precious' (Hick, 1973, p. 196);
- allowing us to see the meaning of a person's life *as a whole*; and
- focusing our attention on what is of real and ultimate value to us – our true 'end'.

Yet the Bible gives some support for the view of death as a curse, rather than part of the good gift of creation, particularly when it is associated with the alienating power of *sin*. But Jesus' resurrection reveals that death does not have the last word in our life-drama, for it is incapable of separating us finally from the saving love of God revealed in Christ (Rom. 5.12–21; 6.20–3; 8.31–9; 1 Cor. 15.20–8, 50–7; Heb. 2.14–18). For Christians, then, though death may still often be an enemy, it is a defeated enemy. For Paul, it is only 'through our Lord Jesus Christ' that this 'sting of death' is removed, and death is 'swallowed up in victory'.

At least part of what belief in life after death is about is the assertion that our transient lives and decisions *matter*. Existentialist writers point out that human existence, unlike other types of being, is a 'being-towards-death' (a translation of Heidegger's word *Dasein*). Our recognition of the inevitability of our death can result in the distinctively human condition of *angst* – existential anxiety, dread or despair of those caught between what they are and what they are obliged to become, in the face of the apparent lack of meaning in the universe. 'Accepting our mortality' may be an essential aspect of overcoming this anxiety; and existentialist thought urges that this is achieved only as we strive for the personal integrity of authentic existence. This involves living responsibly, accepting our limitations and striving to achieve what we can, while avoiding retreating into impersonal conformity.

EXERCISE

Sample some of the things that have been written generally about death, by using the index of a good dictionary of quotations or looking through any comprehensive anthology of poetry. What main themes and concerns emerge, and how should Christians respond to them?

It seems to make spiritual and psychological good sense to say that *in the end* rebellion is less fulfilling of a life than acceptance. Some would say that it is our alienation from the good purposes of God that sours our attitude to death, along with our attitude to many other things (Chapter 6). Human alienation makes an enemy of that which – in the end – we *can only* accept. Acceptance is recognized by many as the last of the 'stages of dying', after we have moved beyond denial, anger, bargaining and depression. Don Cupitt, whose spiritual insights are often independent of his theological non-realism, argues in *Life, Life* that one should 'rejoice in life whilst one can, and one should die without complaint when one must . . . We overcome evil when we do not let it drive us into bitterness or resentment' (Cupitt, 2003, p. 137).

Judgement, Heaven and Hell

The injustice of so much of life forcefully provokes such negative, reactive emotions. Biblical spirituality, which can express intense anger at the flourishing of the wicked (for example Ps. 73), strongly motivated an appeal to God to bring justice in this world – and eventually the next.

God's judgement has been justified by various arguments.

- If God punishes moral evil in a future life, it might restore a 'moral balance' to a universe that is so clearly out of balance during this life.
- The moral and spiritual development cut short at death may somehow continue in the afterlife, until every person attains the full realization of their full moral and spiritual potential.
- The future good of heaven may justify retrospectively all the evils that were a necessary means to this end (cf. Rom. 8.18–23), and perhaps all other evils that 'just happened' along the way.
- Marilyn McCord Adams argues that some evils require 'changing the system' of a material world, and for those who suffer them to flourish as *immaterial souls*, with their meaning-making capacities healed. Then 'the good of beatific face-to-face intimacy with God would *engulf* . . . even the horrendous evils humans experience in this present life here below' (Adams and Adams, 1990, p. 218).

As Christian thinking developed, a tension surfaced between two opportunities for the exercise of God's judgement: (i) a personal, *individual judgement* of the soul at the moment of a person's death; and (ii) a general resurrection and *general judgement* of all who have died, together with those who are still alive (in the creeds, 'the living and the dead'), judged by Christ at his coming again. Much Christian theology has traditionally combined both moments of judgement, and also affirmed the two different beliefs about the nature of the afterlife. So the disembodied soul survives death in preparation for a later resurrection (re-creation) of the physical body that is reunited with, or reanimated by, this soul before the last judgement.

An 'intermediate stage' between death and the final resurrection is suggested by a number of texts (for example Luke 23.43; John 14.2; 2 Cor. 5.1–5; Phil. 1.23; 1 Thess. 4.14–17). If this is regarded as a continuing existence in time, it may be pictured either as a period of conscious 'waiting' or even (as in Luther) of 'sleep', usually 'in paradise' with Christ.

Some theologians have proposed that this interim stage may allow a 'second chance' of salvation, even for those who have rejected God. (Christ's 'descent into hell' in 1 Peter 3.18–20; 4.6 had suggested this possibility for those who had no chance to encounter Christ during their earthly lives.) In Catholic theology, this stage became a purgatorial or purifying experience for those who are saved but who – because of their sins in this life – died in a state that made them unworthy to enter into the divine presence at once. In *purgatory* they could continue to develop spiritually. (On this view, only true saints and those of the baptized who 'were not in need of purification' go directly into the experience of God's bliss.) Eastern Churches regard purgatory as speculation, preferring a simpler restful state for the soul awaiting the last judgement, or the view that the just enter more directly into Christ's presence. Recent Catholic theology has rather downplayed the role of purgatory.

Abuse of the Catholic practice of offering prayers or masses to assist souls in purgatory (cf. 2 Macc. 12.44–5) was one of the sparks that lit the conflagration of the Reformation. Protestants frequently argue that any growth or purification in an intermediate state 'would diminish our historic responsibility in this life', and the 'irrevocable, final and binding' nature of God's judgement (Schwarz, 1984, p. 573). However, a 'moving forward' of heaven and hell to the date of the individual's judgement at the time of death makes the idea of a general judgement of all appear redundant.

Heaven is properly understood as the destination of the righteous after the resurrection and final judgement. It is variously described in Scripture, theology and worship as a banquet, a place of rest, the great sabbath, an unending state of worship, a wonderful city, or a paradisal garden. We should not, of course, interpret any of these metaphors literally (especially where heaven is viewed as eternal in the sense of 'timeless' rather than 'everlasting'). However it is imaged, heaven is the fulfilment or end of salvation. 'For what is our end but to reach that kingdom which has no end?' (Augustine, *City of God* xxii, ch. 30). 'Guesses, of course, all guesses. If they are not true, something better will be. For we know that we shall be made like Him, for we shall see Him as He is' (Lewis, 1964, p. 158).

Most theology insists that heaven is 'not a place but a mode of being . . . the hidden, incomprehensible sphere of God' (Küng, 1993, p. 162). This sort of theology is compatible with claims about God's future plans that envisage a heaven-come-down-to-earth. Wright describes heaven and earth as 'two different dimensions of God's good creation' (Wright, 2007, p. 122). He argues that, in biblical theology, our ultimate destination is not being away from the creation and at 'home with God' – as it is celebrated in so many Christian hymns – but as part of the 'new creation' which 'houses' the resurrected.

Heaven is also sometimes presented as where we may have a vision of God as God is in himself. The concept of this *beatific vision* often includes the notion of God's dwelling within the very essence of the soul, thus being perceived 'from within' by direct contact. This raises the difficulty of whether a person who is so closely united with God remains a distinct entity over against God. Would it still be me, if that is what heaven is like? Interestingly, unlike the experience of unqualified unity that is characteristic of some other faiths, *Christian* mystics tend to speak of a state of intimate union with God which *preserves* our individual, distinct identity.[3] In some cases, it is even expressed in the picture-language of sexual union.

EXERCISE

While 52% of the general population of mainland Britain believe that heaven exists, only 25% accept that there is a hell. Figures from the same study for weekly churchgoers give 89% accepting heaven and 62% hell (Gill, 1999, pp. 70, 128). A survey of committed Anglicans shows that 78% allow that heaven really exists, and 46% that hell does (Francis, Robbins and Astley, 2005, p. 153).

• Which category do you fall into? What arguments would you use to defend your view about the existence or non-existence of hell? If you believe that hell exists, how would you characterize it?

Hell is also portrayed highly metaphorically, and symbolizes a place of despair and separation. The New Testament sometimes draws on the image of a valley south of Jerusalem (*Gehenna* or 'The Valley of Hinnom'), where human sacrifice was once offered and the city's rubbish may have been burned in Jesus' time. The overall impression is thus one of destruction or possibly purification, rather than everlasting *punishment*. It is the 'worms' and 'fire' that are said to last forever (Mark 9.48). 'There is nothing in the traditional doctrine that requires hell to be a place of torture' (Kvanvig, 1997, p. 563); nor does the Bible regard it as the home of the satan, who in his earlier manifestations is an insignificant part of God's court, and whose final fate in the New Testament is in a 'lake of fire'. ('Hades' in the Bible is not hell, but the Greek name for *Sheol*. In Christian

---

3 Mysticism is a particular form of religious experience in *this* life.

thought it is the resting-place of the dead – for some, the pious dead, for others the wicked – pending the final resurrection.) Hell is most significantly portrayed as the place where the felt presence of God is absent.

Hope for All?

Although some texts in the New Testament affirm that God's grace and mercy know no bounds (for example Rom. 11.32; 1 Cor. 15.22; Eph. 1.10; Phil. 2.9–11; Col. 1.19–20; 1 John 2.2), we cannot avoid the fact that many passages endorse a belief in some form of punishment or loss (for example Matt. 13.36–43, 47–50; 25.31–46; Mark 3.29; John 5.28–9; Rom. 2.6–16; 2 Thess. 1.5–10; Rev. 20; cf. Ps. 81.15).

Criticisms of the morality of a doctrine of everlasting punishment tend to centre on the following questions:

- Can punishment ever be justified simply as retribution for wrongdoing, without any hope of further good consequences? Many people argue that punishment *in this life* can only be morally right if it includes, or at least allows, the reformation of the offender (see pp. 127, 129, 131).
- Is it morally justifiable that punishment for sin, which – however great – can only be finite, should last for ever? (If hell is 'everlasting', it must be in time.)

Christ, in Origen's old words, remains on the Cross so long as one sinner remains in hell. That is not speculation: it is a statement grounded in the very necessity of God's nature. In a universe of love there can be no heaven which tolerates a chamber of horrors, no hell for any which does not at the same time make it hell for God. He cannot endure that, for *that* would be the final mockery of his nature. And he will not. (Robinson, 1968, p. 133)

Augustine and others argued that just punishment is itself part of the proper ordering and beauty of God's creation. But it may be closer to the heart of the Christian gospel to see God's judgement, not in terms of judicial proceedings and pronouncements, but as an act – 'the *doing* of justice, the righting of wrong'. And as *Christ* is here the judge, 'our whole conception of that judgement must conform itself to what we know of Christ' (Burnaby, 1959, p. 185).

It is good news ... because the one through whom God's justice will finally sweep the world is not a hard-hearted, arrogant or vengeful tyrant, but the Man of Sorrows ... the Jesus who loved sinners and died for them; the Messiah who took the world's judgement upon himself on the cross. (Wright, 2007, p. 154)

But Wright nevertheless holds that the argument that God will wait until the last soul is converted enables that person 'to exercise in perpetuity a veto on the triumph of grace' (Wright, 2006, p. 91).

The claim that the existence of any sort of hell would be fatal to Christian theodicy often rests on the conviction that a God who condemns some to hell does not bring a good end to every created human life. *Universalism* is the belief that all humankind will ultimately be saved. It has been widely held, both by those Calvinists who say that God predestines all to salvation, and (in more libertarian theological circles) by those who ground it in a firm belief in God's patience. It is sometimes coupled with Augustine's faith that God has made us 'for' ('towards') himself, 'and our hearts find no peace until they rest in you' (*Confessions* i, i). Since *our* end (orientation, purpose) is to love God, in *the* end we shall all eventually do so freely. Origen and others held such a view in the second century, but the majority of the theologians of the Church – including Augustine himself – have rejected universalism, and it was condemned at the second Council of Constantinople in 543.

While writing of 'a truly eternal divine patience and deliverance' that allows us to be open to the possibility of the overwhelming triumph of God's grace in the salvation of all, Karl Barth cautions that we are 'certainly forbidden to count on this as though we had a claim to it, as though it were not supremely the work of God'. *Yet* 'we are surely commanded the more definitely to hope and pray for it' (Barth, 1961, p. 478)

The alternative to universalism is some form of *separationism*. Undeniably, this treats our moral religious choices in this life, as well as our freedom and autonomy, more seriously. Perhaps God *couldn't* ensure the salvation of all without overriding their free will. This has the consequence, however, that God might in the end be unable to save all. (A moderate form of the doctrine could allow that *most* humans will be saved, but not all.) Many who take a separationist view regard hell neither as an arbitrary divine punishment, nor as 'the final retaliation of a vindictive deity', but merely as human 'self-destructive resistance to the eternal love of God' (Migliore, 2004, p. 347). On such a view, hell's gates are 'locked on the inside' (C. S. Lewis). Others have argued that the eternally unrepentant will simply cease to exist, This *annihilationism*, or 'conditional immortality', also implies that not all will be saved. In that case, either there is no need for hell, or hell is the place of destruction that biblical imagery suggests.

John Hick is more hopeful. 'Hell exists, but is empty', he writes. 'It is "there" awaiting any who may be finally lost to God; but in the end none are to be finally lost' (Hick, 1973, p. 72). He counsels, however, that hell can still be regarded spiritually and morally as a real threat. On this understanding, we must all face a 'sort of hell' in the form of a purgatorial experience of 'progressive sanctification after death' – a continuation after death of the soul-making process that inevitably involves some suffering. This vale of soul-making runs through a series of resurrected afterlives (the '*pareschaton*') in other resurrection worlds, in which God may be experienced as more directly present. Hick argues that the *pareschaton* state will continue until each individual finally fulfils her or his full spiritual and moral potential, transcending selfishness and becoming united with God in the *eschaton* or 'unitive state'. This may be a bodiless existence, 'beyond both matter and time, or at least time as we know it' (Hick, 1976, p. 463).

On this view, too, our final end is with the mystery of God.

Suggestions for Further Reading

Introductory

Hebblethwaite, B., 1984, *The Christian Hope*, Basingstoke: Marshall, Morgan & Scott.
McGrath, A. E., 2007, *Christian Theology: An Introduction*, Oxford: Blackwell, ch. 18.
Wright, N. T., 2007, *Surprised by Hope*, London: SPCK.

Advanced

D'Costa, G. (ed.), 1996, *Resurrection Reconsidered*, Oxford: Oneworld.
Hick, J., 1996, *Death and Eternal Life*, Louisville, KY: Westminster John Knox Press.
Ward, K., 1998, *Religion and Human Nature*, Oxford: Clarendon Press, chs 11–14.

Further Reading

Students of doctrine greatly benefit from listening to a variety of voices. Most of the following titles discuss the major doctrines, and their authors represent a wide spectrum of Christian denominations.

Introductory

Barth, K., 2002 [1966], *Dogmatics in Outline*, ET London: SCM Press.

Burnaby, J., 1959, *The Belief of Christendom: A Commentary on the Nicene Creed*, London: SPCK.

Ford, D. F., 1999, *Theology: A Very Short Introduction*, Oxford: Oxford University Press.

Hanson, A. T. and Hanson, R. P. C., 1981, *Reasonable Belief: A Survey of the Christian Faith*, Oxford: Oxford University Press.

Küng, H., 1993, *Credo: The Apostles' Creed Explained for Today*, ET London: SCM Press.

McGrath, A. E., 2008, *Theology: The Basics*, Oxford: Blackwell.

Migliore, D. L., 2004, *Faith Seeking Understanding: An Introduction to Christian Doctrine*, Grand Rapids, MI: Eerdmans.

Norris, R. A., 1979, *Understanding the Faith of the Church*, New York: Seabury.

Pannenberg, W., 1972, *The Apostles' Creed in the Light of Today's Questions*, ET London: SCM Press.

More Advanced or Detailed

Braaten, C. E. and Jenson, R. W. (eds), 1984, *Christian Dogmatics* (2 volumes), Philadelphia: Fortress.

Gunton, C. E. (ed.), 1997, *The Cambridge Companion to Christian Doctrine*, Cambridge: Cambridge University Press.

Gunton, C. E., 2001, *The Christian Faith: An Introduction to Christian Doctrine*, Oxford: Blackwell.

Higton, M., 2008, *SCM Core Text: Christian Doctrine*, London: SCM Press.

Hodgson, P. and King, R. (eds), 2008, *Christian Theology: An Introduction to Its Traditions and Tasks*, London: SPCK.

Lohse, B., 1966, *A Short History of Christian Doctrine*, ET Philadelphia: Fortress.

McGrath, A. E., 2007, *Christian Theology: An Introduction*, Oxford: Blackwell.

McIntosh, M. A., 2008, *Divine Teaching: An Introduction to Christian Theology*, Oxford: Blackwell.

Morse, C., 2009, *Not Every Spirit: A Dogmatics of Christian Disbelief*, London: T. & T. Clark.

Ormerod, N., 2007, *Creation, Grace, and Redemption*, Maryknoll, NY: Orbis Books.

Stiver, D. R., 2009, *Life Together in the Way of Jesus Christ: An Introduction to Christian Theology*, Waco, TX: Baylor University Press.

For Reference

Catechism of the Catholic Church, 2000, ET London: Burns & Oates.

Jones, G. (ed.), 2007, *The Blackwell Companion to Modern Theology*, Oxford: Blackwell.

Mannion, G. and Mudge, L. S. (eds), 2008, *The Routledge Companion to the Christian Church*, London: Routledge.

McGuckin, J. A., 2005, *The SCM Press A–Z of Patristic Theology*, London: SCM Press.

Musser, D. W. and Price, J. L. (eds), 1997, *A New Handbook of Christian Theology*, Nashville, TN: Abingdon.

O'Collins, G., SJ and Farrugia, M., SJ, 2003, *Catholicism: The Story of Catholic Christianity*, Oxford: Oxford University Press.

Olson, R. E., 2005, *The SCM Press A–Z of Evangelical Theology*, London: SCM Press.

Rahner, K. (ed.), 1999, *Encyclopedia of Theology: A Concise Sacramentum Mundi*, London: Continuum.

Richardson, A. and Bowden, J. (eds), 1983, *A New Dictionary of Christian Theology*, London: SCM Press.[1]

Webster, J., Tanner, K. and Torrance, I. (eds), 2007, *The Oxford Handbook of Systematic Theology*, Oxford: Oxford University Press.

---

1 The earlier SCM *Dictionary* (Richardson, 1969) is still useful.

References

Abraham, W., 1989, *The Logic of Evangelism*, London: Hodder & Stoughton.

Adams, M. and Adams, R. M. (eds), 1990, *The Problem of Evil*, Oxford: Oxford University Press.

Allen, D., 1990, 'Natural Evil and the Love of God', in M. Adams and R. M. Adams (eds), *The Problem of Evil*, Oxford: Oxford University Press, pp. 189–208.

Alston, W. P., 1987, 'Functionalism and Theological Language', in T. V. Morris (ed.), *The Concept of God*, Oxford: Oxford University Press, pp. 21–40.

Armstrong, K., 2009, *The Case for God: What Religion Really Means*, London: Bodley Head.

Astley, J., 2002, *Ordinary Theology: Looking, Listening and Learning in Theology*, Aldershot: Ashgate.

Astley, J., 2004a, *Exploring God-talk: Using Language in Religion*, London: Darton, Longman & Todd.

Astley, J., 2004b, 'Religious Non-Realism and Spiritual Truth', in G. Hyman (ed.), *New Directions in Philosophical Theology*, Aldershot: Ashgate, pp. 19–33.

Astley, J., 2007, *Christ of the Everyday*, London: SPCK.

Astley, J., Francis, L. J. and Crowder, C. (eds), 1996, *Theological Perspectives on Christian Formation: A Reader in Theology and Christian Education*, Leominster: Gracewing.

Aulén, G., 1970, *Christus Victor: An Historical Study of the Three Main Types of the Idea of the Atonement*, ET London: SPCK.

Baelz, P., 1968, *Prayer and Providence*, London: SCM Press.

Baillie, D. M., 1948, *God was in Christ*, London: Faber & Faber.

Baillie, D. M., 1957, *The Theology of the Sacraments and Other Papers*, New York: Charles Scribner's Sons.

von Balthasar, H. U., 1989, *The Word Made Flesh*, ET San Francisco: Ignatius Press.

Barr, J., 1973, *The Bible in the Modern World*, London: SCM Press.

Barr, J., 1984, *Escaping from Fundamentalism*, London: SCM Press.

Barrett, C. K., 1971, *A Commentary on the First Epistle to the Corinthians*, London: A. & C. Black.

Barth, K., 1928, *The Word of God and the Word of Man*, ET London: Hodder & Stoughton.

Barth, K., 1933, *The Epistle to the Romans*, ET London: Oxford University Press.

Barth, K., 1956a, *Church Dogmatics*, I/2, ET Edinburgh: T. & T. Clark.

Barth, K., 1956b, *Church Dogmatics*, IV/1, ET Edinburgh: T. & T. Clark.

Barth, K., 1957, *Church Dogmatics*, II/1, ET Edinburgh: T. & T. Clark.

Barth, K., 1958a, *Church Dogmatics*, III/1, ET Edinburgh: T. & T. Clark.

Barth, K., 1958b, *Church Dogmatics*, IV/2, ET Edinburgh: T. & T. Clark.

Barth, K., 1961, *Church Dogmatics*, IV/3, 1, ET Edinburgh: T. & T. Clark.

Barth, K., 1962, *Church Dogmatics*, IV/3, 2, ET Edinburgh: T. & T. Clark.

Barth, K., 1966, *Dogmatics in Outline*, ET London: SCM Press.

Barth, K., 1975, *Church Dogmatics*, I/1, ET Edinburgh: T. & T. Clark.

Black, M., 1962, *Models and Metaphors: Studies in Language and Philosophy*, Ithaca, NY: Cornell University Press.

Bondi, R. C., 1983, 'Apophatic Theology', in A. Richardson and J. Bowden (eds), *A New Dictionary of Christian Theology*, London: SCM Press, p. 32.

Bonhoeffer, D., 1971, *Letters and Papers from Prison: The Enlarged Edition*, ET London: SCM Press.

Borg, M. J., 1997, *The God We Never Knew: Beyond Dogmatic Religion to a More Authentic Contemporary Faith*, San Francisco: HarperSanFrancisco.

Borg, M. J., 2003, *The Heart of Christianity: Rediscovering a Life of Faith*, San Francisco: HarperSanFrancisco.

Borg, M. J., 2006, *Jesus: Uncovering the Life, Teachings, and Relevance of a Religious Revolutionary*, New York: HarperCollins.

Bouteiller, J., 1979, 'Threshold Christians: A Challenge for the Church', in W. J. Reedy (ed.), *Becoming a Catholic Christian*, New York: Sadlier, pp. 65–80.

Braaten, C. E., 1984, 'The Person of Jesus Christ', in C. E. Braaten and R. W. Jenson (eds), *Christian Dogmatics*, Vol. 1, Philadelphia: Fortress, pp. 469–569.

Braaten, C. E. and Jenson, R. W. (eds), 1984, *Christian Dogmatics*, two vols, Philadelphia: Fortress.

Brown, D., 1994, 'Did Revelation Cease?', in A. G. Padgett (ed.), *Reason and the Christian Religion: Essays in Honour of Richard Swinburne*, Oxford: Clarendon Press, pp. 121–41.

Brown, D., 1999, *Tradition and Imagination: Revelation and Change*, Oxford: Oxford University Press.

Brueggemann, W., 1997, *Theology of the Old Testament: Testimony, Dispute, Advocacy*, Minneapolis, MN: Fortress.

Brümmer, V., 1981, *Theology and Philosophical Inquiry: An Introduction*, London: Macmillan.

Brümmer, V., 1993, *The Model of Love*, Cambridge: Cambridge University Press.

Brümmer, V., 2005, *Atonement, Christology and the Trinity: Making Sense of Christian Doctrine*, Aldershot: Ashgate.

Brunner, E., 1934, *The Mediator: A Study of the Central Doctrine of the Christian Faith*, ET London: Lutterworth.

Brunner, E., 1952, *The Christian Doctrine of Creation and Redemption*, ET London: Lutterworth.

Buber, M., 1958, *I and Thou*, ET Edinburgh: T. & T. Clark.

Burnaby, J., 1959, *The Belief of Christendom: A Commentary on the Nicene Creed*, London: SPCK.

Caird, G. B., 1980, *The Language and Imagery of the Bible*, London: Duckworth.

Carroll, R. C., 1997, *Wolf in the Sheep Fold: The Bible as Problematic for Theology*, London: SCM Press.

Catechism of the Catholic Church, 2000, ET London: Burns & Oates.

Christie, A., 2007, 'Who Do You Say I Am? Answers from the Pews', *Journal of Adult Theological Education*, 4, 2, pp. 181–94.

Christie, A. and Astley, J., 2009, 'Ordinary Soteriology: A Qualitative Study', in L. J. Francis, M. Robbins and J. Astley (eds), *Empirical Theology in Texts and Tables: Qualitative, Quantitative and Comparative Perspectives*, Leiden: Brill, pp. 177–96.

Clark, F., 1978, *The Christian Way*, Milton Keynes: The Open University.

Cobb, J. B., 1966, *A Christian Natural Theology: Based on the Thought of Alfred North Whitehead*, London: Lutterworth.

Cottingham, J., 2005, *The Spiritual Dimension: Religion, Philosophy and Human Vocation*, Cambridge: Cambridge University Press.

Cowburn, J., 1979, *Shadows and the Dark: The Problems of Suffering and Evil*, London: SCM Press.

Cranfield, C. E. B., 2004, *The Apostles' Creed: A Faith to Live By*, London: Continuum.

Cullman, O., 1963, *The Christology of the New Testament*, ET London: SCM Press.

Cunningham, D. S., 1998, *These Three Are One: The Practice of Trinitarian Theology*, Oxford: Blackwell.

Cupitt, D., 1980, *Taking Leave of God*, London: SCM Press.

Cupitt, D., 1986, *Life Lines*, London: SCM Press.

Cupitt, D., 2003, *Life, Life*, Santa Rosa, CA: Polebridge Press.

Cupitt, D., 2006, *The Old Creed and the New*, London: SCM Press.

Davis, S. T. (ed.), 2001, *Encountering Evil: Live Options in Theodicy*, Edinburgh: T. & T. Clark.

Del Colle, R., 1997, 'The Triune God', in C. Gunton (ed.), *The Cambridge Companion to Christian Doctrine*, Cambridge: Cambridge University Press, pp. 121–40.

Doctrine Commission of the Church of England, 2005, *Contemporary Doctrine Classics*, London: Church House Publishing.

Drane, J., 2000, *The McDonaldization of the Church: Spirituality, Creativity and the Future of the Church*, London: Darton, Longman & Todd.

Drury, J., 1972, *Angels and Dirt: An Enquiry into Theology and Prayer*, London: Darton, Longman & Todd.

Dulles, A., 2002, *Models of the Church*, New York: Doubleday.

Dunn, J. D. G., 1989, *Christology in the Making: A New Testament Inquiry into the Origins of the Doctrine of the Incarnation*, London: SCM Press.

Dunn, J. D. G., 2003, *The Theology of Paul the Apostle*, London: T. & T. Clark.

Dunn, J. D. G., 2009, *New Testament Theology: An Introduction*, Nashville, TN: Abingdon.

Evans, D., 1979, *Struggle and Fulfillment: The Inner Dynamics of Religion and Morality*, Cleveland, OH: Collins.

Evans, G. R. and Wright, J. R. (eds), 1991, *The Anglican Tradition: A Handbook of Sources*, London: SPCK.

Farley, E., 1983, *Theologia: The Fragmentation and Unity of Theological Education*, Philadelphia: Fortress.

Farley, E., 1988, *The Fragility of Knowledge: Theological Education in the Church and the University*, Philadelphia: Fortress.

Farley, E. and Hodgson, P. C., 2008, 'Scripture and Tradition', in P. C. Hodgson and R. H. King (eds), *Christian Theology: An Introduction to its Traditions and Tasks*, London: SPCK.

Farrer, A., 1966, *Love Almighty and Ills Unlimited*, London: Collins.

Forde, G. O., 1984, 'The Work of Christ', in C. E. Braaten and R. W. Jenson (eds), *Christian Dogmatics*, Vol. 2, Philadelphia: Fortress, pp. 1–99.

Forsyth, P. T., 1909, *The Person and Place of Jesus Christ*, London: Independent Press.

Francis, L. J., 2000, 'The Pews Talk Back: The Church Congregation Survey', in J. Astley (ed.), *Learning in the Way: Research and Reflection on Adult Christian Education*, Leominster: Gracewing, pp. 161–86.

Francis, L. J., Robbins, M. and Astley, J., 2005, *Fragmented Faith: Exposing the Faultlines in the Church of England*, London: Paternoster.

Gadamer, H.-G., 1993, *Truth and Method*, ET London: Sheed & Ward.

Gill, R., 1999, *Churchgoing and Christian Ethics*, Cambridge: Cambridge University Press.

Gorringe, T., 1989, 'Sacraments', in R. Morgan (ed.), *The Religion of the Incarnation:*

Anglican Essays in Commemoration of Lux Mundi, Bristol: Bristol Classical Press, pp. 158–71.

Gunton, C. E., 1978, *Becoming and Being: The Doctrine of God in Charles Hartshorne and Karl Barth*, Oxford: Oxford University Press.

Gunton, C. E., 1988, *The Actuality of the Atonement*, Edinburgh: T. & T. Clark.

Gunton, C. E., 1996, *Theology through the Theologians: Selected Essays, 1972–1995*, London: T. & T. Clark.

Gunton, C. E. (ed.), 1997, *The Cambridge Companion to Christian Doctrine*, Cambridge: Cambridge University Press.

Habgood, J., 1986, 'Discovering God in Action', in T. Moss (ed.), *In Search of Christianity*, London: Firethorn/Waterstone, pp. 108–20.

Hanson, A. T., 1975, *Church, Sacraments and Ministry*, London: Mowbrays.

Hanson, A. T. and Hanson, R. P. C., 1981, *Reasonable Belief: A Survey of the Christian Faith*, Oxford: Oxford University Press.

Hanson, R. P. C., 1983, 'Tradition', in A. Richardson and J. Bowden (eds), *A New Dictionary of Christian Theology*, London: SCM Press, pp. 574–6.

Hardy, D. and Ford, D., 1984, *Jubilate*, London: Darton, Longman & Todd.

Hart, T., 1997, 'Redemption and Fall', in C. E. Gunton (ed.), *The Cambridge Companion to Christian Doctrine*, Cambridge: Cambridge University Press, pp. 189–206.

Hartshorne, C., 1953, 'The Logic of Panentheism', in C. Hartshorne and W. L. Reese (eds), *Philosophers Speak of God*, Chicago: University of Chicago Press, pp. 499–514.

Hartshorne, C., 1976, *The Divine Relativity: A Social Conception of God*, New Haven: Yale University Press.

Hartshorne, C. and Reese, W. L. (eds), 1953, *Philosophers Speak of God*, Chicago: University of Chicago Press.

Hastings, A., 1975, 'Mission', in K. Rahner (ed.), *Encyclopaedia of Theology*, London: Burns & Oates, pp. 967–9.

Haught, J. F., 2007, *Christianity and Science: Toward a Theology of Nature*, Maryknoll, NY: Orbis.

Hebblethwaite, B., 2000, *Evil, Suffering and Religion*, London: SPCK.

Hefner, P. J., 1984a, 'The Creation', in C. E. Braaten and R. W. Jenson (eds), *Christian Dogmatics*, Vol. 1, Philadelphia: Fortress, pp. 265–357.

Hefner, P. J., 1984b, 'The Church', in C. E. Braaten and R. W. Jenson (eds), *Christian Dogmatics*, Vol. 2, Philadelphia: Fortress, pp. 179–247.

Hick, J., 1973, *God and the Universe of Faiths: Essays in the Philosophy of Religion*, London: Macmillan.

Hick, J., 1976, *Death and Eternal Life*, London: Collins.

Hick, J. (ed.), 1977, *The Myth of God Incarnate*, London: SCM Press.

Hick, J., 1983, *The Second Christianity*, London: SCM Press.

Hick, J., 1985, *Evil and the God of Love*, London: Macmillan.

Hick, J., 2005, *The Metaphor of God Incarnate*, London: SCM Press.

Hick, J., 2008, *Who or What is God? And Other Investigations*, London: SCM Press.

Hodges, H. A., 1955, *The Pattern of Atonement*, London: SCM Press.

Hopkins, J., 1995, *Towards a Feminist Christology: Jesus of Nazareth, European Women, and the Christological Crisis*, London: SPCK.

Hordern, W., 1969, 'Creation', in A. Richardson (ed.), *A Dictionary of Christian Theology*, London: SCM Press, pp. 77–9.

Immink, F. G., 2005, *Faith: A Practical Theological Reconstruction*, Grand Rapids, MI: Eerdmans.

Jenkins, D. E., 1987, *God, Miracle and the Church of England*, London: SCM Press.

Jenson, R. W., 1984a, 'The Triune God', in C. E. Braaten and R. W. Jenson (eds), *Christian Dogmatics*, Vol. 1, Philadelphia: Fortress, pp. 83–191.

Jenson, R. W., 1984b, 'The Sacraments', in C. E. Braaten and R. W. Jenson (eds), *Christian Dogmatics*, Vol. 2, Philadelphia: Fortress, pp. 291–389.

Jenson, R. W., 1993, 'God', in A. E. McGrath (ed.), *The Blackwell Encyclopedia of Modern Christian Thought*, Oxford: Blackwell, pp. 234–47.

Jenson, R. W., 1997, 'The Church and the Sacraments', in C. E. Gunton (ed.), *The Cambridge Companion to Christian Doctrine*, Cambridge: Cambridge University Press, pp. 207–25.

Jeremias, J., 1966, *The Eucharistic Words of Jesus*, ET London: SCM Press.

Kelly, J. N. D., 1968, *Early Christian Doctrines*, London: A. & C. Black.

Kelly, J. N. D., 1972, *Early Christian Creeds*, London: Longmans.

Kelsey, D. H., 1975, *The Uses of Scripture in Recent Theology*, London: SCM Press.

Kelsey, D. H., 1992, *To Understand God Truly: What's Theological about a Theological School*, Louisville, KY: Westminster/John Knox Press.

Kelsey, D. H., 1999, *Proving Doctrine: The Uses of Scripture in Modern Theology*, Harrisburg, PA: Trinity Press International.

Kerr, F., 1986, *Theology after Wittgenstein*, Oxford: Blackwell.

King, U., 1997, *Christ in All Things: Exploring Spirituality with Teilhard de Chardin*, London: SCM Press.

Knox, J., 1967, *The Humanity and Divinity of Christ: A Study of Pattern in Christology*, Cambridge: Cambridge University Press.

Koyama, K., 1992, 'Missiology', in D. W. Musser and J. L. Price (eds), *A New Dictionary of Christian Theology*, Cambridge: Lutterworth, pp. 312–4.

Küng, H., 1964, *Justification: The Doctrine of Karl Barth and a Catholic Reflection*, ET London: Burns & Oates.

Küng, H., 1971, *The Church*, ET London: Search Press.

Küng, H., 1977, *On Being a Christian*, ET Glasgow: Collins.

Küng, H., 1993, *Credo: The Apostles' Creed Explained for Today*, ET London: SCM Press.

Kvanvig, J. L., 1997, 'Heaven and Hell', in P. L. Quinn and C. Taliaferro (eds), *A Companion to Philosophy of Religion*, Oxford: Blackwell, pp. 562–8.

Lampe, G. W. H., 1963, 'The Bible Since the Rise of Critical Study', in D. E. Nineham (ed.), *The Church's Use of the Bible: Past and Present*, London: SPCK, pp. 125–44.

Lampe, G. W. H., 1966, 'The Atonement: Law and Love', in A. R. Vidler (ed.), *Soundings: Essays Concerning Christian Understanding*, Cambridge: Cambridge University Press, pp. 173–91.

Lampe, G. W. H., 1977, *God as Spirit*, London: SCM Press.

Langford, M., 1981, *Providence*, London: SCM Press.

Leftow, B., 1999, 'Anti Social Trinitarianism', in S. T. Davis, D. Kendall and G. O'Collins (eds), *The Trinity: An Interdisciplinary Symposium on the Trinity*, Oxford: Oxford University Press, pp. 203–49.

Lewis, C. S., 1952, *Mere Christianity*, London: Geoffrey Bles.

Lewis, C. S., 1955, *The Screwtape Letters*, Glasgow: Collins.

Lewis, C. S., 1964, *Letters to Malcolm: Chiefly on Prayer*, London: Geoffrey Bles.

Lindbeck, G. A., 1984, *The Nature of Doctrine: Religion and Theology in a Postliberal Age*, London: SPCK.

Lossky, V., 1957, *The Mystical Theology of the Eastern Church*, ET Cambridge: James Clarke.

Loughlin, G., 1997, 'The Basis and Authority of Doctrine', in C. E. Gunton (ed.), *The Cambridge Companion to Christian Doctrine*, Cambridge: Cambridge University Press, pp. 41–64.

Mackie, J. L., 1982, *The Miracle of Theism*, Oxford: Oxford University Press.

MacKinnon, D., 1968, *Borderlands of Theology: And Other Essays*, London: Lutterworth.

Macquarrie, J., 1977, *Principles of Christian Theology*, London: SCM Press.

Macquarrie, J., 1990, *Jesus Christ in Modern Thought*, London: SCM Press.

McFague, S., 1983, *Metaphorical Theology: Models of God in Religious Language*, London: SCM Press.

McGrath, A. E., 1997, *The Genesis of Doctrine: A Study in the Foundations of Doctrinal Criticism*, Grand Rapids, MI: Eerdmans.

McGrath, A. E., 2001, *A Scientific Theology: Vol. I. Nature*, Edinburgh: T. & T. Clark.

McGrath, A. E., 2008, *Theology: The Basics*, Oxford: Blackwell.

McIntyre, J., 1998, *The Shape of Christology: Studies in the Doctrine of the Person of Christ*, Edinburgh: T. & T. Clark.

McKeating, H., 1970, *Living with Guilt*, London: SCM Press.

McKeating, H., 1974, *God and the Future*, London: SCM Press.

Mascall, E. L., 1956, *Christian Theology and Natural Science: Some Questions on their Relations*, London: Longmans, Green.

Migliore, D. L., 2004, *Faith Seeking Understanding: An Introduction to Christian Theology*, Grand Rapids, MI: Eerdmans.

Mitchell, B., 1991, 'Philosophy and Theology', in A. Loades and L. D. Rue (eds), *Contemporary Classics in Philosophy of Religion*, La Salle, IL: Open Court, pp. 7–20.

Moltmann, J., 1967, *Theology of Hope: On the Ground and the Implications of a Christian Eschatology*, ET London: SCM Press.

Moltmann, J., 1974, *The Crucified God: The Cross of Christ as the Foundation and Criticism of Christian Theology*, ET London: SCM Press.

Moltmann, J., 1978, *The Open Church*, ET London: SCM Press.

Moltmann, J., 1980, *Experiences of God*, ET London: SCM Press.

Moltmann, J., 1981, *The Trinity and the Kingdom of God*, ET London: SCM Press.

Moltmann, J., 1985, *God in Creation: An Ecological Doctrine of Creation*, ET London: SCM Press.

Moltmann, J., 2000, *Experiences in Theology: Ways and Forms of Christian Theology*, ET London: SCM Press.

Moore, G., 1988, *Believing in God: A Philosophical Essay*, Edinburgh: T. & T. Clark.

Morgan, R. with Barton, J., 1989, *Biblical Interpretation*, Oxford: Oxford University Press.

Morris, Charles R., 1997, *American Catholic: The Saints and Sinners Who Built America's Most Powerful Church*, New York: Random House.

Niebuhr, H. R., 1952, *Christ and Culture*, London: Faber and Faber.

Nineham, D., 1976, *The Use and Abuse of the Bible: A Study of the Bible in an Age of Rapid Cultural Change*, London: SPCK.

Norris, R. A., 1979, *Understanding the Faith of the Church*, New York: Seabury.

Nygren, A., 1932, *Agapé and Eros*, ET London: SPCK.

Otto, R., 1925, *The Idea of the Holy*, ET Oxford: Oxford University Press.

Pannenberg, W. (ed.), 1969, *Revelation as History*, London: Sheed & Ward.

Pannenberg, W., 1972, *The Apostles' Creed in the Light of Today's Questions*, ET London: SCM Press.

Pattison, G., 2001, *A Short Course in the Philosophy of Religion*, London: SCM Press.

Pattison, G., 2005, *A Short Course in Christian Doctrine*, London: SCM Press.

Peacocke, A., 1993, *Theology for a Scientific Age: Being and Becoming – Natural, Divine and Human*, London: SCM Press.

Peacocke, A., 1996, *God and Science: A Quest for Christian Credibility*, London: SCM Press.

Peacocke, A., 1998, 'Biological Evolution – A Positive Theological Appraisal', in R.

J. Russell, W. R. Stoeger and F. J. Ayala (eds), *Evolutionary and Molecular Biology: Scientific Perspectives on Divine Action*, Berkeley, CA: Center for the Natural Sciences, pp. 357–76.

Peacocke, A., 2004, *Creation and the World of Science*, Oxford: Clarendon Press.

Pelikan, J., 1971, *The Emergence of the Catholic Tradition (100–600)*, Chicago: University of Chicago Press.

Phillips, D. Z., 1965, *The Concept of Prayer*, London: Routledge & Kegan Paul.

Phillips, D. Z., 1993, *Wittgenstein and Religion*, Basingstoke: Macmillan.

Phillips, D. Z., 2004, *The Problem of Evil and the Problem of God*, London: SCM Press.

Price, H. H., 1965, 'Survival and the Idea of "Another World"', in J. R. Smythies (ed.), *Brain and Mind*, London: Routledge & Kegan Paul, pp. 1–33.

Rahner, K., 1970, *The Trinity*, ET London: Burns & Oates.

Rahner, K., 1978, *Foundations of Christian Faith: An Introduction to the Idea of Christianity*, ET London: Darton, Longman & Todd.

Ramsey, A. M., 1936, *The Gospel and the Catholic Church*, London: Longmans.

Ramsey, A. M., 1969, *God, Christ and the World: A Study in Contemporary Theology*, London: SCM Press.

Ramsey, I. T., 1957, *Religious Language: An Empirical Placing of Theological Phrases*, London: SCM Press.

Ramsey, I. T., 1963, 'Theological Literacy', *The Chicago Theological Seminary Register*, LIII, no. 5, pp. 1–40.

Ramsey, I. T., 1965, *Christian Discourse: Some Logical Explorations*, London: Oxford University Press.

Ramsey, I. T., 1971, *Our Understanding of Prayer*, London: SPCK.

Richardson, A. (ed.), 1969, *A Dictionary of Christian Theology*, London: SCM Press.

Richardson, A. and Bowden, J. (eds), 1983, *A New Dictionary of Christian Theology*, London: SCM Press.

Richardson, N., 1999, *God in the New Testament*, Peterborough: Epworth.

Ricoeur, P., 1967, *The Symbolism of Evil*, ET New York: Harper & Row.

Ricoeur, P., 1976, *Interpretation Theory: Discourse and the Surplus of Meaning*, Fort Worth, TX: The Texas University Press.

Ricoeur, P., 1981, *Hermeneutics and the Human Sciences*, ET Cambridge: Cambridge University Press.

Ritschl, D., 1986, *The Logic of Theology: A Brief Account of the Relationship Between Basic Concepts in Theology*, ET London: SCM Press.

Robinson, J. A. T., 1962, *Twelve New Testament Studies*, London: SCM Press.

Robinson, J. A. T., 1968, *In the End God*, London: Collins.

Robinson, J. A. T., 1973, *The Human Face of God*, London: SCM Press.

Sabatier, A., 1904, *The Doctrine of the Atonement*, ET London: Williams & Norgate.

Sauter, G. and Barton, J. (eds), 2000, *Revelation and Story: Narrative Theology and the Centrality of Story*, Aldershot: Ashgate.

Schillebeeckx, E., 1968, *The Eucharist*, ET London: Sheed & Ward.

Schleiermacher, F., 1928, *The Christian Faith*, ET Edinburgh: T. & T. Clark.

Schleiermacher, F., 1958, *On Religion: Speeches to its Cultured Despisers*, ET New York: Harper & Row.

Schwarz, H., 1984, 'The Word', in C. E. Braaten and R. W. Jenson (eds), *Christian Dogmatics*, Vol. 2, Philadelphia: Fortress, pp. 257–88.

Selby, P., 1991, *BeLonging: Challenge to a Tribal Church*, London: SPCK.

Shakespeare, S. and Rayment-Pickard, H., 2006, *The Inclusive God: Reclaiming Theology for an Inclusive Church*, Norwich: Canterbury Press.

Smart, N., 1979, *The Phenomenon of Christianity*, London: Collins.

Smart, N., 1996, *Dimensions of the Sacred: An Anatomy of the World's Beliefs*, London: HarperCollins.

Soskice, J. M., 1985, *Metaphor and Religious Language*, Oxford: Oxford University Press.

Stiver, D. R., 2009, *Life Together in the Way of Jesus Christ: An Introduction to Christian Theology*, Waco, TX: Baylor University Press.

Surin, K., 1986, *Theology and the Problem of Evil*, Oxford: Blackwell.

Swinburne, R., 1977, 'The Problem of Evil', in S. C. Brown (ed.), *Reason and Religion*, Ithaca, NY: Cornell University Press, pp. 81–102.

Swinburne, R., 1993, *The Coherence of Theism*, Oxford: Clarendon Press.

Swinburne, R., 1994, *The Christian God*, Oxford: Oxford University Press.

Swinburne, R., 1998, *Providence and the Problem of Evil*, Oxford: Clarendon Press.

Sykes, S. W., 1979, 'The Incarnation as the Foundation of the Church', in M. Goulder (ed.), *Incarnation and Myth: The Debate Continued*, London: SCM Press, pp. 115–27.

Sykes, S. W., 1984, *The Identity of Christianity: Theologians and the Essence of Christianity from Schleiermacher to Barth*, London: SPCK.

Sykes, S. W., 1997, *The Story of Atonement*, London: Darton, Longman & Todd.

Tanner, K., 1997, 'Jesus Christ', in C. E. Gunton (ed.), 1997, *The Cambridge Companion to Christian Doctrine*, Cambridge: Cambridge University Press, pp. 245–72.

Temple, W., 1924, *Christus Veritas*, London: Macmillan.

Temple, W., 1934, *Nature, Man and God*, London: Macmillan.

Tennant, F. R., 1930, *Philosophical Theology*, Vol. II, Cambridge: Cambridge University Press.

Tilley, T. W., 2000, *Inventing Catholic Tradition*, Maryknoll, NY: Orbis.

Tillich, P., 1962, *The Shaking of the Foundations*, London: Penguin.

Tillich, P., 1968, *Systematic Theology: Combined Volume*, London: Nisbet.

Tinsley, J., 1996, 'Tell it Slant', in J. Astley, L. J. Francis and C. Crowder (eds), *Theological Perspectives on Christian Formation: A Reader in Theology and Christian Education*, Leominster: Gracewing, pp. 88–94.

Torrance, A., 2001, 'Jesus in Christian Doctrine', in M. Bockmuehl (ed.), *The Cambridge Companion to Jesus*, Cambridge: Cambridge University Press, pp. 200–19.

Turner, H. E. W., 1976, *Jesus the Christ*, London: Mowbrays.

Vardy, P., 1992, *The Puzzle of Evil*, London: HarperCollins.

Wainwright, G., 1980, *Doxology: The Praise of God in Worship, Doctrine and Life*, London: Epworth.

Wakefield, G. S., 1983, 'Spirituality', in A. Richardson and J. Bowden (eds), *A New Dictionary of Christian Theology*, London: SCM Press, pp. 549–50.

Wallis, A., 1981, *The Radical Christian*, Eastbourne: Kingsway.

Ward, K., 1977, 'Incarnation or Inspiration – A False Dichotomy', *Theology* LXXX, no. 676, pp. 251–5.

Ward, K., 1990, *Divine Action*, London: Collins.

Ward, K., 2007, 'Liberal Theology and the God of Love', in P. Middleton (ed.), *The God of Love and Human Dignity: Essays in Honour of George M. Newlands*, London: T. & T. Clark, pp. 191–201.

White, V., 1991, *Atonement and Incarnation: An Essay in Universalism and Particularity*, Cambridge: Cambridge University Press.

White, V., 2002, *Identity*, London: SCM Press.

Whitehead, A. N., 1926, *Religion in the Making*, Cambridge: Cambridge University Press.

Wiles, M., 1972, 'Does Christology Rest on a Mistake?', in S. W. Sykes and J. P. Clayton (eds), *Christ, Faith and History: Cambridge Studies in Christology*, Cambridge: Cambridge University Press, pp. 3–12.

Wiles, M., 1974, *The Remaking of Christian Doctrine*, London: SCM Press.

Wiles, M., 1982, *Faith and the Mystery of God*, London: SCM Press.

Wiles, M., 1986, *God's Action in the World*, London: SCM Press.

Wiles, M., 1994, *A Shared Search: Doing Theology in Conversation with One's Friends*, London: SCM Press.

Wiles, M., 1999, *Reason to Believe*, London: SCM Press.

Williams, R., 1979, *The Wound of Knowledge: Christian Spirituality from the New Testament to St John of the Cross*, London: Darton, Longman & Todd.

Williams, R., 2000, *On Christian Theology*, Oxford: Blackwell.

Williams, R., 2007, *Tokens of Trust: An Introduction to Christian Belief*, Norwich: Canterbury Press.

Wilson, B. R., 1966, *Religion in a Secular Society: A Sociological Comment*, London:

C. A. Watts.

Wink, W., 1998, *The Powers That Be: Theology for a New Millennium*, New York: Doubleday.

Wittgenstein, L., 1968, *Philosophical Investigations, ET,* Oxford: Blackwell.

Wittgenstein, L., 1974, *On Certainty, ET* Oxford: Blackwell.

Wittgenstein, L., 1980, *Culture and Value, ET* Oxford: Blackwell.

Wolterstorff, N. P., 2002, *Educating for Life: Reflections on Christian Teaching and Learning*, Grand Rapids, MI: Baker Book House.

Wright, N. T., 2006, *Evil and the Justice of God*, London: SPCK.

Wright, T., 2007, *Surprised by Hope*, London: SPCK.

Wright, T., 2009, *Justification: God's Plan and Paul's Vision*, London: SPCK.

Yeats, W. B., 1952, *Collected Poems*, London: Macmillan.

Zizioulas, J. D., 2008, *Lectures in Christian Dogmatics, ET* London: Continuum.

Index of Subjects

Index of Names